Consumer Lending

PAUL BEARES

EDUCATION POLICY & DEVELOPMENT

AMERICAN BANKERS ASSOCIATION

1120 Connecticut Avenue, N.W.
Washington, D.C. 20036

This publication is designed to provide accurate and authoritative information in regard to the subject matter covered. It is sold with the understanding that the publisher is not engaged in rendering legal, accounting, or other professional service. If legal advice or other expert assistance is required, the services of a competent professional person should be sought.

—From a Declaration of Principles jointly adopted by a Committee of the American Bar Association and a Committee of Publishers and Associations.

Printed in the United States of America

1988 Printing

1989 Printing

Acknowledgments

One cannot complete a task such as writing a book without the support of other people. My deepest appreciation is extended to my wife Susan and to my children Sara and David who had to make many sacrifices during the past year. Their love and support made this project possible.

My thanks are also extended to many others who have contributed directly or indirectly to this book, especially Allie Buzzell, Charles Cottrell, Debbie Delinski, Bob Duvall, Jim Pilkington, and Richard Watson. My ultimate gratitude is to the Spirit whose workings have brought me and this project to this point.

Paul Beares
Baltimore, MD
April 1987

Reviewers

The staff of the American Bankers Association wishes to thank the banking professionals whose guidance and insight contributed to the high quality of this textbook. Landon Davis of United Virginia Bank and James Pilkington of the National Council of Savings Institutions served on the advisory committee for *Consumer Lending* and reviewed the manuscript.

These bankers reviewed the manuscript: Robert Duvall, Bank of New York; Robert Georgeson, First National Bank of Lawrence; Beth Cornwall, Seafirst Corporation; Donald Anderson, Security Pacific National Bank, and Arnold Becker, First National Bank of Waukegan.

Carol Penne not only reviewed the manuscript she wrote the excellent glossary.

Table of Contents

List of Exhibits

PART I
CONSUMER CREDIT OVERVIEW

The banking industry—itself in the midst of a sea of change—has watched its consumer credit function swell in importance, from a low-profile source of fixed rate, closed-end loans to a dynamic operation delivering a panoply of products and services to a credit-reliant consumer market. Alongside other retail services, consumer credit has assumed strategic importance in the bank's efforts to stay profitable in a financial services marketplace that has become intensely competitive.

To function effectively in such an environment, today's consumer credit lender needs an impressive store of knowledge, skills, and intuition. These attributes, of course, are not bestowed as if by magic. Instead, they rest on a studied appreciation of the consumer credit business: how it has evolved, the nature of the marketplace, and the legal environment that shapes lending practices. Those are the broadly stated subjects covered in Part I of *Consumer Lending.* Here, you are treated to basic, historical, and regulatory material before being served up the main course in the remainder of the text.

1 Evolution of Consumer Credit

The use of credit has become so pervasive in the United States that it is hard for many of us to imagine a world without it. We use plastic credit cards to purchase everything from airline tickets and zoom lenses for our cameras to household necessities and even medical care. We use credit to help purchase goods that would otherwise be beyond our economic reach. Automobiles costing $20,000, boats costing $75,000, and that sought-after European vacation costing $10,500 are all brought within the reach of many consumers because we have access to credit.

The credit services available to retail customers have evolved over the course of history; however, the pace of change has accelerated in recent years. This evolution has been driven by the desire of consumers to find better ways to meet their financial management needs. Credit products available to today's consumers enable qualified individuals to exercise considerable control over when, where, how, and for what purposes they borrow.

The financial institutions that serve the consumer credit market have been an important part of the evolutionary process. Those serving the market have evolved from an unregulated, ill-defined group of lenders to a specific, legitimate, and highly responsive group of financial institutions. Deregulation of the market in recent years has stimulated greater diversity and sparked the creative energies of lenders seeking to achieve a unique place in the business.

Today's *consumer credit market* presents new challenges and opportunities for consumers and lenders alike. Traditional *product lines* are being joined by new products, and the features available on loan products are expanding and changing. These changes challenge consumers to be knowledgeable and keep up-to-date so they can choose products that best serve their needs. Lenders are likewise challenged to anticipate and be responsive to consumers' needs, while learning to effectively manage an increasingly complex retail credit product line.

Consumer Credit Defined

There are a number of legal definitions of consumer credit that vary depending upon which law you look at. For example, the *Truth in Lending Act* provides the following definitions:

- A *consumer* is a natural person who is primarily or secondarily liable on a credit contract.
- A *consumer credit transaction* is one that is primarily for personal, family, household, or agricultural use, and is not for business or commercial purposes.

This may be contrasted with language from the *Equal Credit Opportunity Act*, which defines an *applicant* as any person who is or may be contractually liable for an extension of credit, other than as a *guarantor, surety, endorser,* or similar secondarily liable party.

In fact, there is no generally accepted legal definition of consumer credit. Rather, a wide variety of laws concern themselves with different aspects of the credit business.

A practical definition of consumer credit is as follows: consumer credit includes all types of credit extended to individuals primarily for the purpose of buying goods and services for their personal consumption. This definition includes both *installment loans,* which are repaid in two or more periodic payments, as well as *single-payment loans,* such as *demand loans* or those that have a specific payment date (a 90-day *note,* for example). This general definition covers credit card transactions; home equity lines of credit; loans to purchase cars, boats, planes, recreational vehicles, and other *durable goods;* as well as loans for bill consolidations, vacations, home improvements, taxes, and other services used by the consumer.

The definition of consumer credit does not include residential, purchase-money, first mortgage loans, the proceeds from which are used to buy a home. These mortgage loans are separated from other forms of credit extended to consumers for a number of reasons. Generally speaking, mortgage loans are governed by different regulations, and the market for such loans is quite different in its composition and operation than the consumer credit market. Mortgage loans are normally handled outside of the bank's consumer credit department due to these differences.

Historical Overview

In looking at history, we hope to learn from the past and to better understand why things are as they are today. We can discover common threads and basic elements that can serve as a focal point for understanding the direction of change and for developing a pro-active position regarding the future.

Our study of the history of consumer credit will focus on how credit has helped consumers meet their financial management needs. We will examine how these needs and consumers' attitudes toward credit have changed over time and how financial institutions have responded to those changes.

Early Examples of Consumer Credit

Consumer credit has had a long and not altogether romantic history. The economic need to borrow is rooted deeply in our culture, and many of the practices, philosophies, and attitudes toward credit have evolved out of thousands of years of history. *Loan sharking* and *usurious interest* were problems in ancient societies, while the very act of borrowing traces back to primitive cultures.

History is rich with quotations that have much to do with some of our society's attitudes and values regarding the issue of being a borrower or a lender. Consider the following:

- *The wicked borrow, and payeth not again: but the righteous showeth mercy, and giveth.*
- *The rich ruleth over the poor, and the borrower is servant to the lender.*
- *Neither a borrower nor a lender be.*
- *Give to him that asketh thee, and from him that would borrow of thee turn not away.*
- *Owe no man anything.*
- *For the love of money is the root of all evil.*

That is not a comforting list of thoughts for those of us involved in the consumer credit business. But two other famous quotations add some flavor to the business:

- *Creditors have better memories that debtors.*
- *He who does not have to borrow lives without care.*

Against this rather pessimistic background, is it any wonder that there has been some stigma attached to borrowing money? Could it be that these thoughts still have an impact on people today? Anyone who has been around the lending business for even a short time can tell you these biases are still alive and active for some people in our society today. But credit can be viewed in a more positive light. Responsible credit use provides many economic and psychological benefits to consumers, such as the knowledge that funds are available to meet short-term emergencies and to enable major purchases, such as automobiles and college tuition. These benefits, plus the responsible provision of credit by financial institutions, have largely changed consumer attitudes and values regarding credit.

Credit extended by merchants and other types of lenders can be traced well back into history. Educator Irving Michaelman noted, in his study of consumer credit, that "Lending money is one of the world's oldest professions."[1] Michaelman traces the development of consumer credit from primitive times through the early 1960s. He further states:

> In the earliest days of primitive societies, lending was purely philanthropic, almost a duty, as tribes owning communal property could hardly conceive of charging anything for the use of such property. . . . In time the concept of private property evolved. . . . Here began the opportunity to offer something of value for loans, namely security, and the story of lending begins. At the same time, those who did not have land to borrow on had conceived the idea of offering themselves in servitude to secure loans. It did not take much ingenuity to substitute the concept of paying interest to replace servitude as recompense to the lender.
>
> The idea of interest, however, was resisted, if not forbidden, in laws calling for loans without interest to the poor and the cancellation of debts every seventh year.[2]

Michaelman also points out that interest rates got pretty high by 1700 B.C. "Babylonia and Assyria had far exceeded the Israelites as traders, and in these countries interest-taking was common practice, at rates of 20 to 360 percent a year."[3] By the time of the Roman Empire, lending took a nationalistic tone: ". . . interest was regulated and even abolished in Rome from time to time, but nonpaying debtors were still subject to imprisonment, slavery or even dismemberment under early Roman law. Interest protection extended only to Roman citizens, and the rulers of the western world thought nothing of imposing harsh interest terms on subjugated nations."[4]

The Romans were among the first to add provisions to loan contracts to cover some of the risks of credit. Selling other services, such as *credit life insurance*, along with providing credit—a practice known as *tie-in selling*—was begun by the Romans. Roman lenders ". . . could add a handsome premium for the peril of shipwreck and additional lesser trivial risks. The practice of tie-in charges thus has a notable genealogy. . . ."[5]

Leaping forward to the 1700s in colonial America, we find that Benjamin Franklin philosophized, "A penny saved is a penny earned," but he also believed in credit. He extended credit liberally in his printing and bookselling business. His personal records show loans made to customers, some *secured* by a pledge of equipment. Thus, the *chattel mortgage*—or loan secured by a pledge of some property—was already well-established in early America.[6] In Franklin's autobiography, he even tells of calling off marriage plans because the bride's parents were unwilling to give him a *dowry* large enough to pay off his printing house debts.

The Industrial Revolution in the United States

The demand for credit received significant impetus with the Industrial Revolution, which reached the United States in the mid-1800s. Technological leaps enabled consumer goods to be mass-produced for the first time in history. This, in turn, required that mass consumer markets be developed to purchase the high volume of goods being produced. It soon became obvious that goods could not be *mass marketed* without first developing a large base of consumers with the ability to purchase a wide variety of goods and services. This need gave rise to a corresponding need for credit programs that would enable consumers to pay for higher priced goods over some period of time.

Many citizens were not ready, however, to accept the idea of credit at this time. Abraham Lincoln voiced concern about rising credit usage, reflecting rural America's lively antagonism for city people: ". . . one of the reasons being that they associated with bankers, loan sharks, and land sharks." The November 1838 issue of *The Cultivator,* a regional newspaper, gave this advice:

> A farmer should shun the doors of a bank as he would the approach of a plague or cholera: banks are for traders and men of speculation, and theirs is a business with which farmers have little to do.

No doubt, many modern-day farmers would agree with these words in the midst of our recent farm crisis.

Lincoln noted that America's usury limits in the 1830s were easily evaded through *note shaving,* the practice of deducting one's expenses from the proceeds of a note bearing the maximum permitted rate. This practice persisted until the time of Truth in Lending legislation in the 1960s.

The consumer credit business received major new impetus in the United States after the Civil War, again according to Michaelman:

> The emergency of the need to borrow on the part of the consumer is often discussed as a by-product of America's new industrialism after the Civil War, which created a wage-earning class that desperately required loans to meet emergencies. This is not particularly borne out by the available statistics, which indicate that lenders themselves preferred to do business with the frayed and genteel middle class and civil servant class which just couldn't live on their meager incomes. . . . Even the lenders who lent on chattels, such as furniture or wagons and horses, dealt with a similar group of customers. . . .[7]

One interesting experiment in banking developed after the Civil War with the creation of The Freedman's Savings and Trust Company, which was chartered on March 3, 1865. The bank, which had branch offices in many eastern U.S. cities, was intended to serve the savings needs of the recently freed slaves and to help mold them into middle-class citizens. Originally chartered as a nonprofit institution, it closely resembled a modern credit union. The bank received consumer deposits and invested them in U.S. bonds.

Freedman's began making loans in 1870, but the loans were limited to those secured by real estate. As a result, few loans were extended to the blacks who made up the overwhelming bulk of the bank's depositors. The bank then began extending loans to white citizens who had little or no security, but did not offer the same loans to its black customers. Discontent ensued. "Finally realizing the errors in their loan policy, the Freedman's Bank trustees persuaded Congress to amend the charter in June 1874, so that money could be returned to the bank communities for investment."[8]

The Freedman's case is an early example of the feelings and attitudes that eventually led to enactment in 1977 of the *Community Reinvestment Act*. The CRA requires banks to invest a portion of their *loan portfolios* back into the communities from which they develop their *deposit bases*. It seems certain that this expectation will continue to be made of the banking business.

The consumer credit business, which began to develop during the 1860–1900 period, was virtually unregulated. It was characterized by very small loans, even adjusting for the inflation that has since eroded the dollar's value. Salary loans of the time were in the $10–$40 range and were designed to help consumers make it from one payday until the next or to meet those inevitable emergencies that arose out of the harsh working conditions of the time. *Chattel loans*—those secured by some form of collateral, usually furniture—were larger, but typically stayed in the $20–$100 range.

Interest rates, on the other hand, were quite high. Customers were often charged 5 cents a week for every dollar they borrowed. This meant that interest rates of 120 percent to 240 percent were common. Not that the rates were advertised that way; but, when proper calculations were made, these were the *effective yields*.[9]

Lenders of the time also used some very strong-handed techniques for collecting debts. Their practices were no doubt effective in recouping money, or at least persuading consumers to refinance their debts with a certain upward adjustment in the interest rate. One particularly onerous practice involved the use of female employees who became nicknamed "bawlerouts." A bawlerout was a person who would go to visit past-due debtors at their places of employment. These women, who were rarely eligible for credit on their own, would loudly confront the delinquent consumer in front of his peers. The resulting bawling out certainly had a strong psychological impact on the debtor.[10]

The following verbiage from an advertisement in the November 23, 1890, issue of the *Chicago Tribune* captures the themes of pre-regulation ads:

Any amount of money from $20 to $10,000 to loan on furniture, pianos, teams, etc.

The property to remain in your undisturbed possession.

At a lower rate of interest than you get elsewhere. Everybody who wants money, call and see us.

We are just as happy to make you a $25 loan as one for $2,500; we will give you plenty of time to pay the money back; in fact, we let you make the payments to suit yourself; as we do not ask for references or make inquiries of your neighbors, the transaction is sure to be private; no fear of losing your goods as we loan money for the interest and not to get the goods; we take up loans from other loan men; if you now have a loan on your goods, call and get our rates.[11]

Now isn't that a reassuring advertisement? You may notice that some of the themes are still present in consumer credit advertising today.

Emergence of Regulated Consumer Lending

A formal, regulated consumer finance market began to emerge around the turn of the century. Finance companies and *Morris Plan banks* were among the earliest financial institutions making significant credit plans available to consumers. In 1900, Arthur Morris founded the first Morris Plan Bank in Norfolk, Virginia. The bank was patterned after similar banks in Europe, and was established with the primary purpose of lending money to people who did not own property. These people had traditionally been denied credit except from loan sharks.

A major step forward came in 1916, when the Russell Sage Foundation—a charitable institution with a goal of improving social and living conditions in the United States—devised the *Uniform Small Loan Law,* which was subsequently enacted in Pennsylvania and New Jersey. This law provided the important early framework for the licensing of consumer lenders, and it established guidelines that provided some credibility for the emerging industry. Other states soon enacted this or similar regulations, allowing legitimate lenders to take a place in the market.

The movement to regulate consumer credit became intense. As the ad in *Exhibit 1–1* illustrates, the loan shark had become a target of the reform effort.

Another significant advertisement, shown in *Exhibit 1–2,* appeared in the April 8, 1916, issue of the *Saturday Evening Post.*

EXHIBIT 1–1
Pass the Loan Shark Bill!

Harry Murphy's great anti-loan shark cartoon, from the *Chicago Examiner* of March 26, 1917.

EXHIBIT 1–2
Time Payments Advertisement

THE SATURDAY EVENING POST

Time Payments

GUARANTY PLAN
AUTOMOBILE Time Payments

Look for this emblem on dealers' windows.

The First Organized National Service To Help Dealers Sell Automobiles

Guaranty Securities Corporation is the first organization of its kind in the world.

Its purpose and service is to directly assist automobile dealers to sell and the public to buy motor cars.

It has no cars of its own to sell.

It has nothing but service to offer automobile dealers.

This service is absolutely free.

And there is virtually no added expense to the car buyer beyond ordinary six per cent interest on the deferred payments.

For months we have been endeavoring to reach every dealer in the cars listed on the opposite page, with the details of the Guaranty Plan.

Hundreds of dealers all over the country are already selling thousands of cars on the Guaranty Plan.

It is sound, secure and safe.

Any dealer (in cars listed on opposite page) who has not received full particulars, may have them promptly for the asking.

The Guaranty Plan enables dealers to sell their cars on time payments—one down payment followed by monthly installments until the car is paid for.

Guaranty Securities Corporation will finance for any dealer (in cars listed on opposite page) any number of sales he makes on this basis.

It makes no difference how large or how small your business is—we will handle it.

Whether you sell one car a week or a hundred cars a month is beside the point.

All you can sell on this liberal installment plan, we will finance for you as fast as the mails will carry the papers to us and our check back to you.

Every dealer knows the tremendous automobile market just waiting to buy cars on the time payment plan.

Every dealer knows that this market is and always has been practically unlimited.

Many dealers have tried to work out their own plans but such a plan takes a lot of money or uses up a lot of bank credit and that in most cases has been the big stumbling block.

So we have worked out a plan for all dealers—large and small.

From now on, with the service of the Guaranty Securities Corporation you will be able to sell as many cars as your factory can supply you with—on this new and practical Guaranty (time payment) Plan.

The Guaranty Plan has been worked out and is backed by a group of capitalists some of whom are among the largest in the country.

Its soundness is vouched for by many of the leading banking and financial institutions in America.

As to the standing of the Guaranty Securities Corporation, we refer you by permission, to the following banks:

Metropolitan Trust Co., N. Y.
Liberty National Bank, N. Y.
First National Bank, Chicago
Corn Exchange National Bank, Chicago
Continental & Commercial National Bank, Chicago

The quicker you adopt this new Guaranty Time Payment Plan, the quicker you and your customers can enjoy its benefits.

Right now thousands of people in every state are waiting to buy cars on the Guaranty Plan.

If you are not fully informed about our service, fill out this coupon, mail it to us and we will send full particulars—or, better yet, telegraph.

Dealers—Send Us This Coupon

Buick —	Chevrolet —	Hudson —	Oldsmobile —	Overland —
Cadillac —	Dodge —	Hupmobile —	Maxwell —	Paige —
Chalmers —	Ford —	Jeffery —	Mitchell —	Reo —
Chandler —	Franklin —	Kissell —	Oakland —	Studebaker —
				Willys-Knight

GUARANTY SECURITIES CORPORATION,
Equitable Building,
New York, N. Y.

I am an authorized dealer in the cars which I have checked (√) in the above list.

Please send me complete information about the Guaranty Plan.

Name
Address
City State

Guaranty Securities Corporation, Equitable Bldg., New York

The first national auto financing advertisement from the *Saturday Evening Post* of April 8, 1916.

This advertisement explained the new concept of *retail installment loan programs* for automobile dealers. Indeed, Henry Ford's mass production of the automobile was to provide the credit industry with its biggest opportunity for growth for the next few decades. Automobile loans became and continue to be a major part of the consumer credit business.

The Post-World War II Era (1946–1965)

The consumer credit market was still in a relatively infantile stage at the beginning of 1945. The faltering world economy of the 1930s, followed by World War II, had held back the emergence of a major consumer products market. Installment *loan outstandings*—the amount of money consumers owed on credit obligations—were estimated by the *Federal Reserve* to be $1.3 billion. Major growth, though, was just around the corner.

The post-war baby boom and the formation and growth of families increased the level of demand for consumer products and credit. Increased demand led to a wider variety of lenders entering the market and to a general increase in the availability of credit. Pent-up consumer demand, combined with industry's need to convert from wartime production, fueled a consumer products explosion unparalleled in history. By the end of 1949, *consumer credit outstandings* had jumped 939 percent to $12.2 billion.

The economy of the 1950s was generally strong. The decade was characterized by themes like: "Be the first person on your block to own . . ." and "Keep up with the Joneses." The desires expressed by these themes helped to bring about a major shift in attitudes regarding credit usage. During the decade, total consumer credit rose 337 percent, reaching $41.1 billion. *Commercial banks,* which had captured the largest share of the consumer credit market in the 1940s, continued to increase their share, reaching nearly 43 percent of the total consumer credit oustandings by the end of the decade.

Social stability encouraged continued market growth. Civilian employment reached high levels and became more steady. No longer did major segments of the population remain unemployed for substantial portions of the year. *Disposable personal income*—the amount of money that consumers have left after paying for basic food, clothing, and shelter needs—also rose. Consumers who would look forward to a gradually rising level of income and could count on steady employment were much more willing to undertake credit obligations. Lenders were also much more willing to lend in an environment where income and employment patterns were stable.

Movement Toward Structural Change (1966–1979)

One of the legacies of the Vietnam War was a dramatic increase in inflationary pressures. Double-digit rates of inflation caused major problems for banks. *Disintermediation*—the flow of funds out of depository institutions to sources paying higher rates—drained funds available for lending and drove up the cost of funds to the banks. This resulted in severe earnings pressures on consumer loans since they were virtually all on a fixed rate basis. Further, banks were not always able to raise rates to match the higher costs of deposits since loan rates were controlled by state law, and state legislators were not anxious to raise rates during a period of high consumer concern with business practices.

Inflation also raised the cost of doing business. Personnel salary costs, a major factor in banking, rose to keep pace with the rate of inflation. Inflation also drove up the cost of the operating systems that support consumer credit products. In the midst of the inflationary spiral, many of these systems were automated to improve productivity and customer service and to control operating costs.

The social upheavals that characterized the 1960s had far-reaching effects. Much of our current consumer protection regulation stems from this time. Truth in Lending, which is a major part of the *Consumer Credit Protection Act* of 1968, signalled the opening bell for many legislative bouts to follow. Major legislation over the next eight years included: *Fair Credit Billing Act, Consumer Leasing Act, Equal Credit Opportunity Act, Real Estate Settlement Procedures Act, Fair Credit Reporting Act*, and the *Fair Debt Collection Practices Act.*

Clearly, the consumer movement was highly successful in bringing about legislation changes within the industry. There is no doubt that many of the earlier practices of loan sharks and poorly disciplined lenders provided the fuel for the fires of change. These changes worked to the benefit of responsible financial institutions and consumers. The industry was able to gain favorable legislation at the state level during this period, allowing lenders to develop new consumer credit products. Lenders also gained the ability to make larger loans, with longer terms and at rates that were both fair and essential to the continued availability of credit.

The soundness of consumer lending and the potential profits available encouraged other financial institutions to increase their activities in the market. *Credit unions* began to spread and grow very rapidly. *Savings institutions* also began to eye consumer credit as an area for growth. However, most *thrifts* were limited by regulations that allowed them to invest only a very small portion of their assets in this type of loan portfolio. *Brokerage firms,* led by Merrill Lynch, also became more active in the consumer credit market. Merrill Lynch's *Cash Management Account* (CMA) was designed to serve a variety of financial service needs for upscale consumers. The CMA provided a line of credit to *account holders* and was one of the first examples of *product packaging*—the practice of marketing a group of financial services as a single product. Other brokers soon began to offer similar products in order to maintain their customer bases and to attract new business.

The Deregulation/Reregulation Movement (1980–present)

Deregulation of the financial services industry broke down many legislative barriers and removed arbitrary market specialization, such as the limitation on thrifts to serving the residential mortgage loan market. Despite claims that nationwide banking did not exist, consumer lending had become a nationwide business for many financial institutions by the beginning of the 1980s. Major banks, such as Citicorp and Bank of America, already marketed their loan products in many states, either through offices bearing their names or through related finance subsidiaries.

Expansion of banks beyond their traditional state boundaries was hastened by a crisis in the thrift industry. Some thrifts were caught in the squeeze resulting from the erratic behavior pattern of recently deregulated deposit rates and the relatively low yielding, fixed rate structure of their assets. Regulators permitted banks to buy failing thrifts and to operate them under a variety of state law provisions. More importantly, state legislators began to respond to the movement toward national banking by passing *reciprocal banking laws,* which allow banks in one state to merge with banks in another state. The movement seemed an inevitable response to the modern economic environment, though there were those who resisted the concept of national and regional banking.

The consumer credit market faced a major trauma in 1980. The Consumer Credit Restraint Program, implemented under the Carter Administration early that year, and a change in Federal Reserve policy, which allowed interest rates to float freely beginning in September 1979, combined to produce a major crisis for the industry. The imposition of credit restraints, at a time when deposit interest rates were skyrocketing toward 20 percent, put an extreme burden on consumer lenders. The restraint program was intended to stem the high rate of growth in consumer borrowing, and it imposed penalties on financial institutions that showed growth in their unsecured consumer credit portfolios.

Banks reacted in many different ways to the restraint program. Actions taken by some banks included—

- discontinuing credit accommodations to marginal indirect dealers (as a result, auto dealer outlets dropped by 3,783 locations during the period from 1979 to 1982, with the biggest drop being domestic auto dealerships);
- discontinuing the issuance of new credit cards and the termination of *lines of credit* for marginal customers;
- ceasing all consumer loans to nonbank customers (this was a common practice among banks);
- discontinuing some loan programs, particularly *unsecured line of credit plans;*
- initiating efforts to relocate portions of consumer credit operations to states with more favorable lending laws.

As the *prime lending rate* soared above 20 percent and the rates paid by banks on *certificates of deposit* climbed into the high teens, fixed rate consumer loans became an albatross around the necks of consumer credit managers. *Exhibit 1–3* depicts the situation in which the cost of funds peaked above the yield on loans. Previously profitable portfolios were suddenly unprofitable.

The negative impact on the consumer credit market was substantial. Financial institutions reacted by increasing pressure on state legislators to provide relief from unrealistic *rate caps.* Banks also sought the freedom to offer a wider variety of products and features, enabling them to meet the changing credit needs of

EXHIBIT 1–3
Fixed Rate Loan Yield Versus Variable Cost of Funds

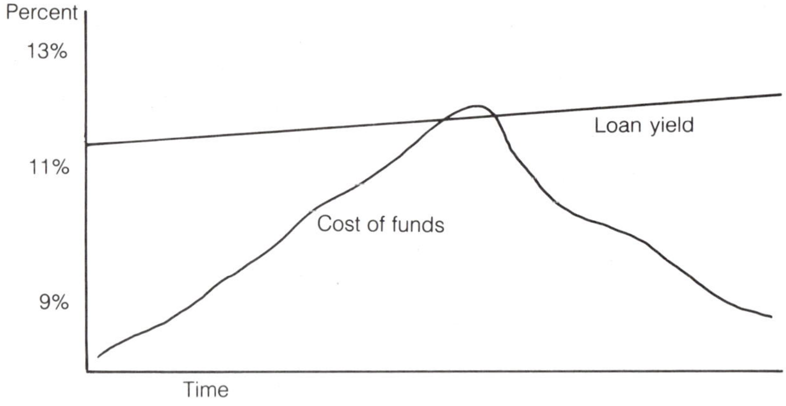

consumers. Legislation authorizing the widespread introduction of home equity line of credit products and variable rate consumer loans, as well as a law providing interest rate relief, were enacted soon after 1980.

Retail Banking Is Redefined

Another significant change that has occurred in recent years is the redefinition of the concept of *retail banking*. Retail banking, once associated only with consumer credit, has been identified in recent years as encompassing all aspects of the bank that relate to individual consumers. This definition suggests a broader perspective on the consumer market and recognizes that there is synergy to be developed if all of a bank's retail areas can work together effectively. For example, the consumer loan application provides a wealth of information about the customer. Sharing this information among departments of the bank can help identify prospects for other retail services, more effectively cross-sell products, and establish a closer relationship with the customer.

Cross sell

Benefits of Consumer Credit

The existence of a well-developed consumer credit market enhances the ability of consumers to purchase goods and services. Consumers can stimulate the economy in a number of ways by borrowing money. First, merchants will order goods to replace items sold, thereby creating demand for manufacturers to produce more goods. Second, purchases by consumers provide income for the merchants. This income may be passed on in the form of wages to employees, purchases for the business, expansion of the business, or creation of more jobs. Or the income may be retained in the business for future use. Third, consumer purchases of services stimulate the economy by providing a similar flow of funds through service-oriented firms such as banks.

As consumers are able to purchase more goods and services, they are able to improve their material standard of living. The possession of certain goods may reduce the consumers' labor and add to their leisure time or enhance their images with themselves or others. As incomes rise further above the subsistence level, borrowing power is increased, and consumers are able to borrow more for the luxuries of life, rather than simply for the necessities. Consumers who have access to credit markets are able to realize enhanced purchasing ability and to raise their standards of living.

The wide availability of credit provides consumers with increased purchasing power throughout swings in the economic cycle. At any given time, some consumers have excess debt, some have an appropriate level of debt, and some have very little debt. Thus, there are always groups within the population that have the ability to increase their debts by increasing their purchasing activity. Some segments of the population even seem to be *recession-proof* and are able to continue consumption levels during fairly substantial economic downturns.

Credit allows consumers to have the goods and services they want or need, without waiting until they can save up the money from their earnings. It allows consumers to enjoy a comfortable standard of living and to pay for it in a convenient and affordable manner. Credit also allows consumers to purchase items today and avoid high costs in the future. This logic is particularly prevalent in periods of high inflation, when delays in purchasing can add significantly to the cost of goods.

The use of credit allows consumers to manage their financial affairs in a planned manner. Purchases can be made when necessary and paid for over subsequent periods. *Debt service* can be effectively managed by maintaining a controllable level of debt in relation to household income.

Government has subsidized and encouraged the use of consumer credit through its tax policy. Tax reform in 1986 changed the rules for deducting interest paid, phasing out the deduction for most consumer loan interest over a five-year period. However, the law retained full deductibility for interest paid on most consumer credit loans secured by real estate. This revision placed public policy firmly in support of consumer loan programs such as home equity lines of credit, residential first mortgages, and second mortgage loans. It is, however, difficult to determine what effect the tax law changes will have on the way consumers will borrow in the future.

Banks and other financial institutions have found that the consumer credit market offers a source of sound loan assets, a base of retail customers who are prospects for other bank products, and an attractive return on the bank's investment. Consumer loans are an important part of the overall portfolio for many banks.

Consumer credit has also been a positive factor in the economic development of the United States. We enjoy one of the highest standards of living in the world, and we have extended credit to a broader segment of the population than any other country. It must not be forgotten, though, that credit also gives rise to problems. Personal bankruptcies, family financial strains, and fraud are problems within the market that will present continuing challenges to the industry. These challenges will be met, and responsible consumers and financial institutions will continue to benefit from the consumer credit market.

Summary

Granting and receiving credit is a practice that has taken place throughout the development of human society. Many of the values, attitudes, and practices associated with modern consumer credit trace their origins to very early history.

The eventual growth of the consumer credit market, though, depended upon the mass marketing of consumer products and services, a base of consumers willing and able to purchase those products, a sound regulatory environment, and the existence of financial institutions committed to the market. As these ele-

Mass Market and Middle Class

ments evolved over time, the market became stronger and larger.

The credit services available to contemporary consumers have also evolved steadily. Today, loan products are available that give consumers a significant amount of control over when, where, how, and for what purposes they wish to borrow. Consumers now have significant flexibility in using credit to meet their financial management needs.

Questions for Review and Discussion

1. Does the term "consumer installment loans" embrace open-end credit products like credit cards? Give a general definition of the term.
2. Why would a saying like "Neither a borrower nor a lender be" gain wide recognition?
3. How have people's attitudes changed toward the granting and use of credit?
4. What historical event first led to the use of credit in the United States? What development specifically gave rise to the need for credit?
5. Give some details about an early banking experiment that ultimately resulted in the notion that a bank has a duty to serve the needs of its depositors and local community?
6. What event in this century is generally attributed with responsibility for a sudden upsurge in consumer credit demand? Why did demand surge?
7. Characterize the consumer movement—especially why it happened and how it affected the banking industry.
8. Has deregulation lightened the compliance burden on your bank? What particular effects of deregulation have you been able to observe?

2 Consumer Installment Credit Market

The consumer installment credit market is a very large and rapidly growing part of the overall retail financial services business. To understand why the market has grown into a multibillion dollar business, we will examine the factors that influence the level of demand for credit. This analysis will help to further our understanding of the historical development of the market.

Next, we will examine the growth of the market, focusing on trends in various types of loans in recent years. We will then discuss the institutions that serve the market. These institutions include commercial banks, finance companies, thrift institutions, credit unions, and retailers. Each of these lender groups has certain advantages and disadvantages in its efforts to compete for the consumer's borrowing business. Our examination of these characteristics will aid in understanding the market and the changes that are likely to take place in the future.

Factors Affecting Consumer Loan Demand

The demand for consumer credit has demonstrated a great deal of strength in recent years; however, the level of demand is never constant. An individual consumer's need for credit is influenced by his income, age, *family life cycle stage*, the community's attitudes and life-styles, and his financial condition at the time.

Consumers are willing to take on debt when they expect to have a regular and steady level of income over the *repayment period*. When the level and regularity of income are not as predictable or favorable, not only will the consumer be less likely to borrow, but lenders will also be less likely to make the loan requested.

The development of a large base of potential consumers living above a subsistence level is essential to the development of consumer credit. Peter Fousek, of the Federal Reserve Bank of New York, notes the following in his study of consumer credit:

> The shift in income distribution toward the lower income groups and the growth of a large middle class was also essential for the spread of installment credit. Among the other fundamental economic prerequisites for installment credit growth, the income security that comes with prosperous times has been a major force in consumer credit expansion.[12]

Income is clearly a major factor in the credit decision-making process. Most banks determine the applicant's maximum borrowing ability by using debt-to-income ratios. For example, many banks stipulate that the consumer's monthly debt payments may not exceed 35 percent of his *gross monthly income*. Thus, a consumer who earns $2,000 per month can have maximum debt payments of $700 per month. The use of such *underwriting guidelines* recognizes that there is a direct relationship between the level of income and the amount of debt a borrower can comfortably handle. Lenders have historically experienced higher loan losses and delinquencies when consumers begin to incur excessive debt obligations. This is the reason why industry observers closely watch the ratio of consumer debt in relation to disposable personal income (DPI). This relationship is depicted in *Exhibit 2–1*. It gives some indication of the ability of consumers to take on additional debt at any particular time.

The consumer's age and family life cycle stage bear a direct relationship to his need for credit. Although the traditional family life cycle has recently undergone some alterations in this country, a large portion of the population still follows the traditional chronological pattern of (1) marriage in the early 20s, (2) one or two children within the next ten years, (3) college for the kids, (4) the "empty nest," peak of career, and income period, and (5) retirement. This life cycle has obvious implications for borrowers and lenders alike.

Demand for consumer credit begins with the desire to purchase some product or service. No one wakes up and says, "Gee, I think I'll borrow some money today." Rather, a person

EXHIBIT 2–1
Consumer Installment Debt Relationship to Disposable Personal Income*

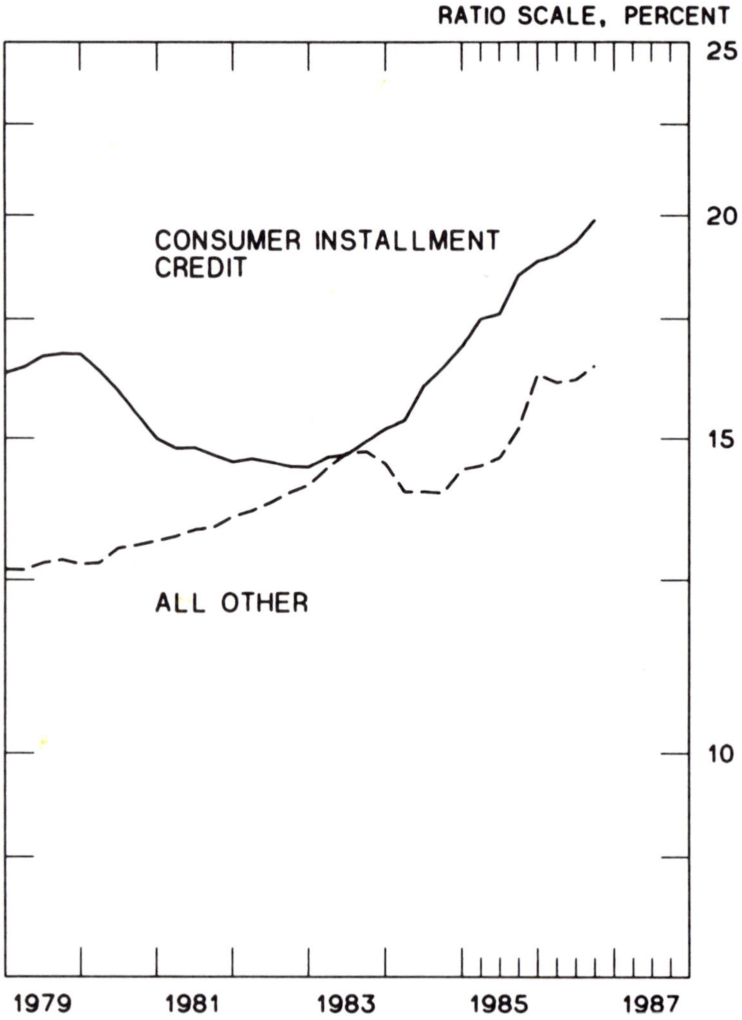

*Credit figure includes credit outstandings of gasoline companies since 1971.
SOURCE: Federal Reserve Chart Book, February 1987

decision to buy

says, "I'm going to go buy that car I've been wanting." The need for credit comes as a *result* of the decision to buy the car.

Consumers usually decide to purchase something first; then they worry about how they are going to pay for the item. This may help explain why consumers typically want rapid credit decisions. The lender taking its time to make a credit decision is delaying the borrower's access to his new car, boat, or European vacation. Clearly, this factor must be taken into consideration when the bank structures its procedures. The failure to give decisions on a timely basis can mean lost loans.

Borrowing needs tend to be heavy at the beginning of the family's life cycle because a new household is being established. New households desire durable goods such as cars, furniture, refrigerators, TVs, computers, VCRs, and all the other "essentials" of modern life.

Children, of course, add an additional burden on family finances. Some experts estimate that it costs in excess of $300,000 to raise a child from birth to college graduation. College, of course, is a very expensive proposition, yet the need for an education in today's highly complex society cannot be overlooked. College costs of $15,000 per year and more are not unusual, and they clearly place a financial burden on the family budget. Some parents say the expense often does not stop there.

Doubtless, many young Americans have read these figures and, after viewing the childrearing experiences of others, have elected not to participate in this part of the traditional family life cycle. This frees up considerable funds for their personal use.

Borrowing needs tend to reach a low point during the "empty nest" years since the typical consumer's income is at its peak and many of his borrowing needs have been satisfied. Many Americans find that this is the ideal time to buy a luxury car or a bigger boat with a much bigger price tag. Generally, though, these are the years when consumers build their savings and investment accounts and plan for a carefree retirement. *Exhibit 2–2* illustrates the relationship between the use of consumer credit and life cycle stage.

We noted in our study of the history of consumer credit in Chapter 1 that there has been a significant shift in the attitudes of consumers regarding the use of credit. This change in attitudes was pointed out by Sylvia Porter in her popular *Money Book*:

EXHIBIT 2–2
Life Cycle Stage and Credit Usage

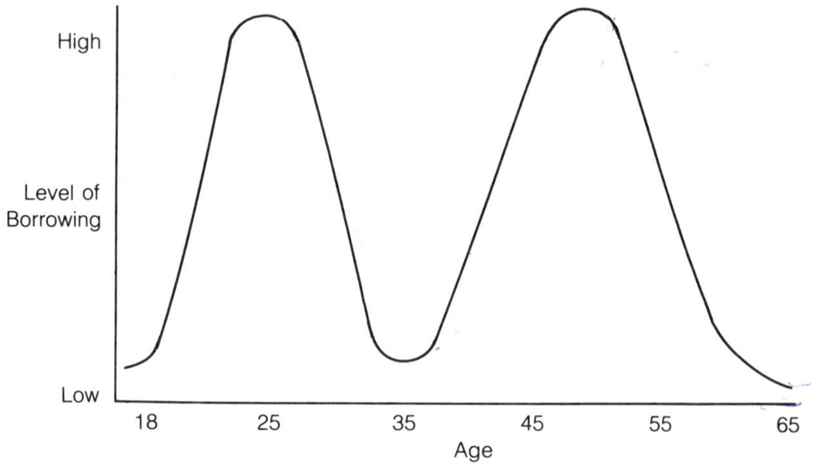

> It is no exaggeration to say that almost uninterrupted buying on the installment plan has become a way of life in American homes to a point where a hefty percentage of families we consider as representing the "ideal" in our nation are never out of debt and another hefty proportion seldom are. In fact, I'll go beyond this and submit that the fundamental reason Americans have been borrowing so much today is precisely because they have had so much. This has intensified your desire to satisfy your aspirations rather than simply finance your needs. And this in turn has led to unprecedented borrowing to achieve your aspirations at once.[13]

Ms. Porter zeroes in on the fact that Americans today, particularly younger citizens, do not want to wait and save up money to buy the things associated with the good life. We want it now and we are willing to borrow to have it. Borrowing has shifted from the basic needs to the luxuries of life. The lender today who is reluctant to lend money for vacations may be considered out-of-date and certainly is not tuned in to the value system of modern consumers.

Consumers tend to exercise self-discipline over their use of credit. This is a particularly important factor if banks are going to continue to grant control of credit use to the consumer in the form of open-end credit programs. Research reveals a tendency to self-control, but with some stretching by consumers of their debt capacities:

> Other things being equal, households with large debts tend to reduce them, and households with small or no debts tend to increase their indebtedness. According to these results, there are certain equilibrium debt levels to which households tend to adjust their debt if their circumstances remain unchanged.[14]
>
> Although families tend to adjust their portfolios toward some desired level of installment credit, there are wide variations about this level over time. Our findings of large year-to-year changes in credit obligations about some longer run level can be interpreted as evidence of potentially destabilizing effects on consumer credit.[15]

These observations help explain some of the variations in consumer credit demand over time. They also focus on a potential problem that can lead to delinquency and credit losses: consumers can let credit use get out of control. Nevertheless, it is important to the banking industry that we have faith in the ability of consumers to discipline their debt load.

The level of consumer demand for credit is also influenced by a number of factors present in the broader economy. Factors like economic stability, inflation, the level of interest rates, and the legal environment all affect the overall demand for credit among consumers. Moreover, consumer credit can only develop when the economy of a country exhibits a level of stability. While credit exists in most cultures, the market remains stunted if there is instability within the government or the national economy. Lenders feel secure when patterns of behavior are highly predictable. Conversely, lending in an unpredictable environment is like playing Russian roulette.

Inflation can be a strong motivating force on consumer borrowing. Consumers often react to high inflation by adopting inflationary psychology, which says to "buy now before prices rise." Inflation drives up the cost of goods, which consumers buy and finance on credit. Another result of inflation is an increase in the average loan size. This results in a never-ending pressure on lenders to increase the length of loan maturities in order to keep the monthly payments at an acceptable level.

This situation is best demonstrated in the automobile credit market. In 1976, the average new car cost $5,414. By 1985, this figure had risen to $11,883—a 120 percent increase. Many banks increased the maximum *term* for a new car loan from an average of 36 months to 60 months to accommodate the increase in selling price. New car loans of up to 84 months, with 100 percent financing were also available in some markets in 1986. Such terms were virtually unheard of previously.

Besides inflation, the cost of credit clearly influences primary demand. Consumers curtailed their borrowing significantly in 1980 and 1981, when interest rates hit peak levels, and they dramatically stepped up borrowing in the 1984–1986 period in response to falling rates. In fact, much of the borrowing in 1986 was to *refinance* high-rate loans from previous years.

Another example of the power of rates to stimulate borrowing has been the use of *interest subvention programs* offered by automobile companies. A subvention program is one in which the manufacturer pays a portion of the cost of credit to the lender in order to offer below-market rates to consumers. These programs are powerful tools used by manufacturers to stimulate product sales, sell slow-moving products, and reduce inventory levels.

The relatively recent implementation of *variable rate loans* will undoubtedly have an impact on consumer lending in the future. Variable rate loans present new challenges and opportunities for both lenders and consumers. For example, when structured to require variable monthly payments, such loans may pose problems for consumers in a rising rate environment. Monthly payments in relation to income may be driven up to levels that strain family budgets, and, in some cases, break them.

The legal environment also affects the consumer credit market because it can either encourage or discourage borrowing and lending activities. In our review of the history of credit in Chapter 1, it was obvious that consumer borrowing was limited when the lending business was dominated by loan sharks. Only when realistic laws were passed could consumers borrow with some confidence.

Unrealistic laws, though, have restrained credit usage from time to time. One classic example is the *usury law* in the state of Arkansas. Until the 1980s, the state's Constitution established a 10 percent usury limit on all consumer debt. The rate was acceptable for many years, but it became a major problem in the inflationary environment of the 1970s. As a result, lenders either discontinued doing business in the state, or severely restricted the availability of credit. Lenders have often limited the availability of credit when usury limits prevented them from being able to achieve the desired return on their investment.

Size of the Market

The size of the consumer credit market is generally measured by (1) the level of outstandings and (2) *loan volume*—the amount of money borrowed by consumers during a given period of time. Since loan outstandings represent *interest-earning assets*, we will look first at the size and trends within that measure during recent years.

Loan Outstandings

Consumer loans may be divided into two major categories—closed-end loans and open-end or revolving loans. *Closed-end loans* are loans in which a fixed amount of credit is extended at the beginning of the transaction and is repaid over a predetermined term. *Open-end* or *revolving loans* are loans in which a commitment is made for a specified amount of credit, which the borrower may use at any time at his own discretion. There is no set *maturity date* and payments vary depending upon the amount of credit being used at any given time.

Exhibit 2–3 shows the size of consumer installment credit outstandings for selected years since World War II. The table shows the growth that took place in the total market and the growth in various types of credit. Revolving loans are shown in a separate category, while closed-end loans are represented in three categories—automobile, mobile home, and other, which includes loans for all other purposes.

The role and importance of major holders of consumer credit have also changed over time. *Exhibits 2–4* and *2–5* show market share data for the major holders, along with trend information.

Loan Volume

Aggregate data for loan volume are not readily available. However, we can identify some of the characteristics and trends in loan volume by examining selected data. *Exhibits 2–6* and *2–7* present selected volume data for commercial bank closed-end loans and for domestic credit card volume for VISA International and MasterCard International.

EXHIBIT 2–3
Consumer Installment Credit Outstandings by Type of Credit, 1945–1985
In Billions of Dollars, Not Seasonally Adjusted

	1945	1950	1960	1970	1980	1985
Total	2.6	15.5	45.1	105.5	313.4	535.1
Automobile	.4	6.0	18.1	36.3	116.3	206.5
Revolving	0	0	0	5.1	59.9	118.3
Mobile Home	0	0	0	2.5	17.3	25.5
Other	2.2	9.5	27.0	61.6	119.9	184.9

SOURCE: Federal Reserve Statistical Release—Series G-19

Exhibit 2–6 reflects the variations in size between different types of closed-end loans. It also demonstrates the trend toward steadily increasing loan size and the mix of loans held in commercial bank closed-end portfolios. *Exhibit 2–7* highlights the very strong rate of growth in volume for the national bank credit cards in recent years.

Recent Growth Rates

The rate of growth of consumer credit during the 1980s is shown in *Exhibit 2–8*. After a virtually stagnant growth rate of .4 percent in 1980 and modest growth in 1981 and 1982, the market resumed double-digit growth rates in 1983 with a 15 percent increase. Growth was very strong in 1984 and 1985, when gains of 20.6 and 18 percent respectively were achieved. Revolving credit products continue to experience the highest rate of growth, though automobile credit too has been strong in recent years.

Competitive Environment

The competitive environment continues to change as the consumer credit market is *deregulated*. Commercial banks, finance companies, credit unions, savings institutions, and retailers have been the primary suppliers of credit. In recent years, the distinctions among various lender groups became less obvious,

EXHIBIT 2–4
Share of Market of Major Holders of Consumer Credit, 1945–1986

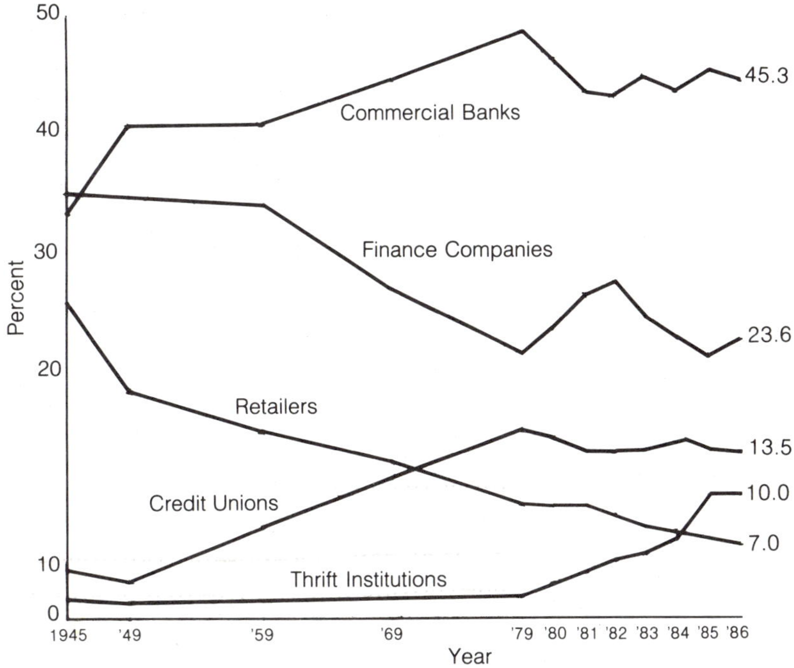

SOURCE: Federal Reserve Statistical Release—Series G-19

and lenders now enjoy greater freedom to develop and market consumer credit products.

Commercial Banks

Commercial banks have held the dominant share of the consumer credit market since 1946. Their market share peaked in 1979 at 51.5 percent, declining to 43.3 percent in 1986. Banks have traditionally dominated the revolving credit market and hold the largest dollar outstandings in each category except in automobiles, where banks rank second to finance companies.

There is a wide divergence in the importance attributed by individual banks to the consumer credit function. Some banks are predominately commercial lenders and have only a very small percentage of their loans with consumers, while other banks have a much larger share of their assets in consumer

EXHIBIT 2–5

Consumer Installment Credit Outstandings by Major Holder, September 1986

In Billions of Dollars, Seasonally Adjusted

	Dollars Outstanding	*Share of Market*	*Percent Change Since 12/79*
Total	585.0	—	97.3%
Commercial Banks	253.5	43.3%	66.0
Finance Companies	144.6	24.7	253.3
Credit Unions	81.6	14.0	76.8
Savings Institutions	61.5	10.5	550.9
Retailers	40.4	6.9	58.2
Gasoline Companies	3.3	.6	(13.2)

SOURCE: Federal Reserve Statistical Release—G-19

loans. A survey prepared by the American Bankers Association revealed that the ratio of consumer loans to total loans was normally less than 30 percent. The percentage of consumer loans in banks tends to decline as the size of the bank increases. Thus, small banks often have ratios in excess of 30 percent, while larger banks typically have less than 20 percent of their loan outstandings with consumers.

Reflecting their market share and performance, banks have enjoyed several advantages in the consumer credit market. These include a positive image, a large base of retail customers, and a responsive branch distribution system.

The banking industry's image, in particular, has contributed to the major competitive advantages enjoyed by commercial banks. Banks are viewed in a positive light by most consumers, and their trustworthy image helps overcome the stigma often attached to borrowing. Branch personnel are often viewed as experts in personal finance and may have more credibility than some other lenders.

The base of checking and savings account customers held by banks also represents an important asset and a competitive advantage. Retail customers are prime targets for the bank's lending efforts. In fact, research consistently proves that satisfied customers are highly responsive to other marketing efforts by the bank, much more so than noncustomers.

EXHIBIT 2–6
Portfolio Distribution of Loan Volume[1] by Type of Loan, 1983–1985

	1983			*1984*			*1985*		
	Percent Distribution		*Average*	*Percent Distribution*		*Average*	*Percent Distribution*		*Average*
Type of Loan	*Number*	*Dollar*	*Amount*	*Number*	*Dollar*	*Amount*	*Number*	*Dollar*	*Amount*
Personal—direct and indirect	30.1%	16.5%	$3,444	26.7%	14.1%	$3,714	25.9%	14.6%	$3,786
Automobile—direct	17.6	16.6	5,907	18.4	17.5	6,624	18.3	18.6	6,849
Automobile—indirect	29.0	36.6	7,944	32.1	41.6	9,013	29.5	39.9	9,093
Home Improvement, Own Plan—direct and indirect	3.2	3.5	6,995	3.8	3.6	6,486	4.2	4.3	6,825
Home Improvement, FHA Title I—direct and indirect	0.5	0.5	6,800	0.4	0.4	7,248	0.2	0.2	6,424
Mobile Home—direct	0.6	1.3	13,846	0.5	0.7	9,953	0.5	0.9	10,840
Mobile Home—indirect	0.6	1.9	21,526	0.8	2.3	20,559	0.6	1.3	15,984
Farm Equipment—direct and indirect	0.2	0.6	18,643	0.2	1.1	19,636	0.1	0.1	8,470
Recreational Vehicle—direct and indirect	2.3	3.6	9,591	2.1	3.5	11,204	2.0	2.8	11,528
Student (Federal or State Programs)	12.1	5.9	3,087	11.7	6.0	3,604	15.1	6.9	3,114
Installment, Small Business—direct and indirect	1.4	4.2	18,595	1.4	3.3	16,955	1.5	3.7	16,793
Aircraft—direct and indirect	0.1	0.4	65,120	0.1	0.3	44,783	0.2	0.3	29,375
Second Mortgage—direct and indirect	2.3	8.4	22,818	1.8	5.6	21,322	1.9	6.4	22,818
Total Installment Loan Volume[2]			$ 6,369			$ 6,667			$ 6,712

1. Volume—new loans made during the year.
2. Excluding floorplan and open-end credit.

SOURCE: American Bankers Association. 1986 Retail Bank Credit Report

The branch distribution system is another important element in developing direct loan business and marketing other credit products. Much of the growth of bank loan outstandings can be traced to the expansion of the branch network, as banks followed consumers into the suburbs. Consumers prefer borrowing from convenient loan sources, and many are willing to pay a premium, such as higher interest rates, in order to gain convenience.

Despite the significant advantages they enjoy, commercial banks also face some challenges and problems in the consumer credit market. The wide variety of products offered by banks

EXHIBIT 2–7
Selected Statistics for VISA and MasterCard
In Millions

	1983	1984	1985	Change 1984–1985
Cardholders	123.8	142.8	160.9	+12.7%
Dollar Volume	$80,152	$103,404	$126,357	+22.2%
Retail sales	72,336	91,691	110,456	+20.5%
Cash advances	7,816	11,713	15,901	+35.8%

SOURCE: American Bankers Association, 1986 Retail Bank Credit Report

creates a problem of priorities. Branch staffs are expected to wear many hats and are called upon to balance an ever-changing list of priorities. Consumer lending—sometimes a low priority for the bank—may not receive the amount of management time and attention necessary to optimize lending opportunities.

Another variable is the degree of risk-taking, which varies widely from bank to bank. Some banks are extremely conservative in their lending practices. They accept only low-risk loans and offer new products only after thorough testing by others in the market. The result of this conservative stance may be a loss of market share, a failure to maximize profits, and the need to play catch-up with more aggressive competitors.

Still another problem that consumer lenders in banks may face is the lack of consistent management support. Some banks occasionally cut off or substantially reduce certain types of loans, only to aggressively pursue these loans at other times. This practice generally reflects a short-term rather than a long-term market perspective, and it can adversely affect future lending efforts.

The nature of consumer loans themselves may pose some problems for banks. The *fixed rates* and relatively long *maturity structures* of many types of consumer loans tend to erode their profitability. As a result, variable rate lending has now become an important part of many banks' consumer loan programs. Variable lending programs have helped overcome concerns about protecting profit margins in both rising and falling cost-of-

EXHIBIT 2–8
Consumer Credit Outstandings Growth, 1979–1986
In Billions of Dollars, Seasonally Adjusted

Period	*Total Market*	*Automobile*	*Revolving Credit*	*Mobile Home*	*Other*
1979	296.5	112.5	53.4	18.2	112.4
1980	297.7	112.3	54.9	19.1	111.4
1981	314.3	120.0	60.8	20.4	113.2
1982	328.2	125.4	66.0	22.0	114.8
1983	376.5	145.9	78.4	22.2	130.0
1984	453.6	173.1	98.5	24.2	157.8
1985	535.1	206.5	118.3	25.5	184.9
9/86	585.0	236.6	126.4	24.9	197.1

SOURCE: Federal Reserve Statistical Release—Series G-19

funds environments. In addition, banks have become more adept at matching the funding for their consumer credit portfolios with the types of loans generated, and *secondary markets* have been developed to give increased *liquidity* to the loan portfolio. In recent years, a few banks have sold off credit card, automobile, boat, and mobile home portfolios to a variety of investors. This practice, while not widespread at this time, may develop as a viable alternative for more banks in the future.

Finance Companies

Finance companies can be divided into a number of different groups, depending upon who owns them. *Captive finance companies*—such as GMAC, Chrysler Credit, Ford Motor Credit, and General Electric Credit—were originally formed to help manufacturers sell the goods they produced. In recent years, these companies have moved to tighten their grip on the automobile segment of the consumer credit market and to broaden the type of loans they make. GMAC, for example, now offers a full range of loan services, including home mortgages, boat loans, and unsecured loans, to customers throughout the country.

Another important group of finance companies are those owned by commercial banks. Citicorp, Bank of America, Wells Fargo, Fleet Bank, and many other banks have purchased finance companies during the last fifteen years. The finance company subsidiaries constitute a branch network outside of the bank's home state, providing a natural transition for regional or national banking. The finance company subsidiaries also allow banks to reach a segment of the market not fully served by commercial banks. For example, finance companies might make loans to customers who pose higher credit risks than most banks would normally accept.

A third group of finance companies consists of *independent finance* or *personal loan companies*, such as Beneficial Finance, Household Finance, Commercial Credit, and CIT and Associates. Most of these have either merged with other finance companies, have been purchased by banks, or have bought banks in a number of states and gone into the banking business. Beneficial, for example, has aggressively acquired credit card portfolios through its Beneficial National Bank subsidiary. The differences between banks and finance companies are likely to continue to blur in the future as both types of entities cross state lines and engage in a full range of consumer financial services.

Looking back, though, we find that finance companies had been on a long downhill slide until 1980. Their negative trend in market share has been reversed, though, by a combination of aggressive activity and the industry's ability to obtain banking charters. Finance companies, for example, as a result of the efforts of captives to control domestic automobile financing through rate subsidy programs, had the largest increase in automobile outstandings over the one-year period ending September 1986, with a gain of 39.7 percent (compared to a 5.7 percent gain by banks). Overall, finance companies had the highest growth rate compared to other lenders during that time period, with a 26 percent increase.

The ability to specialize gives finance companies a competitive advantage over many other lenders. This specialization has led to the development of highly efficient operational systems, skilled lending and collection personnel, and aggressive marketing practices.

Moreover, many finance companies are able to open branch offices throughout the country. State laws limit branching to some extent, but restrictions are far less severe than those faced by most banks. The freedom to branch allows the companies to locate branches in desirable market areas and to optimize convenience for consumers.

The biggest competitive disadvantage faced by the finance company industry has been its poor image. This problem undoubtedly stems from the fact that finance companies generally used to charge higher rates and, for the most part, dealt with higher risk consumers. The industry also continues to be associated with some unacceptable credit practices that, in the past, were used by a few of its members, tending to tarnish the image of all finance companies.

Another major problem for the finance company industry is its reliance on borrowed funds, rather than savings deposits, to fund loan portfolios. This results in a higher *cost of funds*, which must be passed on to customers in the form of higher rates. Borrowed funds are also subject to problems of availability and greater volatility. Funds raised in the short-term money market—an important source of finance company funds—can be volatile and were squeezed very hard in the early 1970s, forcing many finance companies to curtail their activities in many states.

Savings Institutions

Until 1980, savings and loan associations and mutual savings banks, now referred to as *savings institutions or thrift institutions*, were only permitted by regulation to invest a small percentage of their assets in consumer loans. This constraint prevented most savings institutions from taking an active role in the market. Since this restriction has been relaxed, thrifts have had the highest rate of growth in the consumer credit market. Thrift institutions' outstandings rose nearly 550 percent after 1979, leading all other groups by a significant amount.

Thrifts, like banks, have a large base of retail customers. These customers represent a significant advantage in efforts to diversify loan portfolios. Thrifts also have a base of branch offices from which to develop their direct loan business and *cross-sell* other loan products and related retail services. The relatively short maturities and high rates offered by consumer loans represent major attractions for savings institutions bogged down with large portfolios of fixed rate mortgage loans. The fact that their current customer base already includes many potential customers for a variety of consumer loans can only serve to enhance growth prospects during the next decade.

The troubled financial condition of many thrifts—a legacy of soaring interest rates in the late 1970s and early 1980s—has prevented many of them from embarking on the development of new product lines, though the recent overall gain in market share proves that many thrifts are very healthy and aggressive. Nevertheless, implementation of a consumer credit program requires a significant up-front commitment, as well as a commitment of management time and resources. These demands have slowed the entry of many thrifts into the market.

Thrifts also had little experience to apply in building a consumer credit market. They are beginning to import expertise from other lender groups in order to avoid the pitfalls and capitalize on the benefits a consumer credit program can offer.

Credit Unions

Credit unions are associations of individuals with some common bond. They offer a wide variety of consumer financial services to their members, operating on a not-for-profit basis. This means that any profits are distributed to the members in a variety of ways, primarily in the form of higher rates on savings accounts and lower interest rates on loans.

Credit unions have experienced a slight decline in market share in recent years. Their previous 14 percent share ranked third among major holders of consumer credit. Low-rate financing offered by captive finance companies and open-end credit programs offered by other lenders have cut into the market share previously enjoyed by credit unions. Additionally, some credit unions have experienced funding problems that have restrained their growth potential.

Some of the largest credit unions are those associated with a particular company—for example, United Airlines, AT&T, IBM, and Westinghouse—those associated with the military service—including the largest credit union in the country, the Navy Federal Credit Union—and those associated with state and local governments. The association between the credit union member and the organization the credit union represents is generally very strong. This relationship is a definite advantage in developing and maintaining a strong consumer loan program.

Credit unions have access to relatively low-cost funds since they raise funds primarily from the savings accounts of their members. They are able to offer their members a level of convenience generally not available to other lender groups. For example, both savings deposits and loan payments can be handled on a *payroll deduction* basis by many credit unions. This feature is the ultimate in payment convenience and a positive feature from the standpoint of personal financial management. It also helps to reduce delinquencies and losses.

The major disadvantage facing credit unions is their restricted customer base. Credit unions are limited to serving their memberships, and they must serve all of their members without being able to tap other desirable consumer groups. Many credit unions have attempted to overcome this restriction by more widely defining the common bond that forms the basis for membership.

Many credit unions do not have the resources to offer a full range of consumer credit products, particularly the popular open-end products. Small credit unions are often staffed by part-time or volunteer employees. As a result, they may not offer the privacy, convenience, and level of service that many customers want.

Retailers

Retail merchants were among the first groups to extend credit terms to individual consumers. They entered the business for the primary purpose of increasing the sale of goods and services above the level that could be attained from cash sales alone. Today, retailers in almost every product field extend some type of credit plan to their customers.

Among the major issuers of retail credit accounts are large department stores such as Sears, Roebuck and Co., J.C. Penney, and Montgomery Ward. Many major department store chains still offer a private brand credit plan, though many also accept *VISA®*, *MasterCard®*, and some regional credit cards. Small retailers also provide less formal credit accounts for their customers to accommodate purchases, especially of large items like major home furnishings and appliances. Most gasoline companies still offer their own credit card programs, though some have discontinued their plans, and most have encouraged cash purchases by offering discounts. Some major gasoline retailers have begun to accept the national bank cards in addition to their own private brand credit accounts.

The market share held by retailers has been on a steady decline for the last several decades, though actual dollar outstandings have continued to rise. Much of the activity in retailer accounts has shifted to the major national bank card programs—VISA and MasterCard—which provide consumers with greater flexibility and convenience, while relieving merchants of the need to tie up funds in carrying the customer's credit accounts.

Regardless of the overall trends, many retailers continue to promote their own credit programs in the hope of tying the consumer more closely to their stores. Consumers often patronize a store where they can obtain credit in preference to one where they cannot. Therefore, some retailers maintain their proprietary credit programs, even while also widening their markets by accepting major credit cards as well. Sears, for example, has the largest base of credit card customers in the world; even so, it has chosen to market its Discover card in an effort to broaden its position and reach beyond its current retail customer base. It is important to note that the Discover card is handled through a commercial banking subsidiary of the Sears organization.

One decisive advantage that retailers enjoy is the fact that their customers are ready to buy. Thus, their ability to provide credit at the point of sale enables them to package the sale of goods or services conveniently with the sale of credit. Retailers also tend to offer more flexibility in credit arrangements than are available from most other lenders. Plans such as 90 days with no payments or "no payments until next year" are designed to maximize the sale of goods. There is, however, the expense to the retailer of carrying the account for a period of time.

Many retailers, though, are unable to tie up funds in customer accounts receivable. They have neither the financial strength to carry the accounts nor the wherewithal to *service* the accounts. Retailers that offer their own credit plans must be able to process loan applications, make credit approvals, and handle the processing of payments and collection activities relating to the accounts. These functions represent an additional cost that must be covered by the interest income generated from the accounts or subsidized by the price of the goods sold.

As American society became more mobile and the number of retailers mushroomed, it simply became a burden for the consumer to establish individual credit arrangements with each retailer with whom he wished to do business. The demand for convenience and the flexibility to be able to purchase goods and services using a multipurpose national card provided strong motivation for consumers to sign up for the national bank card programs. As a result, there has been a dramatic growth in the national bank card programs and a corresponding decline in retailer market share.

Other Credit Sources

Credit has long been provided by families and friends. For the borrower, this may be the best possible source since the terms are likely to be informal ("Pay me when you have the money") or may be more in the form of a gift than a credit transaction ("Pay me back whenever you are able to, but if you can't, don't worry about it"). However, there can be significant psychological costs associated with borrowing from one's family or friends. The transaction can be used as an attempt to control the borrower or to induce a "guilt trip" on him. In the long run, it may be far more comfortable to borrow the money from a bank than to opt for the more flexible terms, with strings attached, available from one's family.

Loans may also be obtained from insurance companies. Individuals who own an insurance policy that builds cash value can borrow against the policy, usually at very favorable rates and with extremely flexible terms. A sample cash value table is shown in *Exhibit 2–9*.

The policyholder may borrow against the cash value at an annual percentage rate set forth in the insurance policy, as long as the policy is in force. As the cash value builds, the consumer has a source of loan funds available at a rate of interest that is usually below market rates. The consumer must repay the interest on the borrowed funds; the principal may be repaid at his discretion, or it will be paid out of the policy proceeds if it is still outstanding at the time of the policyholder's death.

Other sources of loans include employers, some of whom are willing to lend money to employees. Loans of this nature are particularly common in small companies where the owner has a close working relationship with his employees.

Loans may also be obtained from *real estate brokers*, who may provide *short-term equity advances* to facilitate the purchase of a new home; *securities brokers*, who provide *margin accounts* and other loan services to their customers; and trades people, many of whom provide short-term credit to facilitate specific purchases for home improvements or other needs.

EXHIBIT 2–9
Cash Value—Universal Life Policy

End of Policy Year	Cash or Loan Value
1	$ 81.90
5	3,007.02
10	6,854.21
15	10,411.09
20	12,470.02

Summary

Demand for consumer credit is influenced by a number of variables. The consumer's income, age, life cycle stage, life-style, attitudes about borrowing, and personal financial condition all have some effect on his use of credit. Likewise, credit usage is affected by circumstances in the economy at large. Economic factors, such as inflation and the general level of interest rates, influence the level and timing of credit usage.

Consumer credit is a rapidly growing, multibillion dollar market. Loan outstandings, the amount of money owed by consumers on credit obligations, has maintained a relatively strong, though not steady, rate of growth since World War II. Automobile loans are the largest group of consumer loan outstandings, while revolving credit products have achieved the highest rate of growth over the last decade.

The major lenders serving the consumer credit market are commercial banks, finance companies, credit unions, savings institutions, retailers, and gasoline companies. Commercial banks hold the largest share of the market, with over 43 percent of the total market. Savings institutions have had the highest rate of growth during the early 1980s, followed by finance companies.

Questions for Review and Discussion

1. Choose one of the family life cycle stages and characterize it in terms of credit usage.

2. Describe generally the typical attitude toward credit of today's consumer.

3. What general trend is observable in consumer loan size and loan maturities? Can you pinpoint a reason for the trend?

4. Despite the fact that commercial banks have traditionally emphasized their business loan portfolios, what do the statistics say about their share of the consumer credit market?

5. Why have banks exhibited an interest in acquiring or forming finance company subsidiaries?

6. Why do retailers offer credit to their customers, and how has the market share of retailer credit plans fared over time?

7. How intense is the competition in your bank's market area? What types of credit providers compete directly with your bank? Talk to your consumer credit manager to find out the answers.

8. Try to locate some statistics from your consumer credit department that show installment credit outstandings for your bank. How have they changed over time? Can you identify a trend?

3 Regulation of Consumer Credit

A sound legal environment is essential to the growth and stability of consumer credit. Laws that result in fair trade practices and provide for an equitable distribution of credit help build a relationship of trust between consumers and financial institutions, foster market acceptance of consumer credit products, and encourage responsible credit usage.

Consumer lending has undeniably had its share of problems. The temptation to charge unreasonably high rates and use undue pressure on consumers when attempting to collect delinquent payments were once chronic problems among lenders. However, most financial institutions have attempted to be good corporate citizens and have recognized that fair practices help their efforts to build a sound consumer credit portfolio.

Consumer credit laws and regulations are developed at the state and federal level. Each state develops its own set of lending laws that govern permissible types of loans, rates, and contractual terms. Legislative and regulatory action at the federal level was relatively limited until the 1960s when social concerns over equality, discrimination, and fair treatment led to a series of federal consumer credit laws. The two primary areas of focus for federal laws have been the requirement for uniform disclosures of important credit features and the provision of credit on an equal basis to all qualified consumers.

In this chapter, we will discuss the major federal laws that affect consumer lending: the Equal Credit Opportunity Act, Truth in Lending Act, Fair Credit Reporting Act, Community Reinvestment Act, Real Estate Settlement Procedures Act, Fair

Housing Act, Home Mortgage Disclosure Act, and Flood Disaster Protection Act. Next, we will discuss how banks can establish a consumer compliance program to ensure conformance with all applicable statutory and regulatory requirements.

An Overview of the Regulatory and Legislative Environment

The regulatory environment can be described as a roughly cyclical process. Laws are passed that govern the marketplace. Based on the laws, regulators issue regulations and monitor financial institutions for compliance. Violations and problems may be resolved administratively, or they may require intervention by the courts, which interpret the laws and resolve issues in dispute. Changes in the market or in the regulatory and legislative environment itself may ultimately lead to further legislative activity.

Federal Regulation and Enforcement

The federal legislative process begins with the U.S. Congress. Congress is charged with the responsibility of enacting laws, many of which govern consumer credit. Federal law generally is concerned with the industry's trade practices, the fairness of the credit allocation system, and the manner in which disclosures are made to consumers.

As *Exhibit 3–1* indicates, federal laws are monitored and enforced by a number of regulatory agencies. These agencies develop rules and regulations that specify how laws are to be implemented and then monitor the institutions under their purview for compliance. Some institutions are subject to review by more than one federal agency. For example, national banks are regulated by the *Comptroller of the Currency*, the *Federal Reserve Board*, and the *Federal Deposit Insurance Corporation*.

State Regulation and Enforcement

Each state has its own laws regulating consumer credit. The state laws have primary control over the rates lenders charge, the contract provisions that may be used in credit transactions, maximum loan maturities, and the fees that can be imposed on loans. There is a wide variety of legislation at the state level,

EXHIBIT 3–1
Federal Agencies and the Institutions They Supervise

Institutions Supervised	*Primary Federal Supervisory Agency*
National banks	Comptroller of the Currency
State member banks	Federal Reserve Board
Nonmember insured banks	Federal Deposit Insurance Corporation
Insured savings institutions and members of the Federal Home Loan Bank System	Federal Home Loan Bank Board
Federal credit unions	National Credit Union Administration
Consumer finance companies, mortgage bankers, and certain other creditors	Federal Trade Commission

which often makes it difficult for lenders from different states to communicate. Some states do not allow lenders to charge variable rates or to secure loans with second mortgages on a consumer's home. Others dictate restrictive interest rates.

Each state has regulatory agencies that monitor financial institutions chartered under state law. For example, the state banking commissioner regulates state-chartered banks. These banks may also be regulated by the Federal Reserve Board if they are members of the Federal Reserve System.

Federal Consumer Credit Laws

As already noted, federal laws focus primarily on providing uniform disclosures of important credit features and ensuring that credit is provided on an equal basis to all qualified consumers. While there have been many consumer credit laws passed since 1968, we will focus on the major laws relating to these primary themes.

The Equal Credit Opportunity Act

The Equal Credit Opportunity Act (ECOA) was passed by Congress in 1974 as Title VII of the Consumer Credit Protection Act. It was substantially amended and took its current form in 1976. The act, implemented by the Federal Reserve Board's *Regula-*

tion B, covers all types of credit, including consumer and business credit.

The primary objective of the ECOA is to prohibit discrimination regarding any aspect of a credit transaction on the basis of the applicant's race, color, religion, national origin, sex, marital status, or age. A lender may not treat one borrower or prospective borrower less favorably than another on the basis of these characteristics. The act also prohibits discrimination because all or part of the applicant's income is from a public assistance program, or because the applicant has in good faith exercised any rights under the Consumer Credit Protection Act.

Provisions of the ECOA affect all aspects of consumer credit transactions, including the bank's procedures for taking loan applications, credit evaluation criteria, adverse action notifications, and record-keeping requirements. Thus, ECOA is probably the most pervasive of all consumer credit laws. The rationale for an antidiscrimination law is obvious: people were denied credit for all of the reasons specified in the ECOA. Unfounded biases and undesirable practices did exist, and it was necessary to take strong action to change them.

Application Requirements

ECOA and Regulation B provide specific rules to define when an application is made, who is an applicant, and what other parties are covered. Specifically, the ECOA protects—

- any person who makes an oral or written request for an extension of credit made in accordance with procedures established by a creditor for the type of credit requested
- persons who have already had credit extended to them, as well as individuals currently applying for credit
- any person who is or may be contractually liable for an extension of credit, other than as a guarantor, surety, endorser, or similar secondarily liable party.

Furthermore, the ECOA says that an application is considered to have been made when—

- a request for an extension of credit has been made in accordance with the procedures established by a creditor for the type of credit requested, or
- when a conversation between an individual and a creditor turns to a discussion of that person's creditworthiness and the creditor offers any opinion on the subject.

These definitions have an impact on the bank's policies and procedures. For example, if the bank has a policy of not accepting applications for credit over the phone, a consumer could not claim to have made an application in that manner. Indeed, to avoid potential ECOA problems, many banks have adopted such a policy without having evaluated the broader marketing implications. By requiring all applicants to complete and sign a written application form, the bank may be losing loan business.

The second part of the definition of when an application has been taken poses some additional concerns. If a woman, for example, tells a loan officer that she has just gotten divorced and asks if that would affect her ability to obtain a loan, and the officer offers an opinion, an application has been made under the terms of the act, whether or not an application form has been completed. This particular provision was included to help prevent discouraging a potential applicant from applying for a loan.

Discouraging applications from protected groups is not permitted under the ECOA. Lenders could be deemed to have discouraged an applicant in several situations: by offering adverse opinions regarding the applicant's creditworthiness; by creating barriers to allowing a potential applicant to complete a loan application; and by selectively advertising to avoid major groups within the bank's primary market area. An example of creating barriers includes the failure of a bank located in an ethnic area to provide application forms in the language predominantly spoken in the market area—Spanish language documents in parts of Florida, Texas, and California, for example—or the failure to employ loan personnel who speak the language of the area.

ECOA concerns itself with the types of questions asked of consumers on loan application forms and the order in which questions may be asked. To ease compliance, the Federal Reserve provides model forms.

Credit Evaluation Requirements

The ECOA requires lenders to eliminate some of the criteria they may have previously used to evaluate the creditworthiness of applicants. Prior to the act, some lenders denied credit because: (1) the applicant was not white; (2) the applicant was divorced, separated, or unmarried; (3) the applicant was over the age of 65 or would be during the course of the loan; (4) the applicant was female; (5) the applicant was on welfare or public assistance; or

(6) the applicant was a member of a particular religious denomination. Basing a credit decision on these criteria is considered unfair discrimination under ECOA. The specific prohibited evaluative criteria are as follows:

- race and color—Questions regarding race may not be asked, except for government monitoring purposes on a credit request for loans secured by residential property. This exception allows regulators to monitor lenders' compliance with credit availability requirements contained in equal housing regulations. Under no circumstances is race or color to be considered in the decision-making process.
- religion—Questions regarding religion are not permitted under any circumstances, nor is this factor to be considered in the credit decision.
- national origin—The same rules apply to this category as for race and color. However, the creditor "may consider whether an applicant is a permanent resident of the United States, the applicant's immigration status, and such additional information as may be necessary to ascertain its rights and remedies regarding repayment." Thus, national origin may be considered in the decision-making process to some extent. Aliens who are likely to return to their native country and could avoid being held accountable for the debt may be refused credit based upon their citizenship status.
- age—Lenders may request the applicant's age and consider it in the decision-making process "when such age is to be used to favor the elderly applicant in extending credit." Other rules state that age may be used as a variable in credit-scoring systems, provided that elderly applicants are not assigned a negative value. For example, age may be used if applicants over the age of 55 receive the highest score possible for this characteristic.

Creditors are subject to several rules regarding income that may be related to age. For instance, lenders may take into account the level and probable continuity of income over the term of the loan. Thus, if an applicant is eligible for retirement during the term of the loan, the creditor may evaluate the applicant's ability to pay based upon his likely post-retirement level of income. If the applicant would be unable to meet the bank's *debt-to-income ratio* after retirement, the loan could be denied based upon insufficient ability to pay, but not due to age.

- marital status—Whether a creditor may ask an applicant's marital status depends on the applicant's state of residency and the type of credit being sought. In a *community property state,* creditors may always inquire about the marital status of an applicant, no matter what type of credit is sought. In a *noncommunity property state,* creditors may not inquire about an applicant's marital status if the applicant is applying for an individual, unsecured credit account. Marital status may be asked if the applicant requests secured credit, and on all requests for joint, unsecured credit.

  In cases where inquiries about marital status are permitted, only the terms "married," "unmarried," and "separated" are permitted. Additionally, questions about a spouse may be asked if: (1) the applicant resides in a community property state; (2) the spouse will use the account; or (3) the applicant is relying on income from a spouse or former spouse to qualify for the credit.

- income—The ECOA prohibits lenders from disregarding income from alimony, child support, or separate maintenance payments and from welfare or similar public support programs. The regulation also prevents lenders from disregarding income from part-time employment and the income of a woman of child-bearing age. These provisions were intended to correct practices that were used by lenders to judge an applicant's creditworthiness. Indeed, before ECOA, lenders regularly asked what a woman's child-bearing intentions were, and they did not count the wife's income when figuring a family's ability to pay because of the possibility that she might become pregnant and leave the job.

  The act does allow lenders to consider the probability that these protected sources of income will continue over the term of the loan and to judge the reliability of the income source. This provision allows lenders to examine documents—such as divorce decrees and separation agreements—that verify income and show how long it is expected to continue. And, of course, lenders are also allowed to investigate the borrower's employment, income, and credit history.

- sex—The sex of the applicant may not be considered in making a credit decision. Given the trend toward more single-person households, more working women, and modern life-styles, few lenders have difficulty with this provision.

Credit Scoring

ECOA recognizes the development of *credit-scoring programs* as a legitimate means of evaluating credit risk. Accordingly, it sets forth guidelines for how the programs are developed, the criteria that may be included in the system, and how the system is to be maintained. Scoring systems must be demonstrably and statistically sound and empirically derived. A system must be developed from the bank's own base of applicants and periodically monitored to validate its predictive ability.

Adverse Action

An *adverse action* is the refusal of a lender to grant credit to an applicant on the basis requested. An applicant might request an unsecured loan, for example, but the lender denies the loan request or decides that the loan can be made, but only on a secured basis. In the latter case, the lender might make a *counteroffer*, meaning that it would offer credit on a basis other than that requested by the consumer. Both decisions—to reject a loan request or to make a counteroffer—are covered under the regulation's adverse action provisions. (If the consumer accepts the counteroffer, no special disclosures need be made. On the other hand, if the terms of the counteroffer are not accepted by the consumer, the bank must send an adverse action notice.)

Regulation B states that lenders must notify applicants of an adverse action within 30 days after receiving a completed application or after taking adverse action regarding an existing account (for example, terminating a line of credit). A sample adverse action notice is shown in *Exhibit 3–2*. Lenders have up to 90 days to send a formal adverse action notice when the applicant has been made a counteroffer and has not notified the bank of his acceptance or refusal of the offer.

From a practical standpoint, the ECOA and Regulation B are concerned with the need to tell consumers why they failed to qualify for a loan. Knowing the reasons for a loan denial allows the applicant to correct a problem or at least to better understand why he does not qualify. Indeed, this is an area where lenders have traditionally provided financial counseling to consumers. Rejected applicants are not always the friendliest people, but sometimes the lender can provide them with information that will help them qualify for credit in the future, thereby preserving their goodwill.

EXHIBIT 3–2
Sample Adverse Action Notice

Federal Reserve Board's Model Notice of Action Taken and Statement of Reasons

Statement of Credit Denial, Termination, or Change

[Date]

Applicant's Name: ______________________________

Applicant's Address: ______________________________

Description of Account, Transaction, or Requested Credit: ______________

Description of Action Taken: ______________________________

____

Part I—PRINCIPAL REASON(S) FOR CREDIT DENIAL, TERMINATION, OR OTHER ACTION TAKEN CONCERNING CREDIT. This section must be completed in all instances.

_____ Credit application incomplete

_____ Insufficient number of credit references provided

_____ Unacceptable type of credit references provided

_____ Unable to verify credit references

_____ Temporary or irregular employment

_____ Unable to verify employment

_____ Length of employment

_____ Income insufficient for amount of credit requested

_____ Excessive obligations in relation to income

_____ Unable to verify income

_____ Length of residence

_____ Temporary residence

_____ Unable to verify residence

_____ No credit file

_____ Limited credit experience

_____ Poor credit performance with us

_____ Delinquent past or present credit obligations with others

_____ Garnishment, attachment, foreclosure, repossession, collection action, or judgment

_____ Bankruptcy

_____ Value or type of collateral not sufficient

_____ Other, specify

Part II—DISCLOSURE OF USE OF INFORMATION OBTAINED FROM AN OUTSIDE SOURCE. This section should be completed if the credit decision was based in whole or in part on information that has been obtained from an outside source.

_____ Our credit decision was based in whole or in part on information obtained in a report from the consumer reporting agency listed below. You have a right under the Fair Credit Reporting Act to know the information contained in your credit file at the consumer reporting agency. The reporting agency played no part in our decision and is unable to supply specific reasons why we have denied credit to you.

EXHIBIT 3–2 continued

Name: ____

Address: ____

Telephone number: ____

_____ Our credit decision was based in whole or in part on information obtained from an outside source other than a consumer reporting agency. Under the Fair Credit Reporting Act, you have the right to make a written request, no later than 60 days after you receive this notice, for disclosure of the nature of the information.

If you have any questions regarding this notice, you should contact:

Creditor's name: ____

Creditor's address: ____

Creditor's telephone number: ____

NOTICE: The federal Equal Credit Opportunity Act prohibits creditors from discriminating against credit applicants on the basis of race, color, religion, national origin, sex, marital status, age (provided the applicant has the capacity to enter into a binding contract); because all or part of the applicant's income derives from any public assistance program; or because the applicant has in good faith exercised any right under the Consumer Credit Protection Act. The federal agency that administers compliance with this law concerning this creditor is (name and address as specified by the appropriate agency).

Violations

ECOA violations can be extremely costly to the bank since the act provides for civil penalties and class action suits. A successful class action suit can cost the bank $500,000, or one percent of its net worth, whichever is less.

Truth in Lending Act

The Truth in Lending Act, enacted in 1968, was the first in a series of consumer credit protection laws. This act is implemented by *Regulation Z.* It was changed significantly in 1982 when Congress passed the *Truth in Lending Simplification and Reform Act*. The revisions were a response to the deregulation movement of the early 1980s and were passed in order to correct some of the complexities of the earlier law.

The Truth in Lending Act is intended to protect consumers involved in a *credit transaction* (one that is primarily for personal, family, or household use in amounts less than $25,000) by requiring uniform and detailed credit disclosures. Primary emphasis is placed on disclosures that allow consumers to determine the exact cost associated with a credit transaction and to compare rates and other credit costs in order to make informed decisions. The Truth in Lending Simplification and Reform Act sought not only to preserve the key disclosure criteria, but also to allow lenders a little more flexibility in the way in which the data are presented in loan documents.

Annual Percentage Rate

The Truth in Lending Act requires that all lenders disclose the effective rate of interest on a loan in one standard manner. Rates must be quoted as an *annual percentage rate* (APR) using formulas contained in Regulation Z. The APR represents the cost of a loan, including the finance charge and any other mandatory charges.

Finance Charges

The *finance charge* is defined as the dollar amount that the credit will cost the consumer. This item, along with the annual percentage rate, is regarded as essential for the consumer who wishes to compare the costs of different financing arrangements. One of the main things the finance charge reflects is how much will be paid in interest over the full term of the loan. For example, a $3,000 loan for 36 months at an annual percentage rate of 15 percent will incur interest charges of $744. Reducing the term to 24 months reduces the interest to $491.04, a reduction of $252.96.

Lenders must disclose the APR and finance charges, along with the amount financed and total of payments, in a section known as the *"federal box"* (see *Exhibit 3–3*). These disclosures must be more conspicuous than other disclosures since they are the primary factors that the borrower can use to compare credit costs.

Closed-End Loan Disclosures

Truth in Lending disclosures must be made before a closed-end loan is consummated. *Consummation* is defined as the time when the consumer becomes contractually liable on a credit transaction. In addition to the disclosures shown in the federal box, Regulation Z requires that the consumer have the option of receiving a detailed explanation of the items that make up the *amount financed,* which is the amount of money loaned to the consumer and subject to a finance charge. *Exhibit 3–4* shows a sample itemization of the amount financed.

EXHIBIT 3–3
Federal Box Disclosures

DISCLOSURE STATEMENT

CREDITOR
Originating Office

Preparation Date:
Borrower(s)

Loan Type:

ANNUAL PERCENTAGE RATE	FINANCE CHARGE	AMOUNT FINANCED	TOTAL OF PAYMENTS
The cost of your credit as a yearly rate	The dollar amount the credit will cost you	The amount of credit provided to you or on your behalf	The amount you will have paid after you have made all payments as scheduled
%	$	$	$

Your payment schedule will be:

Number of Payments	Amount of Payments Varying From	To	Payments are due monthly beginning

Security: You are giving a security interest in:
☐ the property being purchased
☐ ______________________________

Collateral securing other loans with us may also secure this loan

Filing Fees: $______________

Insurance: You may obtain property insurance from anyone you want that is acceptable to the creditor.

Late Charge: If a payment is late, you will be charged __________% of the payment.

Assumption: Someone buying your house may, subject to conditions, be allowed to assume your loan on the original terms.

Prepayment: If you pay off early you ☐ will not have to pay a penalty ☐ may have to pay a penalty.
If you pay off early you ☐ will not be entitled to a refund of part of the finance charge ☐ may be entitled to a refund of part of the finance charge

Demand Feature: ☐ If checked, this obligation has a demand feature

Variable Rate:

See your loan documents for any additional information about nonpayment, default, prepayment penalties and refunds, and required repayment in full before the scheduled date, and other matters pertaining to this credit transaction.

☐ If checked, a RESPA Good Faith Estimate has been provided.
☐ If checked, an Itemization of Amount Financed is provided on a separate form.

The undersigned acknowledge receipt of a copy of this disclosure:

______________________ ________ ______________________ ________
Borrower Date Borrower Date

DATE MAILED, IF APPLICABLE ______________ BY ______________________

MCP - 0406 (6/85) ORIGINAL TO BORROWER

EXHIBIT 3–4
Sample Itemization of Amount Financed

Itemization of the Amount Financed of $____________
$____________ Amount given to you directly
$____________ Amount paid on your account with the bank

Amount paid to others on your behalf
$____________ To (public officials, credit bureau, appraiser, and/or insurance company)
$____________ To (name of other creditor)
$____________ To (other)
$____________ Prepaid finance charge

Disclosures for variable rate loans must also conform to provisions in Regulation Z. Sample disclosures are shown in *Exhibit 3–5*. They specify the various changes that could occur on loans with variable rates.

The intent of the variable rate disclosures is to give consumers a clear understanding of the effect a change in rate will have on the loan. Because of the wide variety of variable rate programs, it is very difficult to develop one disclosure to cover all programs. For example, some programs fix the monthly payment at the time the loan is made, passing rate changes along to the consumer in the form of more or fewer monthly payments. Other variable rate programs pass on rate changes in the form of higher or lower monthly payments.

Truth in Lending also establishes specific requirements for advertising credit products. It requires sets of disclosures if certain triggering terms are used in the advertisement. These *triggering terms* include: (1) the amount or percentage of any down payment required; (2) the amount of any installment payment; (3) the dollar amount of any finance charge; (4) any reference to the rate; (5) the number of monthly payments required; or (6) the period of repayment. No advertisement can give any triggering term without providing all other required credit terms. These disclosures must meet the requirements for clarity and conspicuousness specified by Regulation Z.

Open-End Credit Disclosures

Since open-end accounts remain open for an indefinite period of time and allow future credit usage, different disclosure require-

EXHIBIT 3–5
Sample Variable Rate Disclosures

The annual percentage rate may increase during the term of this transaction if:
(the prime interest rate of (creditor) increases)
(the balance in your deposit account falls below $__________)
(you terminate your employment with (employer).)

The interest rate will not increase above __________%
The maximum interest rate increase at one time will be __________%
The rate will not increase more than once every (time period)

Any increase will take the form of:
(higher payment amounts)
(more payments of the same amount)
(a larger amount due at maturity)

If the interest rate increases by __________% in __________ (time period) your regular payments will increase to $__________

ments apply. The Truth in Lending Act requires that disclosures must be made when the account is opened and periodically during the life of the account.

The initial disclosures must be made before the first transaction. This is a flexible provision that allows banks to use a wide variety of marketing approaches without being overburdened with the need to make lengthy disclosures. The consumer must also be provided with all necessary disclosures before ever using the account. If he does not like the information in the disclosures, he may cancel before incurring any expense. The required open-end disclosures include—

- a statement of when finance charges begin to *accrue*, including an explanation of whether or not any period exists during which credit may be used and repaid without incurring a finance charge
- a disclosure of each *periodic rate* that may be used to compute the finance charge, the range of balances to which it is applicable, and the corresponding annual percentage rate; when different periodic rates apply to different types of transactions—some banks charge more for cash advances than for merchandise purchases on credit cards—the type of transaction to which the periodic rate applies shall also be disclosed
- an explanation of the method used to determine the balance on which the finance charge may be computed

- an explanation of how the amount of any finance charge will be determined, including a description of how any finance charge other than the periodic rate will be determined
- a statement of the consumer's rights and a notice of procedures to be used to resolve a billing error.

The disclosures must state any *security interest*—claims against the property purchased under the account or otherwise pledged as collateral—that the bank will have. For example, in the case of a home equity line account, the fact that the creditor is taking a security interest in the customer's residence must be disclosed.

Periodic disclosures are required for each billing cycle in which there is activity on the account or a remaining balance. These disclosures, generally contained on the customer's billing statement, are illustrated in *Exhibit 3–6*.

The *periodic statement* must contain—

- *account balance* at the beginning of the *billing cycle*
- an identification of each credit transaction and any credit to the account during the billing cycle
- each periodic rate and corresponding annual percentage rate and the balances to which each applied during the billing cycle
- the finance charge
- the minimum payment due and the date it is due
- the closing date of the billing cycle
- the outstanding balance as of the closing date.

Consumers entitled to a periodic statement must be notified at least 15 days prior to the effective date of any change in credit terms. This provision is frequently triggered by changes in state law or the bank's marketing program. For example, if the bank decided to raise its rates, customers would need to be notified 15 days in advance of the change. The customer must be given the option to pay off the balance on the account under the old terms or to accept the new terms. The customer may accept the new terms and continue to use the account, either by signing a new agreement or by using the account after the effective date of the change. If the customer uses the account after the new terms go into effect, he is generally subject to all of the new terms.

Special Credit Card Provisions

The Truth in Lending Act prevents banks from mailing *unsolicited credit cards* to consumers, a practice that flourished in

EXHIBIT 3–6
Sample Monthly Billing Statement

AMOUNT ENCLOSED

MAKE CHECK PAYABLE TO BANK

REVOLVING CREDIT ACCOUNT STATEMENT

ACCOUNT NUMBER

H

CLOSING DATE	PAYMENT DUE DATE
02/15/85	03/10/85
MINIMUM PAYMENT DUE	NEW BALANCE
$54.87	$1,848.00

PLEASE RETURN THIS PORTION OF THE STATEMENT WITH PAYMENT.

PERSONAL LINE:

FINANCE CHARGE CALCULATION

FINANCE CHARGE		AVERAGE DAILY LOAN BALANCE		DAILY PERIODIC RATE		NO. OF DAYS	**ANNUAL PERCENTAGE RATE**
$23.95	=	$1,819.33	X	.042465%	X	31	15.500%
NEXT BILLING PERIODS RATE				.040410%			14.750%

POSTING DATE		REVOLVING CREDIT ACTIVITY 01/15/85 TO 02/15/85	DEBITS/ADVANCES CREDITS/PAYMENTS
01/21	ADVANCE		93.24
01/23	ADVANCE		49.09
02/06	PAYMENT	THANK YOU	51.70-

SUMMARY

ACTIVITY	PREVIOUS BALANCE	PAYMENTS CREDITS	ADVANCES DEBITS	FINANCE CHARGE	NEW BALANCE
LOAN ADVANCES	1,713.33	31.61	142.33	.00	1,824.05
FINANCE CHARGE	20.09	20.09	.00	23.95	23.95
OTHER CHARGES	.00	.00	.00	.00	.00
TOTALS	1,733.42	51.70	142.33	23.95	1,848.00

PRINCIPAL PAYMENT	CURRENT CHARGES			OTHER/PREVIOUS UNPAID PAYMENTS	MINIMUM PAYMENT DUE
	INTEREST	INSURANCE	LATE CHARGES		
30.92	23.95	.00	.00	.00	54.87

ACCOUNT NUMBER	CREDIT LIMIT	AVAILABLE CREDIT	CLOSING DATE	PAGE
	2,000	175	02/15/85	1 OF 1

NOTICE: SEE REVERSE SIDE FOR IMPORTANT INFORMATION

the late 1960s. The act also states that a customer must sign a specific request form before an account can be opened.

Credit cardholders may be held liable for up to $50 of any *unauthorized transaction* if the bank advises the consumer of this liability and provides him with a telephone number and/or address to be contacted in the event of loss, theft, or other unauthorized use.

Rescission Rights

The provisions of the Truth in Lending Act apply to all loans in which the lender takes a security interest in the borrower's primary residence. A *primary residence* can be a mobile home, boat, trailer, or traditional housing, but the term does not include vacation and second homes.

Each borrower who owns and lives in the residence securing the loan must be given the required disclosures. The right to *rescind*—cancel—the loan lasts until midnight of the third business day following consummation. Any of the borrowers eligible to rescind may rescind the transaction by notifying the lender that they are exercising that option. This provision is designed to give consumers the opportunity to examine all of the disclosures in greater detail before becoming legally obligated on the loan.

One effect of the right to rescind is to delay the funds disbursement until the rescission period has elapsed. If any party to the loan executes his right to rescind, the entire contract is void. The bank must cancel the transaction and is not entitled to receive any finance charges on the loan.

The consumer may waive the right to rescind only under the following conditions:

- the consumer determines that the extension of credit is needed to meet a bona fide financial emergency, *and*
- the consumer provides a signed and dated *statement of waiver* or modification explaining the nature of the emergency.

Fair Credit Reporting Act

The Fair Credit Reporting Act (FCRA) is Title VI of the Consumer Credit Protection Act. Effective since 1971, the FCRA is directed primarily at *credit reporting agencies*—firms that supply credit information to third parties like banks and other lending institutions.

The FCRA has four primary objectives:

- to establish acceptable purposes for which a consumer credit report may be obtained
- to define consumers' rights regarding credit reports, with particular emphasis on giving consumers access to their reports and a procedure for correcting inaccurate information
- to establish requirements for handling any adverse credit decision that resulted in whole or in part from information contained in a credit report
- to define the responsibilities of a credit reporting agency.

A *consumer credit report* is defined as information on an individual's handling of his credit accounts. The information is gathered by a credit reporting agency and passed to third parties with a legitimate business need for the information. When a bank reports factual information to another bank or to a credit reporting agency regarding its experience with its own customers, it is not covered under the definition. If the bank passes along information regarding the customer's accounts with another bank, it would then be in the business of supplying consumer reports, according to the FCRA's definition.

Creditors may obtain a credit report from a credit reporting agency only when they have received a bona fide application for credit, have an open loan account with the consumer, or are legitimately considering offering credit. A report may be obtained on all the individuals who are applying for a loan. Randomly obtaining credit reports, though, just to check on friends, adversaries, neighbors, relatives, and fellow employees is prohibited. Such uses of credit reports violate the right of privacy guaranteed to all consumers.

The FCRA does not prohibit banks from using prescreening programs to market credit products. *Prescreening* is a process in which the bank matches a list of names against a credit bureau file to identify consumers who meet certain predetermined credit characteristics. As a result of the prescreening process, the requesting bank receives a list from the credit reporting agency of the names of potential customers who meet the bank's qualification criteria. The bank does not see the individual credit reports for these consumers, though, so the practice does not fall within the scope of the FCRA.

If the bank obtains an actual credit report and the report contributes to an adverse action, it must disclose the source and nature of the adverse information to the consumer. This information must be communicated to the consumer within 30 days from the date of the application.

Consumers have the right to see their credit bureau file and to have corrected any erroneous information. Credit reporting agencies may charge for this service.

Community Reinvestment Act

The Community Reinvestment Act (CRA) was passed in 1977 as Title VIII of the *Housing and Community Development Act*. While it has no direct effect on individual loan decisions, it does affect the bank's overall loan strategy and lending policies.

CRA is designed to encourage regulated lending institutions to make available enough funds to meet the full and legitimate credit needs of all communities, and all segments of those communities, within their market areas. Emphasis is placed upon serving low- and moderate-income areas.

The CRA requires the bank's board of directors to develop a written plan outlining objectives and strategies for meeting the credit needs of its communities. The bank is also required to take steps to inform the public of its general plans and performance in areas covered by CRA, and to invite the public to review relevant bank documents for comment.

The clout in the CRA consists of the ability of supervisory agencies to deny the establishment of new branches or to block acquisitions and mergers planned by banks found not to be in compliance with the requirements of the act. As a practical matter, the existence of CRA is a reminder that banks have a special relationship with their communities and that it is not acceptable to serve the credit desires of foreign countries or remote businesses while neglecting the borrowing needs of local businesses and individual customers.

Real Estate Transactions

The consumer movement of the 1960s and 1970s led to the passage of a number of laws directed at real estate lending. *Purchase-money, first mortgage lending* provided the focus for most of the laws, although second mortgage lending, nonpurchase-money first mortgages, and home improvement loans were also affected to some degree. In particular, eliminating the practice of *redlining*—refusing to make any loans in designated geographic areas—was given emphasis.

Real Estate Settlement Procedures Act

The Real Estate Settlement Procedures Act, known as RESPA, was enacted in 1974 and implemented through *Regulation X*. The act was substantially amended in 1975 in response to concerns expressed by the mortgage lending industry.

RESPA requires that mortgage lenders give disclosures to applicants similar to those required by the Truth in Lending Act. The required disclosures included a good faith estimate of *closing costs* and a special information booklet covering the various aspects of mortgage loans. These disclosures provide the consumer with a much better understanding of all of the costs associated with the impending mortgage loan transaction. In addition, RESPA gives borrowers some control over those costs by allowing them to select the title company that will be used.

RESPA applies to any loan secured by a residence intended for one to four families and that involves the *transfer of title*. Its coverage does not extend to nonpurchase-money first mortgages or to second mortgage and equity line accounts.

The act places some restrictions on the amount of money mortgage lenders can require in an *escrow account*. It also prohibits *kickbacks* and *fee-splitting*—the practice of paying people for referring potential loan customers—on covered transactions. According to the provision, no person can give or accept any fee or kickback for referring business to or from a specific person incidental to the transaction. For example, an attorney may not offer to pay a lender for business referred to him for services such as title checks.

Fair Housing Act

The *Fair Housing Act* was passed as Title VIII of the *Civil Rights Act* of 1968. It prohibits discrimination in the sale or rental of housing, the financing of housing, and the provision of brokerage services.

In framing the Fair Housing Act, Congress was concerned about two practices that were prevalent at the time: *blockbusting* or *steering,* which involves directing groups of consumers into specific neighborhoods and away from others; and discrimination in providing real estate loans to protected groups. Discrimination took the form of—

- refusing to sell or rent a dwelling to members of certain groups
- discrimination in the terms or conditions of sale or rent
- falsely informing a person a dwelling was not available
- denying a loan for purchase, construction, or repair of a dwelling.

The Fair Housing Act affects consumer credit lenders inasmuch as they extend loans for home improvements and home maintenance. Lenders covered by the Fair Housing Act are required to display the *Equal Housing Lender poster* and to submit reports to regulators regarding their real estate loans. They must maintain a log of all covered applications and provide required data to regulatory agencies as requested. Those agencies monitor the portfolios of banks under their jurisdiction to ensure they are not discriminating or engaging in the practice of redlining.

Home Mortgage Disclosure Act

The *Home Mortgage Disclosure Act* (HMDA) was adopted in 1975 and implemented by *Regulation C.* Revisions were implemented in 1980.

The HMDA is strictly a disclosure law. It requires banks to report the geographic area where real estate loans have been made. This information is then used by regulators to evaluate a bank's compliance with the Community Reinvestment Act and to evaluate whether or not the bank is engaging in discriminatory lending practices. Information is furnished to regulators showing the number of real estate related loans—mortgages, second mortgages, equity lines, and home improvement loans—made by census tract. If, from the data, it is evident that certain areas are not being served by the bank, redlining or other unacceptable practices may be present. The HMDA helps detect and, therefore, control illegal mortgage lending practices.

Flood Disaster Protection Act

The Flood Disaster Protection Act, passed in 1973, established the National Flood Insurance Program. The purpose of the program is to provide reasonably priced flood insurance to persons residing in flood-prone areas. Enactment followed a particularly difficult year in which hurricanes and other natural disasters destroyed millions of dollars' worth of homes.

The act requires banks to determine whether or not a property is located in a flood hazard zone before making a loan secured by real estate or a mobile home. If the home is in a flood zone, the bank must disclose this fact to the consumer and, if the property is in a community participating in the National Flood Insurance Program, it must require that the consumer obtain federal flood insurance.

Consumer Credit Compliance Program

The rash of consumer credit regulation that occurred from the late 1960s through the early 1980s made it necessary for banks to develop an ongoing *compliance program*. The complexity of many of the regulations, combined with the ongoing requirements for reporting and record retention, imposed significant additional costs and administrative burdens on all financial institutions.

Compliance programs are designed to achieve a variety of purposes. These include—

- improving customer service by having procedures in place to resolve inquiries and problems in an efficient manner
- increasing bank efficiency by standardizing some tasks and providing clear direction regarding actions to be taken
- ensuring compliance with all applicable regulations
- avoiding costly penalties and litigation resulting from regulatory violations.

Responsibility for compliance begins with the bank's board of directors and extends to tellers and customer service representatives. Without a commitment from all employees, the bank may be exposed to compliance problems.

Some of the key steps involved in developing and maintaining a compliance program are to document the bank's policies, develop formal procedural manuals, train lenders and support personnel in the requirements of the law, and conduct internal audits. The importance of well-documented policies and procedures and an effective compliance program is spelled out clearly in the following excerpt from Regulation B:

> Failure of compliance. A failure to comply with this section shall not constitute a violation when caused by an inadvertent error; provided that, on discovering the error, the creditor corrects it as soon as possible and commences compliance with the requirements of this section.

The compliance program helps to ensure that the bank remains in compliance by subjecting it to periodic formal review.

If an inadvertent error or violation is detected, it can be corrected before major problems develop.

Summary

Consumer lending is a highly regulated business. Lenders are subject to a variety of federal and state laws governing trade practices, provisions in credit contracts, and the distribution of credit. Compliance with these laws is monitored and enforced by a variety of regulatory agencies, and the judicial branch of government is instrumental in interpreting the law.

There has been a series of federal laws directed at the consumer credit market since 1968. These laws have focused primarily upon the need to provide consumers with uniform disclosure of key credit features and to ensure that credit is provided on an equal basis to all qualified consumers. These laws have resulted in significant changes in the policies, procedures, and practices within the industry.

Questions for Review and Discussion

1. Give some examples of practices that led to the development of consumer credit laws and regulations.

2. What types of consumer loan matters do state laws generally regulate?

3. Name the nine bases on which a provider of credit may not discriminate under the Equal Credit Opportunity Act.

4. How are federal laws implemented and enforced? Give some examples.

5. A creditor may not discriminate on the basis of age. What is the practical impact of this law when evaluating an application from a 19-year-old? From a person approaching retirement?

6. What is the basic intent of the Truth in Lending Act?

7. A credit card account stays open for an indefinite period, so when must disclosures be made? How does the bank know what to disclose and when?

8. Does your bank have a formal consumer credit compliance program? Take a look at your bank's compliance policy statement or talk to the compliance officer and find out the organization and scope of the program. Write a brief summary of your findings.

PART II
CONSUMER CREDIT PRODUCTS AND SERVICES

The universe of consumer credit products and services offered by commercial banks is always expanding. But it was until only recently that the word "universe" could have been applied at all. Once limiting themselves to a small inventory of loan products, banks looked to other areas like commercial lending as a focus for bringing in profits. That has all changed now, and consumer credit operations have taken a prominent place in the family of financial services offered by modern commercial banks.

This part of *Consumer Lending* introduces you to the many types of consumer credit products and services being marketed today. Consumer installment loans are divisible into two broad product groupings: closed-end and open-end loans. *Closed-end loans,* as the name implies, have a term that ends at a stated time, when the principal and interest payments agreed upon have been made in full. Closed-end loans are further divisible into direct loans and indirect loans. A *direct loan* is a loan transaction in which the consumer deals directly with the bank; an *indirect loan,* on the other hand, involves a third party, like an automobile dealer, who acts as an arranger of credit between the borrower and the bank. The other broad product grouping is *open-end loans,* sometimes known as revolving credit. This kind of credit, once approved, remains available to the borrower up to a certain limit for as long as he makes regular, periodic payments. Thus, the term of an open-end credit account is indefinite.

Within these broad groupings are numerous individual products and services, including credit-related products like leasing and credit insurance. Besides imparting specific knowledge about their features and operation, this part gives you an appreciation of the vastness and diversity of the universe of consumer credit products.

4 Closed-End Loans

Closed-end loans have historically been the dominant form of consumer credit. Loans in this category accounted for nearly 70 percent of the dollars outstanding on consumer installment credit accounts at the end of 1985. At that time, Federal Reserve estimates show that the total dollar outstandings in closed-end loans reached $426.8 billion. Banks held the largest share of this market, but other financial institutions, such as finance companies, credit unions, and savings institutions held large closed-end loan portfolios.

In this chapter, we will discuss the characteristics common to all closed-end loans. We will then examine different unsecured and secured loans and discuss the implications that collateral has on the lending process. Finally, we will focus on the characteristics of direct loan products and the advantages and disadvantages these loans offer consumers and lenders.

Characteristics of Closed-End Loans

Closed-end loans are most easily recognized by the fact that they have a predetermined term. Loans run for 24, 36, 60, and even up to 240 months. Competitive conditions and the ever-increasing price of items consumers purchase on credit have led to a seemingly endless stretching of maturities. It should be noted that one of the central reasons for extending maturities is to keep monthly payments at a level affordable and attractive to consumers, and the amount of monthly payments is a primary consideration for consumers shopping for a loan.

Other contract provisions for closed-end loans are also set for the life of the loan. Closed-end loans have predetermined monthly payment schedules and specific collateral arrangements. The fixed nature of a closed-end loan contract allows the consumer to plan his budget, knowing exactly what amount must be set aside for loan payments, when the payments are due, and how long the loan will be open.

Another characteristic of closed-end loans is that they are directly related to a specific purpose or borrowing need, for example, purchasing a car, consolidating bills, or making home improvements. The close association between the loan request and a specific need injects the *purpose* of the loan as a variable often evaluated in the decision-making process. Lenders are in a position to evaluate whether or not the loan purpose is acceptable. Many lenders want to have some control in this area, while others are content to give consumers almost complete control over the purposes for which they wish to borrow.

Types of Closed-End Loans

A common approach to grouping loans is based upon the purpose for the loan, examples of which are shown in *Exhibit 4–1*. This approach is helpful in monitoring diversification within the portfolio and the performance of specific loan types.

Another approach to grouping loans is based upon the type of collateral securing the loan and the behavior pattern of the collateral's value over the loan term. For example, the value of a car *depreciates* from the moment the car is sold. Grouping loans by type of collateral is helpful in understanding some of the elements of risk on a loan and the lending policies used by the bank.

The mix of closed-end loans varies widely from bank to bank. However, *Exhibit 4–1* points out some of the key characteristics and trends for each loan type. Personal, unsecured loans and student loans often account for a high percentage of the number of loans in the portfolio but a lower percentage of dollar outstandings. This is because the loans are typically for smaller amounts. On the other hand, second mortgage, aircraft, and mobile home loans are larger, accounting for a relatively high percentage of the dollar outstandings and a lower percentage of the number of loans.

EXHIBIT 4–1
The Portfolio Distribution of Closed-End Loan Outstandings by Type of Loan, 1983–1985

	1983			1984			1985		
	Percent Distribution			*Percent Distribution*			*Percent Distribution*		
Type of Loan	*Number*	*Dollar*	*Average Amount*	*Number*	*Dollar*	*Average Amount*	*Number*	*Dollar*	*Average Amount*
Personal—direct and indirect	20.8%	10.5%	$ 2,590	20.7%	10.3%	$ 2,762	18.8%	11.2%	$ 3,283
Automobile—direct	17.4	14.3	4,141	19.2	16.4	4,746	18.6	16.9	5,003
Automobile—indirect	28.8	29.9	5,331	29.8	33.8	6,290	32.3	36.5	6,246
Home Improvement, Own Plan—direct and indirect	5.0	6.0	6,268	4.7	5.0	5,892	4.7	4.8	5,719
Home Improvement, FHA Title I—direct and indirect	1.3	1.3	5,095	0.9	0.9	5,182	1.1	0.5	5,164
Mobile Home—direct	1.1	2.6	12,056	0.9	1.5	8,852	0.9	1.5	9,526
Mobile Home—indirect	1.8	4.8	14,079	1.9	4.6	13,349	1.6	3.8	13,297
Farm Equipment—direct and indirect	0.2	0.5	11,619	0.2	0.7	12,296	0.2	0.2	8,883
Recreational Vehicle—direct and indirect	3.0	3.8	6,622	2.5	4.5	10,095	2.0	2.9	9,047
Student (Federal or State Programs)	14.8	8.7	3,031	14.3	8.6	3,352	14.9	8.4	3,097
Installment, Small Business—direct and indirect	1.5	3.8	13,333	1.6	3.9	13,595	1.6	3.6	12,669
Aircraft—direct and indirect	0.1	0.9	54,118	0.1	0.3	28,576	0.1	0.3	31,936
Second Mortgage—direct and indirect	4.2	12.9	15,784	3.2	9.5	16,302	3.2	9.4	16,271
Total Installment Loan Outstandings[1]			$ 5,292			$ 5,546			$ 5,778

1. Excluding floorplan and open-end credit.

SOURCE: American Bankers Association, 1986 Retail Bank Credit Report

Unsecured Loans

This category of loans is comprised of the many loans made to consumers in which the lender relies on the individual borrower to honor his debt obligation without the requirement for collateral. Many banks follow very conservative practices regarding unsecured loans, also known as *personal loans.* Other banks take a much more aggressive posture and have learned how to effectively manage the unsecured part of their loan portfolios.

Unsecured lending is based on trust in the honesty and integrity of the consumer. The borrower pledges to repay the loan under the terms set forth in the loan agreement. In the event the borrower encounters problems that culminate in *default* or *charge-off*, the bank must work with the customer rather than take action against collateral to resolve the problem.

Comaker Loans

A special category of loans, which may be unsecured or secured, are those involving comakers. A *comaker* is someone who signs the loan documents along with the applicant in order to strengthen the loan request and induce the bank to make the loan. Comakers receive no direct benefit from the loan; that is, they do not receive any of the funds from the loan proceeds, nor do they acquire any ownership interest in collateral that may be purchased with the loan proceeds. The comakers' status may be contrasted to the status of co-applicants. A *co-applicant* is an equal party to the loan, sharing in the proceeds from the loan and typically receiving a share of ownership in goods purchased with the loan funds.

The fact that a comaker receives no benefit from the loan has significant implications for the decision-making process. Since the comaker is simply assuming an obligation, he may have a strong tendency not to accept responsibility for the loan when problems develop in collecting payments from the *primary borrower*. For this reason, banks tend to confine their comaker loans only to those situations in which they want to add some strength for an applicant who has very limited credit experience or limited stability due primarily to age. When they approve such loans, lenders prefer to have comakers who are closely associated with the applicant, such as parents, rather than casual acquaintances.

Home Improvement Loans

Unsecured loans are often made for the purpose of making improvements to the borrower's residence. It is normal practice for lenders to try to secure large home improvement requests with a *second mortgage, home equity line of credit*, or some other collateral. Smaller requests and requests from very strong customers may be unsecured.

Home improvement loans, in particular, are generally perceived to be sound loans since the funds will be used to improve the borrower's residence, which will, in turn, increase the value of his home. Banks often have special policies that recognize the favored status of home improvement loans over other types of unsecured loans. Maturities are often longer and rates lower than comparably sized personal and comaker loans.

Secured Loans

Collateral is customarily taken on many types of consumer loans to reduce the level of risk in a transaction. If the consumer encounters problems and is unable to repay the loan under its contractual terms, the lender may take possession of the collateral, subject to provisions in the *loan contract,* and sell it in an effort to satisfy the debt.

We will analyze the various types of secured loans by grouping them according to the behavior pattern of the collateral's value. The four basic behavior patterns are: *depreciating value, fluctuating value, stable value,* and *appreciating value.* Each group has unique considerations that should be addressed when setting the bank's lending policies and procedures.

Depreciating Value Collateral

Depreciating value collateral includes all loans secured by goods that decline in value from the moment they are sold. Goods in this group include automobiles, boats, trucks, airplanes, recreational vehicles, mobile homes, motorcycles, and equipment.

The illustration in *Exhibit 4–2* shows the relationship between the depreciating value of an item of collateral and the *balance* on a loan. The gap between the collateral value and the loan balance represents the area of credit risk on a secured loan. It is apparent from the graph that a credit problem early in the life of the loan can lead to a loss by the bank.

Individual units within each category of goods may decline in value at different rates. For example, a Chevrolet Citation may decline in value faster than a Ford LTD. This difference in the rate of depreciation is a factor affecting risk in the loan. Obviously, units that depreciate more rapidly represent greater credit risk. The rate of depreciation is also affected by factors such as market demand, unit condition, color, image, and intrinsic value.

An important consideration when securing a loan with depreciating value collateral is the determination of the item's

EXHIBIT 4–2
Depreciating Value Collateral: Credit Risk

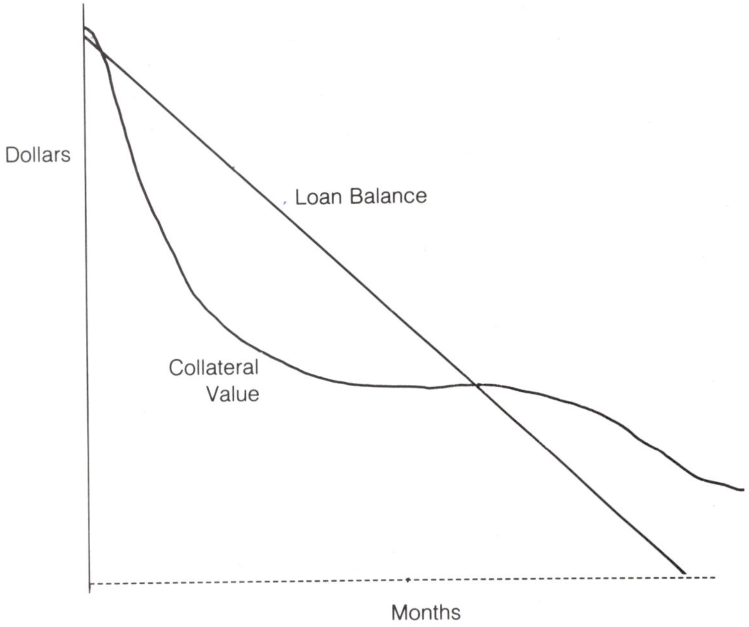

value at the time the loan is made. The value is usually determined by referring to *valuation guidebooks*. Automobile values may be obtained from *NADA* or *Black Book* publications, while new car values may be determined directly from dealer invoices or from services such as Automotive Invoice Service. Boat values can be obtained from *BUC Book* or, in some cases, from a marine survey. Values for mobile homes, recreational vehicles, motorcycles, and airplanes may also be obtained from similar publications. The valuation of goods is not a precise science, however, and the credit analyst should be aware of the limitations of each valuation source used. *Exhibit 4–3* shows sample pages from commonly used collateral valuation guides.

Fluctuating Value Collateral

The value of some forms of collateral rises and falls over time. These fluctuations increase collateral risk and make risk man-

EXHIBIT 4–3
Samples from Valuation Guides

42 **FORD 1986-85**

DOMESTIC CARS

Av'g. Trd-In	BODY TYPE	Model	Av'g. Loan	Av'g. Retail
1986 LTD CROWN VICTORIA-Continued				
225 Add	Brougham Roof		225	300
150 Add	2-Tone Paint		150	200
850 Deduct	W/out Air Cond		850	850
1986 THUNDERBIRD-AT-PS-AC				
THUNDERBIRD-V6				
8000	Coupe 2D	46	7200	9175
9200	Coupe 2D elan	46	8300	10500
THUNDERBIRD-V8				
8200	Coupe 2D	46	7400	9400
9400	Coupe 2D elan	46	8475	10725
THUNDERBIRD-4 Cyl.-AT/5 Spd.				
9100	Turbo Coupe 2D	46	8200	10400
400 Add	Power Sunroof		375	475
150 Add	AM/FM Stereo/Tp.		150	200
75 Add	Power Door Locks		75	100
100 Add	Power Windows (Std. elan & Turbo)		100	125
100 Add	Power Seats		100	125
75 Add	RearWindDefroster		75	100
75 Add	Cruise Control		75	100
75 Add	Tilt Strg. Wheel		75	100
100 Add	Wire Wheel Covers		100	125
200 Add	Leather Seats		200	250
100 Add	2-Tone (Std. Turbo)		100	125
650 Deduct	W/out Air Cond		650	650
1985 ESCORT/EXP-AT-PS-FWD				
ESCORT-4 Cyl.				
3250	H'back 2D	04	2925	4075
3350	H'back 4D	13	3025	4175
3450	H'back 2D L	04	3125	4275
3550	H'back 4D L	13	3200	4400
3700	Sta Wgn 4D L	09	3350	4550
3725	H'back 2D GL	05	3375	4575
3825	H'back 4D GL	14	3450	4700
3975	Sta Wgn 4D GL	10	3600	4850
3975	H'back 4D LX	15	3600	4850
4125	Sta Wgn 4D LX	11	3725	5000
4125	H'back 2D GT	07	3725	5000
4200	H'back 2D Turbo GT	07	3800	5075

Av'g. Trd-In	BODY TYPE	Model	Av'g. Loan	Av'g. Retail
50 Add	AlumWheels (StdTur)		50	75
125 Add	Sunroof		125	150
75 Add	AM/FM Stereo*		75	100
100 Add	AM/FMStereo/Tp**		100	125
50 Add	Power Door Locks		50	75
25 Add	Tilt Strg. Wheel		25	50
125 Add	Luxury GL Pkg.		125	150
75 Add	Squire Option		75	100
25 Add	Luggage Rack		25	50
75 Add	2-Tone Paint**		75	100
500 Deduct	4Cyl.DieselEng.		500	500
200 Deduct	Manual Trans.		200	200
100 Deduct	Convent. Steer.		100	100
	*Std. EXP Luxury			
	**Std. EXP Turbo			
1985 TEMPO-AT-PS-AC-FWD				
TEMPO L-4 Cyl.				
4200	Sedan 2D	18	3800	5075
4300	Sedan 4D	21	3875	5200
TEMPO GL-4 Cyl.				
4300	Sedan 2D	19	3875	5200
4400	Sedan 4D	22	3975	5300
TEMPO GLX-4 Cyl.				
4450	Sedan 2D	20	4025	5350
4550	Sedan 4D	23	4100	5475
75 Add	AM/FM Stereo*		75	100
100 Add	AM/FM Stereo/Tp.		100	125
50 Add	Power Windows		50	75
50 Add	Power Door Locks*		50	75
50 Add	Power Seats		50	75
50 Add	Cruise Control		50	75
25 Add	Tilt Strg. Wheel*		25	50
25 Add	RearWindDefroster		25	50
75 Add	2-Tone Paint		75	100
50 Add	Leather Seats		50	75
250 Add	Luxury GL Pkg.		225	325
200 Add	Sport GL Pkg.		200	250
300 Add	Luxury GLX Pkg.		275	375
500 Deduct	4Cyl.DieselEng.		500	500
325 Deduct	Manual Trans.		325	325

Sample Boat Valuation Guide

BERIRAM YACHT
DIV OF WHITTAKER CORP
3663 NW 21 STREET
MIAMI FL 33142

COAST GUARD MFG ID BER

LOA FT	LOA IN	NAME AND/OR MODEL	TOP RIG	BOAT TYPE	HULL MTL	HULL TP	ENGINE TP	ENGINE # HP	ENGINE MFG	ENGINE MODEL	BEAM FT	BEAM IN	DRAFT FT	DRAFT IN	LIST PRICE
26	2	26 II SPORT CONV	OP	SPTCR	FBG	DV	OB				10		3		32350
26	2	26 II SPORT CONV	OP	SPTCR	FBG	DV	IB	T185	CRUS		10		2	4	43085
28	6	BAHIA-MAR	OP	SDN	FBG	DV	IB	T230	MERC	MIE 230	11		2	8	67655
28	6	BAHIA-MAR	OP	SDN	FBG	DV	IB	T260	MERC	MIE 260	11		2	8	69310
28	6	FLYBRIDGE CRUISER	FB	SDN	FBG	DV	IB	T230	MERC	MIE 230	11		2	8	72670
30	7	EXPRESS CRUISER	OP	EXP	FBG	DV	IB	T350	CRUS	350	11	4	3		93920
30	7	EXPRESS CRUISER	OP	EXP	FBG	DV	IB	T215D	GM	8.2T	11	4	3		119895
30	7	FLYBRIDGE CRUISER	FB	SDN	FBG	DV	IB	T350	CRUS	350	11	4	3		95150
30	7	FLYBRIDGE CRUISER	FB	SDN	FBG	DV	IB	T215D	GM	8.2T	11	4	3		120485
33		FLYBRIDGE CRUISER	FB	SDN	FBG	DV	IB	T350	CRUS	350	12	6	3		115310
33		FLYBRIDGE CRUISER	FB	SDN	FBG	DV	IB	T270D	CUM	VT-555-M	12	6	3		160435
33		FLYBRIDGE CRUISER	FB	SDN	FBG	DV	IB	T270D	CAT	3208T	12	6	3		164015
33		SPORT FISHERMAN	FB	SDNSF	FBG	DV	IB	T350	CRUS	350	12	6	3		112595
33		SPORT FISHERMAN	FB	SDNSF	FBG	DV	IB	T270D	CUM	VT-555-M	12	6	3		154555
33		SPORT FISHERMAN	FB	SDNSF	FBG	DV	IB	T270D	CAT	3208T	12	6	3		159715
35	4	CONVERTIBLE 35 II	FB	CNV	FBG	DV	IB	T350	CRUS	350	13	3	3	2	136550
35	4	CONVERTIBLE 35 II	FB	CNV	FBG	DV	IB	T215D	CUM	V-555-M	13	3	3	2	174750
35	4	CONVERTIBLE 35 II	FB	CNV	FBG	DV	IB	T300D	CAT	3208T	13	3	3	2	186630
38	5	CONVERTIBLE 38 III	FB	CNV	FBG	DV	IB	T355D	CAT	3208TA	13	3	4	1	232845
38	5	CONVERTIBLE 38 III	FB	CNV	FBG	DV	IB	T425D	CUM	VT-903-M	13	3	4	2	254330

SOURCE: *NADA Used Car Guide*, May 1987
SOURCE: 1985 *BUC Book*—New Boats (Fall Edition)

agement difficult. Collateral in this category includes corporate *stocks, bonds,* and other types of *securities.* The value of securities changes constantly, making careful analysis and control essential.

Many banks only handle securities as collateral on *demand loans,* which allow the bank to call the balance due in full at any time. This gives the bank the ability to protect itself from a decline in the value of the securities. Under the usual arrangement, if a stock declines in value, the bank can ask the customer to provide more stock to secure the loan, or it can demand that the loan be paid off.

To aid in evaluating fluctuating value collateral, one can determine the value of actively traded stocks and bonds from data published in most newspapers. The value of privately held securities, those not traded in public markets, is more difficult to determine.

Loans made for the purchase of securities must comply with the Federal Reserve's *Regulation U,* which states that the loan advance may not exceed 50 percent of the purchase price of the stocks or bonds securing the loan. Loans secured by stocks or bonds already held by the consumer, while not subject to the margin requirements, should certainly provide for fluctuations in the value of the collateral during the course of the loan.

Unless the bank includes a *call provision* in its loan documents, the bank is subject to collateral risk should the value of the stocks or bonds deteriorate during the term of the loan. This could create a risk exposure such as that shown in *Exhibit 4-4.*

To manage the risk, the bank must clearly define which types of securities, if any, it is willing to accept as collateral for closed-end loans. Stocks and bonds that are actively traded on large secondary markets (for example, the New York Stock Exchange) are somewhat safer than securities that do not have well-established markets. However, the risk associated with any individual security varies greatly and must be evaluated carefully at the time the loan request is received.

Stable Value Collateral

Taking a security interest in stable value collateral significantly reduces the level of risk on a loan. Collateral in this category includes savings accounts, certificates of deposit, and *cash value life insurance.* The value may be determined directly from the account record, passbook account, or insurance policy. Loans

EXHIBIT 4–4
Fluctuating Value Collateral: Credit Risk

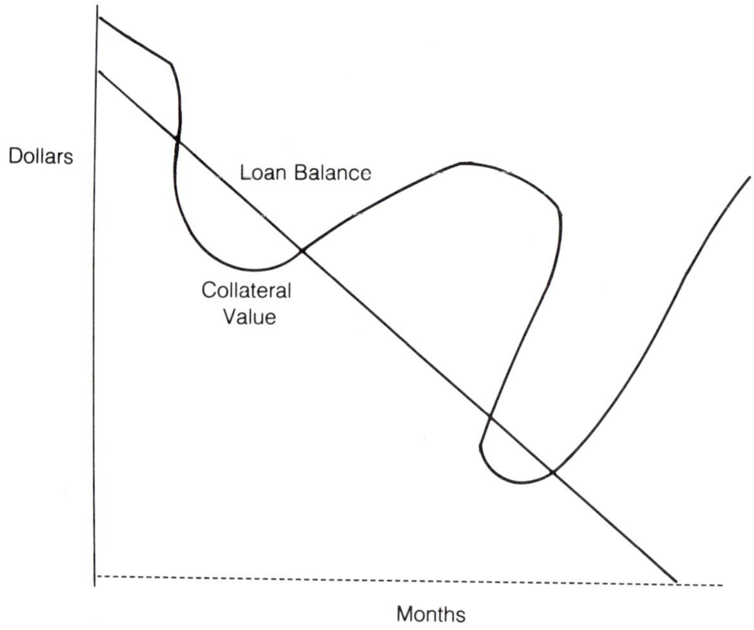

secured by this form of collateral are generally regarded as loss-free, although lenders can attest to the fact that losses do sometimes occur due to operational errors. For example, if the *hold* imposed on a savings account because it is serving as collateral is accidentally released, a customer may take advantage of the opportunity to remove all of the funds from the account, leaving the bank in an unsecured position.

Barring operational errors, this category of loans has a very low risk, a fact that helps explain why loans secured by stable value collateral generally carry the lowest interest rates of all types of consumer loans. *Exhibit 4–5* shows the credit risk on loans secured by stable value collateral.

Appreciating Value Collateral

Some collateral actually appreciates—increases—in value over time. This category of secured loans is usually confined to real

EXHIBIT 4–5
Stable Value Collateral: Credit Risk

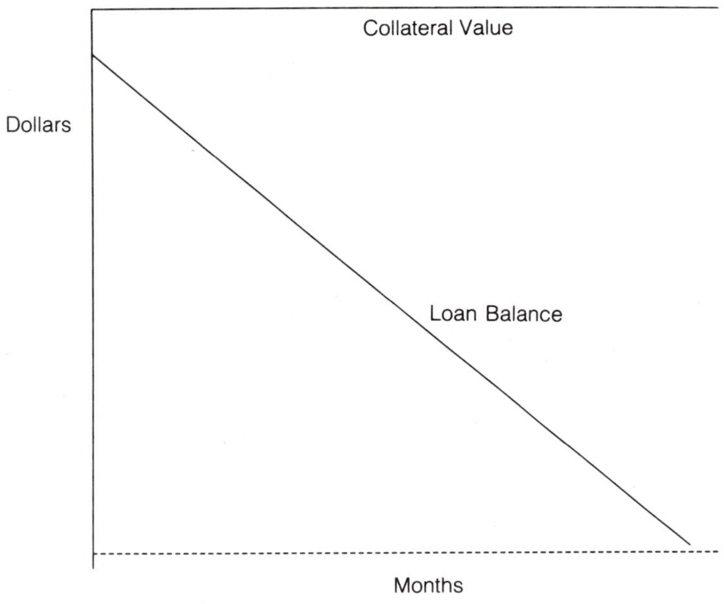

estate collateral. Real estate, particularly an individual's residence, provides the best potential source for increasing the amount of credit a consumer can obtain. The build-up of *equity*, due to rising home values, is the source of most of the *net worth* reflected on the average consumer's *balance sheet*.

The value of appreciating value collateral is usually obtained from an appraisal performed by a qualified appraiser. In theory, loans made using appreciating value collateral would exhibit the relationship to the loan balance illustrated in *Exhibit 4–6*.

There are no guarantees that all real estate will appreciate in value. In fact, some properties go down in value due to neglect, adverse changes in the surrounding community, and natural or man-made disasters. Further, loan collectors can tell you that homes and other collateral sold under quick sale situations—auctions and foreclosures—do not usually bring their full value. These facts demonstrate that even loans secured by appreciating value collateral are not completely risk-free.

EXHIBIT 4–6
Appreciating Value Collateral: Credit Risk

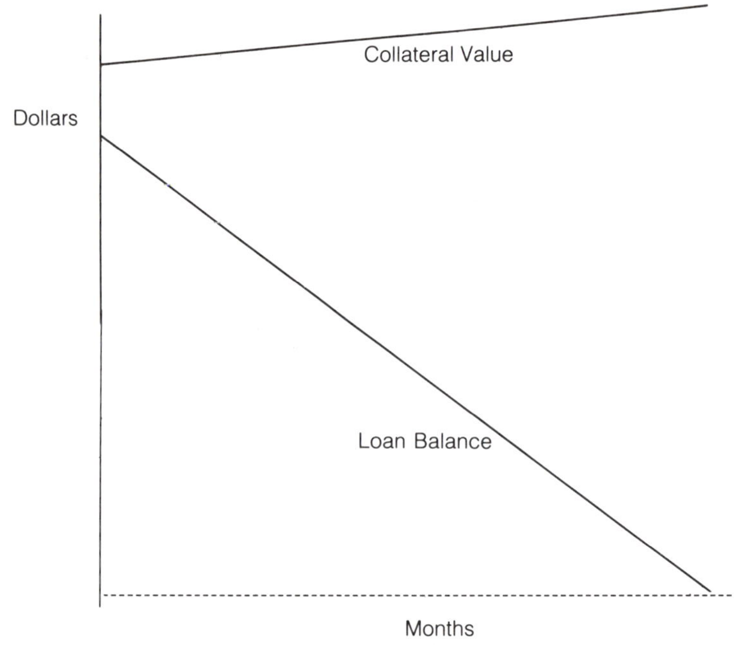

Guaranteed Loan Programs

Numerous governmental and quasi-governmental organizations offer specialized loan programs to meet the borrowing needs of certain groups. The level of risk varies among the programs, as do the specific program requirements.

Guaranteed student loans designed to help students finance a college education are the most common type of guaranteed loans handled by consumer credit departments. One of the best known is the Department of Education's Guaranteed Student Loan (GSL) Program. Loans are guaranteed up to established dollar limits as long as the bank fully complies with the program's operational requirements. GSLs also enjoy a very active secondary market made up of banks and other institutions that are willing to buy loans from the originating lender. This allows banks to pursue a wide variety of strategies with regard to student loans, and it provides a high degree of portfolio liquidity.

Other *guaranteed loans* often handled by a bank's consumer credit department include programs offered by state and local governments, Farmers Home Administration and Department of Housing and Urban Development programs, and loans offered through the Small Business Administration. Some of these programs provide for full protection against loan losses, while others, such as the SBA loan program, provide partial guarantees.

In most cases, lenders do not compromise their credit requirements for guaranteed loans since the potential for collection problems and losses still may exist. And, while they do not generally offer high yields for the bank, making guaranteed loans plays an important part in fulfilling the bank's obligation to serve the legitimate borrowing needs of its community. In particular, participation in programs that benefit the community and serve the needs of the less fortunate help a bank meet its obligations under the Community Reinvestment Act.

Direct Loans

Direct loans—one of the general categories of closed-end loans—provide the bank with the greatest amount of control over the lending process. The consumer deals directly with bank personnel at all stages of the process, and the resulting personal contact presents many opportunities and challenges for those involved.

A convenient location and a close customer-bank relationship are very important factors in developing a successful direct loan program since most direct loans are *closed* in the bank's offices. This reliance on the bank's facilities has obvious implications regarding the market reached with direct loans and the manner in which these loans are marketed. It is difficult to get consumers to drive past competitors to obtain a direct loan from the bank unless the bank has something special to sell, such as lower rates, better services, or better loan products. The close relationship between branch location and the ability to attract direct loan customers at least partially explains the proliferation of bank branches between 1950 and 1980.

Direct lending, as already noted, involves the customer in direct personal contact with bank employees. Answering inquiries regarding credit products, taking applications, communicating the credit decision, *loan structuring* (tailoring the loan to provide the best possible loan for the customer), selling efforts, the loan closing, and consummating the loan, are typically handled on a one-on-one basis with the customer. This means that the bank must train and develop its personnel to be able to handle the loan functions in a customer-oriented, efficient manner.

The Bank's Perspective on Direct Loans

Direct lending offers financial institutions a number of advantages. The high level of control over the loan process, personal contact with the customer, and loan structuring and selling opportunities can be helpful in building a sound consumer credit portfolio.

The absence of third parties and the use of bank personnel at all stages of the lending process give the bank more control than it has for any other type of consumer credit. The quality of the application, the extent and quality of the credit investigation, the *loan decision*, and the loan structuring flexibility are controlled by the bank. The result of this higher level of control is normally better quality *loan decisions*, which, in turn, enhance profit opportunities and minimize credit losses. Nevertheless, as *Exhibit 4–7* shows, losses tend to be somewhat higher for some types of direct loans than for indirect loans (to be covered in Chapter 5). This can be partially explained by the fact that dealers often share some of the risk on indirect loans they originate, thereby reducing the bank's *loss exposure*. It may also reflect a tendency of some lenders to compromise *credit standards* when making direct loans to customers they know. The inevitable result is that some weak loans are made because of a personal relationship rather than on the basis of individual merits.

As previously noted, the opportunity to establish a personal relationship with the customer is an important benefit of direct lending. Many individual lenders build up a following of customers who are loyal, not necessarily to the bank, but to them. This relationship develops from providing high-quality service to people over a period of time, and it can be a very powerful tool in building a solid customer base.

Consumers tend to be more receptive to marketing efforts by individuals and organizations with whom they have already had a satisfactory experience and in whom they trust. If the bank

EXHIBIT 4–7
Installment Credit Dollar Losses, 1983–1985

	Percent Dollar Losses		Percent Dollar Losses		Percent Dollar Losses	
	Gross	*Net*	*Gross*	*Net*	*Gross*	*Net*
Type of Loan	*1983*		*1984*		*1985*	
Personal—direct and indirect	1.71%	1.27%	1.42%	.93%	1.36%	% .97
Automobile—direct	.64	.42	.40	.27	.54	.39
Automobile—indirect	.46	.32	.35	.21	.40	.29
Home Improvement, Own Plan—direct and indirect	.67	.36	.46	.31	.55	.43
Home Improvement, FHA Title I—direct and indirect	.35	.20	.48	.40	.25	.21
Mobile Home—direct	.92	.36	.63	.34	.78	.66
Mobile Home—indirect	.81	.29	.55	.38	.33	.25
Farm Equipment—direct and indirect	2.64	1.19	5.24	4.95	1.82	1.55
Recreational Vehicle—direct and indirect	.77	.49	.46	.27	.60	.45
Student (Federal or State Programs)	.13	.05	.20	.04	.05	.04
Installment, Small Business direct and indirect	1.31	.96	1.21	.70	1.34	1.14
Aircraft—direct and indirect	2.55	.83	2.08	1.71	2.20	1.92
Second Mortgage—direct and indirect	.23	.11	.21	.14	.39	.35
Other—direct and indirect	1.05	.63	.85	.58	.96	.72
Total Installment Loan Losses[1]	.60	.36	.44	.28	.53	.39

1. Excluding floorplan and open-end credit.

SOURCE: American Bankers Association, 1986 Retail Bank Credit Report

can offer high-quality personal service in its direct lending program, it may be able to enhance its total retail banking effort. Traditional direct lending is a natural fit with the concept of the *personal banker* being implemented by many banks today to serve their affluent clientele.

Direct loan applications also make it possible for the lender to recommend a variety of borrowing structures to the consumer. This ability is not possible at all with indirect loans, and it is significantly restricted in most forms of open-end credit. Once the application is taken, the lender may first wish to *qualify* the borrower for the specific loan requested, but he may then proceed with a full analysis of the applicant's financial needs and creditworthiness in order to recommend the best loan for the customer and the bank. This may involve recommending a different type of loan and a substantially different loan size and structure than those initially requested.

For example, suppose an applicant requests a small $1,000 loan to pay for college expenses. The lender might determine in the interview that this will be an ongoing need since the applicant's daughter is entering her freshman year. An analysis of the facts may lead the lender to recommend an equity line of credit account, rather than the $1,000 loan. The equity line account, where permitted by state law, allows the applicant not only to meet his immediate borrowing need but also to provide a flexible source of funds and repayment terms to meet future borrowing needs. This type of structuring provides numerous benefits to both the bank and the consumer. Moreover, it is an example of how lenders can provide valuable financial advice.

Another advantage of a direct loan program is that it gives the bank the opportunity to stress a total banking relationship with the retail customer. When an applicant's credit request is approved, a positive environment in which to cross-sell the bank's other services is created. The credit analyst also has the benefit of having more information available to him concerning the customer's financial practices and needs than he does in any other type of account relationship with the bank. When a customer opens a checking account, the bank knows his name, address, and employer. In contrast, when a customer applies for a loan, the bank knows those facts plus the customer's income, credit history, debts, age, number of dependents, and other personal information. The extra information gained from the loan application can be used to target more specific and more effective cross-selling efforts.

There are a number of disadvantages for financial institutions offering direct loans. The labor-intensive nature of the process, as well as its reliance upon skilled lenders and attractive branch locations, poses significant management challenges. There is an obvious trade-off between the advantages of personal contact and the costs associated with using bank personnel. Personnel costs represent a large element of expense for banks, and it is essential that consumer credit managers be sensitive to identifying products and procedures that will increase the staff's productivity. Several options for reducing employee costs and/or enhancing productivity are to—

- automate as much of the process as possible
- emphasize indirect loans to shift some of the loan functions to the dealers
- emphasize open-end credit products, which reduce the costs of handling future borrowing needs.

The recent emphasis placed upon creating a sales culture within banking has significant implications for consumer credit. As consumer credit personnel develop higher levels of selling skills and begin to focus more clearly on the importance of delivering products and services designed to meet the financial service needs of consumers, they will be able to sell the bank's credit services more effectively.

The Consumer's Perspective

Retail customers also benefit in several ways from borrowing on a direct loan basis. Financial counseling provided in connection with the lending process can be helpful in managing the borrower's personal financial situation. The direct lending process also gives the borrower the opportunity to become aware of other financing options available, as well as any other services that might suit him. This opportunity is particularly important in the current market, where new products are constantly being developed and greater product differentiation confronts the customer. Counseling by the lender might simply be in the form of suggestions regarding a particular loan, or it might involve advice regarding debt structuring, other bank products, or how to build savings.

Positive, well-informed counseling is a vital element in developing customer relationships. It is a far more effective tool for developing customer goodwill than the less demanding practice of order-taking. Effective counseling requires a high level of product knowledge and communication skills. It is a mistake to assume that the customer is aware of all of the financial alternatives available in today's rapidly changing banking environment. It is hard enough for bankers to keep up with new products, and that is our job.

In addition to the financial counseling opportunities that arise, the flexibility to structure loans inherent in the direct loan process can benefit the customer by—

- lowering monthly payment requirements on outstanding loans

- reducing the number of debts
- lowering interest rates on loan accounts
- increasing borrowing flexibility in the future through the use of more versatile open-end credit programs.

These benefits can be very significant to consumers. In some cases, the lender's ability to structure the loan means that a loan can be made rather than rejected. In many cases, it means enhanced profits for the bank at the same time that the consumer enjoys the benefits just noted.

The primary disadvantages of direct loans from the consumer's perspective are the possible inconveniences inherent in the process and the exposure to lender biases. The direct loan process requires the customer to make one or more trips to the bank during office hours. The time spent is in addition to the time it took to shop for the goods or services being financed. Direct loans are not as convenient for the consumer as indirect loans, where the dealer handles both the sale of goods and arranges for financing, nor are they as convenient as open-end credit lines which, once opened, allow the customer access to credit when, where, and for whatever purpose he deems appropriate.

Exposure to lender bias is a more subtle disadvantage. Many lenders subscribe to the "lending is an art" philosophy, which holds that the lender weighs *all* of the tangible and intangible variables and comes up with a decision regarding the loan request. While there is obvious merit in this philosophy, it must also be recognized that such an approach allows individual biases to creep in; even prohibited criteria, such as age, race, and marital status, can enter into the decision-making process. Lender biases can work to the benefit of some consumers, such as those who are well-known by the lender, but to the disadvantage of others. Biases against bill consolidation loans, people who borrow from finance companies, applicants who don't bank with your bank, divorced people, women, truck drivers, and so on, occasionally are asserted. And often, if not most of the time, these variables have nothing to do with whether or not applicants repay their loans. To some extent, lender bias is an unavoidable element in the direct lending process. It is being gradually rooted out, however, by means of better education of loan personnel.

Summary

Closed-end loans are classified in a number of different ways. The broadest categories are direct loans—loans in which the consumer deals directly with the bank—and indirect loans—loans in which the consumer deals with a third party who arranges credit through a lender. Loans may be further divided into groups based upon the type of collateral securing the loans. These distinctions are helpful in monitoring the bank's loan portfolio and establishing lending policies.

Collateral behavior patterns are an important consideration when analyzing risk on loans. The lender should know how to determine the value of the collateral at the outset of the loan, and understand how its value is likely to change over the loan term. While there is some collateral risk on all secured loans, risk is greatest on collateral that depreciates or fluctuates in value over the loan term.

Direct loan programs provide financial institutions with the greatest amount of control over the lending process. This control can be helpful in maintaining credit quality, developing other retail account relationships with the consumer, and structuring the best loan for the customer and the bank.

CONSUMER CREDIT AT WORK

The Annapolis Boat Show

Each year, the boating industry holds one of its largest in-water boat shows in the charming city of Annapolis, Maryland, home of the United States Naval Academy. On alternating weekends, dealers display sailboats, then powerboats, ranging from $500 inflatable craft to $1 million-plus luxury yachts. The shows attract thousands of visitors, many of whom are ready to buy the boat of their dreams.

The Annapolis boat shows are also popular with financial institutions seeking to develop retail boat loans. Banks and other lenders obtain display space on the grounds of the show, where they can vie for direct loan business. The shows are the culmination of loan development plans that were drawn up nearly a year before and are fine-tuned in the weeks just prior to the event.

One regional bank developed a multifaceted marketing plan for the boat show. The plan included direct mail and telemarketing efforts to potential retail customers and marine dealers, a cocktail party for all dealers participating in the show, and a booth at the show that offered one-hour credit approval. The direct mail and telemarketing for retail customers were directed to the bank's current boat loan customers and to boat owners whose names were obtained from a variety of mailing lists. The mailing offered consumers the opportunity to be preapproved for a specific dollar amount before they went to the show. This would allow customers to shop, knowing they had a loan and how much they could afford. The direct mailing effort and the cocktail party for dealers emphasized the bank's commitment to the marine industry and encouraged dealers to refer both direct and indirect boat loans to the bank's booth.

The week before the show, the bank's consumer credit marine specialists, supported by marketing department personnel, conducted training for the employees who would be working at the bank's booth. The training covered everything from how to dress—nautical but professional—to product knowledge and how to manage the booth. The final plan, including rates, maximum loan maturities, and down payment requirements, was set at the last possible moment to ensure that no competitors would find out and thereby gain an unfair advantage. The final rate was not set until the morning the show began, and then only after carefully checking the rates offered by competitors.

To accommodate one-hour loan approvals, a telephone and terminal for obtaining credit reports were located in the booth. Behind the scenes were lenders and support personnel who could be called into service as needed. Those handling the booth were skilled and highly motivated salespeople.

Once the show gates opened, a crush of consumers began the constant flow of opportunities that would last for three days. Many consumers came ready to buy and prepared to apply for credit, some carrying copies of their tax returns and personal financial statements. Once an application was taken at the booth, a support person would begin the process of investigating the application. A lender would then review the application and make a credit decision. If higher lending authority was needed, senior lenders were on call to handle that need. Customers could return to the booth within an hour, assured that they would have a decision.

At the end of the first show, the bank counted the results: millions of dollars in new direct and indirect boat loans, an enhanced image with marine dealers and consumers, and a sense of pride among the employees who contributed to the success of the show. The bank subsequently used this same kind of marketing program in other marine trade shows, as well as in other trade shows sponsored by home improvement dealers, recreational vehicle dealers, and automobile dealers.

Questions for Review and Discussion

1. Name as many characteristics as you can that are peculiar to closed-end loans. What advantage do these characteristics hold for the borrower?

2. What intangible factor does unsecured lending depend on?

3. Does the requirement for a comaker on a loan really make a risky loan less risky? What type of applicant usually prompts a bank to ask for a comaker?

4. Why are home improvement loans, though often not secured, considered a relatively safe investment for the bank?

5. Identify the four categories of secured loans and discuss their effect on risk.

6. Name an advantage of direct lending for a bank and then name an offsetting disadvantage. Do the advantages and disadvantages overall balance out?

7. Does your bank offer guaranteed loans, for example, guaranteed student loans? What percentage of your bank's consumer credit portfolio is guaranteed by a government or quasi-government agency?

8. What is your bank's policy about the types of collateral it will accept on a personal, secured loan?

5 Indirect Loans and Related Credit Products

Indirect loans have constituted a significant part of the consumer credit business since the first national dealer plan was announced by the Guaranty Securities Corporation in 1916. These loan programs were developed to help retailers optimize sales by providing a ready source of credit for their customers, and to help financial institutions attract loan customers beyond the reach of their office distribution system.

In recent years, captive finance companies have captured a growing share of the indirect loan market. This gain has been achieved, in large part, through the use of *interest subsidy programs*. These programs, along with the widespread offering of leasing plans, have significantly changed the automobile finance market.

Floorplan lines of credit—loan programs in which the bank finances the dealer's inventory—are an important part of the indirect lending business. A bank that extends a floorplan line of credit generally has a closer relationship with the dealer. This relationship gives the bank some control over the dealer's retail loans and enhances the possibility of obtaining other banking business from the dealer.

Characteristics of an Indirect Loan Program

An indirect loan involves three parties: a lender who provides the loan; a dealer who sells goods or services; and a consumer. Their relationship is depicted in *Exhibit 5–1*. A contract is signed by the consumer in order to purchase goods or services and is

EXHIBIT 5–1
Indirect Lending Relationships

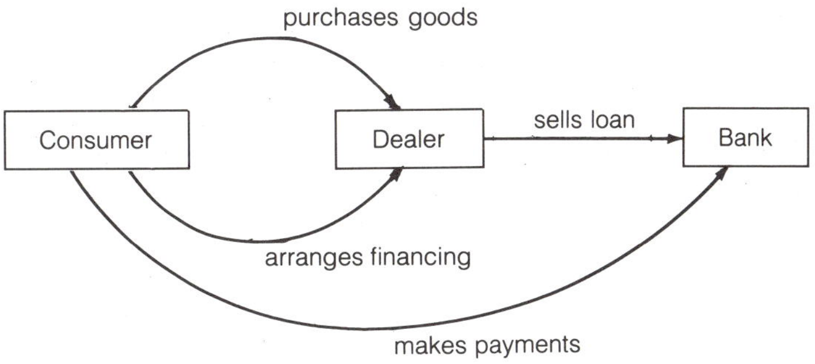

subsequently assigned to the bank that approved the loan. These contracts impose certain rights and responsibilities on all parties to the contract. Additionally, the bank and the dealer execute a separate agreement defining the terms and conditions to be used in handling the dealer's retail accounts.

The bank does not have any direct contact with the customer until the loan has been made. The dealer takes the application and does the *loan documentation* and closing. Consumers often do not know, nor are they particularly concerned about, who is providing the loan. The first contact the bank has with the customer usually occurs when a billing statement or coupon book is mailed. Some lenders never try to establish any further relationship with their indirect loan customers, while others seek to build on these lending relationships by marketing other products to them.

The potential sources of indirect loans are as broad as the variety of retailers that sell goods and services to individual consumers. Primary sources are dealers selling expensive tangible goods such as automobiles, boats, mobile homes, recreational vehicles, and other depreciating value collateral. Other sources include home improvement dealers and appliance dealers, although most borrowing for appliances is now done through credit cards.

A bank normally limits the types of its indirect loan sources based upon the types of goods sold, the quality of dealers available, and its specific objectives for this product line. Strategies are then developed to attract and maintain the desired base of dealers. For example, in the face of strong competition from captive finance companies, many banks focused their efforts on developing a base of foreign car dealers. These dealers were attractive because many of them had high volumes and dealt with attractive segments of the consumer market.

Another important characteristic of indirect loans is that they are related to a specific sale. This characteristic is a key difference between direct and indirect loans. The credit analyst reviewing an indirect loan request may not consider any significant loan structuring options since the bank is unable to offer alternative loan arrangements. As a result, the analyst reviews only the terms of the particular sale—rate, maturity, down payment, and dealer add-ons—and makes a decision or counteroffer within those constraints. For example, the lender might approve the loan subject to receiving a larger down payment, but he could not suggest a *bill consolidation* to the customer.

The Indirect Lending Process

An indirect lending relationship with a dealer is developed as a result of sales efforts by bank personnel. The bank determines which type of dealers it wishes to deal with and which particular dealers within that group it will seek for an indirect relationship. Particular care is taken at this stage to solicit only dealers who will produce the kinds of loans desired by the bank, and who maintain an image and selling practices that are acceptable to the bank.

The bank may seek to diversify its portfolio by targeting dealers who handle different types of products and by seeking dealers who handle different brands of those products, such as Toyota and Chrysler automobile dealers, or powerboat and sailboat dealers. The type and number of dealers desired vary depending upon the bank's objectives, the type of dealers available in the bank's market area, and the competitive environment.

A successful sales effort results in the establishment of a formal business agreement. The terms of the relationship are set forth in contracts covering the specific services the bank will provide for the dealer. The contract covering indirect retail loans is often referred to as the *dealer plan of operation*.

This dealer agreement covers a wide range of topics relating to the business relationship including: provisions for any income the dealer will receive from interest income on retail loans; and the bank's rates, maturities, down payment requirements, and other terms for individual contracts. The agreement also details the dealer's rights and responsibilities regarding the loan program.

Exhibit 5–2 shows some of the kinds of information normally covered on a retail plan of operation. Note that the plan establishes: (1) the rate the bank will charge on loans purchased from the dealer, called the *retention* or *buy rate*; (2) the maximum rate the dealer can charge retail customers; (3) the maximum loan term; (4) the down payment requirement; and (5) the dealer recourse and dealer reserve option selected. These features will be discussed in a moment.

It is common practice for dealers to have indirect lending agreements with many different banks. Whichever bank is able to establish the closest relationship with the dealer, or is able to offer the lowest rates or most liberal credit availability at any given time, is likely to obtain most of the dealer's business.

Once a dealer agreement is signed, the dealer may begin directing business to the bank. The dealer takes applications in the normal course of business and sends them to potential lenders. These applications are often transmitted electronically, which allows the dealer to send the application to the bank—or to a number of banks—in a matter of minutes. Small dealers typically rely on more traditional methods, such as calling the application directly into the bank.

Once transmitted to a bank, the indirect loan applications are generally processed by centralized credit departments that specialize in these types of loans. The loans are investigated and a credit decision is made by bank personnel. The decision is then communicated by telephone to the dealer. Given the highly competitive nature of indirect lending, it is usually necessary for

EXHIBIT 5–2
Sample Retail Automobile Dealer Plan of Operation

Year Model	*Bank Retention (Buy) Rate*	*Maximum Customer Rate*	*Term*
New cars	10.00%	13.00%	48 months
	11.00%	14.00%	60 months
Current used	12.00%	15.00%	48 months
One-year-old	13.00%	16.00%	48 months
Two-year-old	13.00%	16.00%	42 months
Three-year-old	13.50%	16.50%	36 months
Four-year-old	14.00%	17.00%	30 months
Older models	16.00%	18.00%	24 months

Down payment: The minimum downpayment on all vehicles is 20%.
Recourse option. All loans are on a nonrecourse basis.
Dealer reserves: Reserves are paid monthly on an earn-as-we-earn basis.

loan decisions to be communicated as quickly as possible, generally within hours of receiving the application.

The dealer prepares the legal documents for all approved loans. Large dealers usually prepare the documents on sophisticated equipment, and the loans are closed by finance specialists. Smaller dealers, on the other hand, usually prepare the forms for closing manually, using salespeople or an office manager. Whoever prepares the loan documents might also attempt to sell credit insurance and *warranty* services as part of the loan. The dealer alone benefits from any income generated from such sales.

Next, the dealer sends the completed loan documents to the bank. The original application and contract are sent along with any other documents required for the loan. The contract is reviewed to ensure that it is properly prepared and that the loan complies with the conditions of approval noted on the bank's records.

The final step in the process is for the bank to book the loan and *disburse* the loan proceeds to the dealer. Soon thereafter, the bank sends a coupon book or billing statement to the customer, sometimes along with a thank-you letter. The bank may also attempt to cross-sell other services at this time.

The Bank's Perspective on Indirect Loans

Dealers perform a number of tasks associated with the lending process, providing benefits for the bank. The most important benefit is the role the dealer plays in selling the bank's credit services. The dealer handles some of the lending tasks and may accept some responsibility for the performance of individual loans, elements of indirect lending that are also beneficial.

The bank's dealer base can be a powerful extension of its own sales force. The dealer can offer the bank's services to consumers at a time and place at which they are ready to borrow. Dealers are able to reach market areas that are out of reach of the bank's offices, which enables the bank to build a base of customers in a geographic area beyond its primary market for direct loans.

The effectiveness of dealers in generating loan business has been clearly demonstrated over the years. There are several reasons for their success. First, they provide substantial time and place convenience to the loan customer. They are in a position to satisfy both the consumer's desire for a product and the need for credit at the same time. Second, large dealers usually employ sales professionals to handle the credit sales function. These salespeople are frequently paid on a commission basis and are rewarded for selling credit-related insurance products. This method of compensation provides a high degree of incentive for optimizing sales results.

In addition to the promotional costs saved as a result of the dealer's sales efforts, lenders also realize cost savings because the dealer handles some of the time-consuming aspects of the loan process. The dealer takes the application, prepares loan documents, and closes the loan. This allows the bank to handle more applications with a smaller staff and helps increase productivity levels.

The bank may also be able to reduce the level of risk on indirect loans if the dealer is willing to accept some responsibility for loan performance. This responsibility is usually referred to as *dealer recourse,* meaning the bank has recourse to the dealer to recover all or a portion of any loss it may suffer on a retail loan.

There are four basic recourse options:

- *nonrecourse* or *no-liability*—dealers agreeing to this option have no responsibility beyond normal warranties

- *recourse* or *full recourse*—dealers agreeing to this option are responsible for reimbursing the bank the full amount of any losses on its accounts
- *repurchase*—dealers agreeing to this option are responsible for the full amount of any losses if the bank returns the collateral to them within 90 days of delinquency on the loan
- *limited recourse*—this option may be used on a selective basis. Dealers may agree to reimburse the bank for a flat dollar amount, for example, $1,000, or for a specific period of time, for example, full recourse for the first 12 months; any loss suffered above the dollar amount or beyond the agreed time is absorbed by the bank.

Note that our sample dealer plan of operation, shown in *Exhibit 5–2,* provides for a nonrecourse arrangement. There has been a steady trend away from the other recourse options due to competitive pressures, though such plans are still prevalent in some markets and may be found, at least occasionally, in most markets.

The value of a given recourse plan depends upon a number of factors. The most important factor is the strength and reliability of the dealer. If the dealer goes out of business or has no regard for its obligations, the bank can lose the benefits of any recourse provisions. At best, recourse can help the bank avoid credit losses and allow it to accept some marginal customers; at worst, it can lure the lender into a false sense of security.

Dealer relationships offer other benefits to banks as well. Banks often enjoy a full financial relationship with their dealers. This may include depository accounts, commercial loans, credit card merchant accounts, investment accounts, and the personal accounts of the dealer's owners and employees. These other account relationships help to strengthen the bond between the retailer and bank, and they represent an excellent source of business and profits for the bank.

Indirect lending also allows the bank to diversify into markets for products such as automobiles, boats, mobile homes, recreational vehicles, and home improvements, and to diversify within those markets, that is, to tap the markets for foreign versus domestic cars, or powerboats versus sailboats. *Diversification,* the strategy of generating a variety of loan types from a variety of sources, is desirable because it helps reduce the level of risk within the portfolio.

Another important feature of indirect lending is that it enables the bank to adjust its loan volume quickly. New dealers, particularly high-volume auto dealers, can generate hundreds of loans and millions of dollars in loan volume in a very short period of time. This volume can help the bank invest available funds quickly but, of course, can be both an advantage and a disadvantage. For example, in 1980, many banks elected to dramatically curtail their consumer loan business due to a severe profit squeeze. One response was to cut off loans channeled through high-volume indirect dealers, thus slowing new loan volume. On the down side, the action may have had a negative impact on later efforts to serve the automobile market.

As already suggested, the indirect market presents some disadvantages and challenges for banks. First, banks and other financial institutions not affiliated with domestic automobile manufacturers have faced a major handicap in the new car lending market in recent years. The frequent use of *interest subvention programs* by major domestic car manufacturers has channeled a substantial share of new car loans to their captive finance subsidiaries. Under these financing programs, the manufacturer subsidizes the lender's rate by making up the difference between the buy rate and the customer rate. This marketing strategy has benefitted consumers, who have access to below-market rate financing, but it has severely cut domestic new car loan volume during program periods and has forced banks to reassess their positions in the indirect and direct auto loan markets.

Second, indirect lending has the disadvantage of providing no direct contact with customers. This fact makes it somewhat more difficult for banks to build customer relationships, though many banks do achieve customer relationships through a program of targeted marketing to indirect loan customers. Other banks seem content with the indirect loans and do not make any extra effort to convert them to fuller banking relationships. This latter approach, though, is becoming less common as more banks emphasize the desirability of building account relationships.

A third problem that may develop under an indirect loan program is pressure exerted by the dealer to induce the bank to make marginal loans. To some extent, a conflict of interests is an inevitable part of the indirect lending relationship. The dealer is concerned primarily with selling goods and generating profits from sales. The dealer is far less concerned about, or aware of, any credit problems that could arise in the future. If the dealer is sending a lot of good business to the bank, an expectation sometimes arises that the bank should be willing to take a few marginal-risk customers along with the good ones. This expectation is greater when the dealer accepts some recourse on the loans.

Banks have adopted a number of strategies for tempering dealer pressure. These include: (1) requiring a lender to seek higher authority for approval of nonstandard credit risks, (2) requiring dealer recourse endorsements on all high-risk applicants, and (3) discontinuing relationships with dealers who apply undue pressure.

A fourth disadvantage is that banks may experience problems with the selling practices of some dealers. Dealers with sound selling practices can help create a positive image for the bank, while dealers with high pressure, deceptive, or otherwise unacceptable practices reflect poorly on the bank. In some cases, banks might even suffer credit losses due to poor selling practices by dealers. Care should be taken to determine that a particular dealer's practices are acceptable before a relationship is established, and the situation should be monitored on a continuing basis by the bank. Indications of problems, such as customer complaints, failure to correct documentation problems, high delinquency among the dealer's loans, and discrepancies between the terms disclosed on the loan papers and information provided by the dealer, should be carefully reviewed by the bank and the necessary corrections made.

A fifth issue of concern regarding indirect loan programs is the level of loyalty in the relationship. Dealer loyalty is a relative measure of the closeness of the relationship between the bank and the dealer. The ideal relationship is one in which the bank gets first offer on all of the dealer's business and receives the loan contracts on all of the loans it approves for the dealer. The least desirable relationship is one in which the dealer sends the bank only applications that have already been rejected by its other loan sources. In the latter case, the bank must spend a lot of time and effort, usually just to develop a high-risk credit portfolio.

Dealer loyalty is a function of the extent to which the bank continually provides the dealer with a competitive retail plan, delivers high-quality service, has other relationships with the dealer, and is loyal to the dealer throughout the economic cycle.

Dealers want a financing source they can count on. They do not want to be subject to major shifts in programs that revolve around the short-term needs of the bank. Indeed, this issue is a legitimate one for dealers, as many banks have been inconsistent in their indirect lending strategies. Others, though, have remained loyal to their dealer base, even at the expense of short-term profits.

A sixth issue of concern is the fact that serious problems can arise in handling retail paper. These include fraudulent practices on the part of dealers. Fictitious loans, double financing, the misrepresentation of terms, and straw purchases might occur if the dealer is under financial strain or as a result of poor selling practices. Fraud generally does not go on very long, but it can result in considerable exposure for the bank.

Fictitious loans are applications and contracts submitted for nonexistent individuals or on real people who did not, in fact, enter into a contract with the dealer. This type of fraud can be detected by sound investigation practices, which verify the existence of the consumer, and audit confirmation programs, which detect any discrepancies on loan contracts.

Applications and contracts may also be submitted to and approved by more than one lender, resulting in the dealer being paid twice for one sale. This practice, known as *double financing,* usually surfaces quickly since the customer receives two coupon books or bills. A quick response is necessary when such complaints arise.

Dealer personnel may also misrepresent some of the terms on a loan request to make a loan application appear more favorable. Selling prices, down payments, and other terms may be misrepresented, making it appear the customer has invested more into the sale than the dealer actually received. This problem may be minimized by relying on sound collateral valuation guides to determine the amount the bank will lend for various collateral. Random audits to verify loan terms also help curb *misrepresentation.*

Another fraudulent practice that can arise is the use of straw purchasers. A *straw purchaser* is an individual who allows his name and credit information to be used to obtain a loan for someone who does not qualify for the loan. While the straw purchaser actually signs the loan documents, he receives no direct benefit from the loan. This practice is extremely dangerous since it normally arises when the user of the goods does not qualify for credit due to a bad credit history or some other significant problem. Straw purchasers, like comakers, often do not pay for loans if the primary user fails to make payments.

The Dealer's Perspective on Indirect Loans

The availability of an indirect financing program helps dealers close sales on the spot, enables them to offer monthly payments, and increases dealer profits.

First, dealers are anxious to close sales to interested consumers as quickly as possible because it eliminates the possibility of losing a customer who either finds a better deal elsewhere or decides to postpone making a purchase. This is one reason why fast credit approvals are so important to the indirect lending process.

Second, the availability of credit programs allows the dealer to offer monthly payments, which can bring the purchase of large-ticket items within the reach of more consumers. Since consumers generally have an idea of how much they can afford in the way of monthly payments on loans, the dealer has some latitude to structure a loan payment within an acceptable range. The availability of a long-term repayment plan also enables dealers to sell customers up to higher priced models, or, if necessary, down to less expensive models in order to make sales.

The extra profit dealers earn from credit sales, consisting of income from loans and insurance, is very important to them. Banks pay the dealer a portion of the interest charges on loans developed by the dealer. These funds compensate the dealer for its sales role and for the tasks it performs in connection with taking the application and closing the loan.

The dealer's portion of the finance charge income is calculated by determining the difference between the rate charged to the retail customer and the bank's buy rate. For example, if the dealer charges the customer 13 percent and the bank's buy rate is 10 percent, the dealer earns the difference—3 percent—over the term of the loan.

Dealers also earn income from the sale of services related to the credit sale, including credit insurance income and warranty policies. These sources of revenue can make a significant contribution to the dealer's total income. *Exhibit 5–3* shows the income a dealer might receive from a typical retail transaction.

EXHIBIT 5–3
Dealer Income from a Retail Contract

Customer is purchasing a new Pontiac Firebird—48-month term.

		Dealer Income
Amount financed	$9,000.00	
Bank retention rate	12.00%	
Customer rate	13.50%	
Total finance charge	$2,822.66	
Bank's retention	2,484.87	
Dealer share of finance charge		$ 337.79
Life insurance premium	144.00	
Dealer commission—32%		46.08
Accident & health premium	276.70	
Dealer commission—32%		88.54
Warranty policy	585.00	
Cost to dealer	300.00	
Dealer profit on warranty		285.00
Total dealer earnings on this retail contract		$ 757.41

The dealer earns the income from a loan over the term, for example, over a 48-month period. This arrangement parallels how banks earn interest on a loan account. If the loan is paid in full prior to the end of the contract, some of the funds are *rebated* to the bank. The dealer's share of the finance income—$337.79 in the sample transaction detailed in *Exhibit 5–3*—goes into a reserve account with the bank. The dealer reserve account is a checking account established for the dealer but controlled by the bank. Funds are added to the account during the month as new loans are booked. Funds may be disbursed to the dealer from the reserve account at the end of the month on two basic schedules:

- *earn as bank earns*—Under this schedule, the dealer receives income in the same manner as the bank receives its income. As payments are made, the interest income is split between the bank and the dealer based upon their appropriate share.
- *reserves paid up-front*—Under this schedule, the dealer receives the full amount of its share of the finance charge income for all

loans booked the prior month. This amount is reduced by any income on prior loans that must be rebated when an account pays out ahead of time. For example, if a customer with a 48-month loan pays the loan off at the end of 24 months, the bank and dealer will not earn all of the interest anticipated on the loan. The dealer must, therefore, be charged for the unearned portion that has already been paid to it.

The Consumer's Perspective on Indirect Loans

Retail consumers may derive several benefits from an indirect loan. Many consumers place a high value on convenience, and some are willing to pay extra for it. Indirect lending programs have traditionally emphasized the convenience element. High-volume dealerships frequently sell a vehicle, close the loan, and send the happy customer on his way before even attempting to get the loan approved. The consumer does not need to deal separately with the financial institution to arrange a loan because the purchase and loan are handled in one transaction.

Another benefit to consumers of indirect loans is that the terms may be more flexible than they are on a direct loan. The fact that lending policies for indirect loan programs are often liberal compared to direct loan programs has developed because of competitive pressures in the indirect loan market and the existence of dealer recourse under some dealer agreements. Therefore, dealers frequently offer credit for longer terms with lower down payments than the bank offers on direct loans.

Interest rate subsidy programs also benefit some indirect loan customers. For example, if the manufacturer is offering a rate of 2.9 percent for certain car models, the consumer would pay a 2.9 percent rate on his loan. The difference between that rate and the financial institution's buy rate would be paid by the manufacturer to eligible lenders:

9.5% Bank buy rate
2.9% Customer rate
6.6% Difference paid by manufacturer

The difference in finance charges between the two rates represents a cash savings to the consumer.

Finally, consumers who lack a good credit record or the stability characteristics normally required for loan approval are occasionally able to obtain financing through a dealer. This benefit results primarily from either the dealer's willingness to accept some degree of recourse on the loan, thereby reducing the bank's risk, or from the pressure exerted on the bank by important dealers to take some marginal paper.

On the negative side, indirect lending may not be the best loan alternative for a particular consumer if viewed from a total financial management perspective. Each loan request must stand on its own, and there is no provision for restructuring the borrower's debts. The lender is not able to provide any financial counseling for the borrower, though this role is sometimes assumed by the dealer's finance and insurance representative. Information provided by these individuals, however, is usually concerned with figuring out ways to make a sale and not necessarily with what is the best loan for the customer.

Another drawback of the easy availability of credit through an indirect loan program is that credit and product comparison shopping might not occur. This is because consumers tend to develop a strong urge to buy a product. A familiar scene is a car shopper falling in love with a car he just saw and wanting to take it home immediately. Salespeople are trained to recognize these strong urges and to help the consumer realize his dream without further ado. This common behavior pattern leads many consumers to commit to large purchases without shopping for the best possible deal. The decisions often come under closer scrutiny after it is too late. People usually do a good job of rationalizing their decisions, but sometimes they direct their anger at the nearest scapegoat. In the case of an indirect loan, the bank may be a convenient scapegoat for the disgruntled customer who realizes, too late, that he signed for a loan that he should not have.

Finally, consumers may be harmed by unfair or deceptive selling practices by dealers. High-pressure sales approaches, deals packed with unwanted or unnecessary credit insurance or warranty policies, and misquoted interest rates are all examples of sales practices that frequently come to light only after the contract is signed and the customer has gone home. Consumers are sometimes told that the bank requires them to take insurance or that the bank sets the rate on the loan. Worse yet, consumers occasionally sign blank contracts or contracts that are not complete, only to be surprised later by the interest rate and terms.

Banks clearly have a responsibility to themselves and their customers to monitor the selling practices of dealers with whom they contract. Abuses may occur even in well-managed, reliable dealerships. They should be addressed as quickly as possible.

Floorplan Financing

Floorplanning is a form of commercial lending to dealers with whom the bank has an indirect retail lending relationship. The bank establishes a line of credit for the dealer so it can purchase a representative inventory of goods for display purposes. For example, automobile dealers maintain relatively large inventories of vehicles on their lots. These vehicles may be sold immediately or may be used to show prospective buyers the options available to them. This allows consumers to pick just the right car to meet their desires.

Some dealers own all of the inventory on their floors or lots, but most dealers borrow money from banks or other financial institutions so as to carry an effective level of inventory. Using a bank floorplan line has the additional advantage of freeing the dealer from tying up cash in a large inventory. Floorplan financing is also known as *inventory financing* or *wholesale line of credit programs*.

The Floorplan Process

The operation of a floorplan line is illustrated in *Exhibit 5–4*. We will discuss each of the steps in the process in turn.

Line of Credit Is Established

After the bank has successfully attracted a dealer to its financing program, and the dealer has been approved by the appropriate individual or committee, a floorplan account is established. The bank then advises the manufacturers that supply goods to the dealer that it will now be providing floorplan financing for the dealer. A dealer may have several sources for handling its retail loans, but it normally has a floorplan line with only one bank.

The amount of the line depends upon the dealer's sales volume, the variety of units available, the time it takes for the manufacturer to deliver ordered units to the dealer, and seasonal demand patterns. A general rule of thumb is that dealers should maintain an inventory equivalent to 60 days of sales volume. Naturally, this should be adjusted in accordance with seasonal demand patterns. For example, boat dealers in the

EXHIBIT 5–4
Operation of an Automobile Dealer Floorplan Account

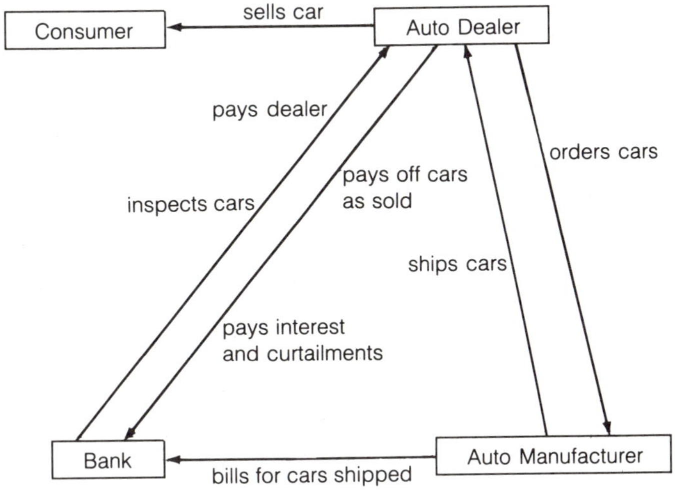

northeastern part of the country experience their heaviest sales volume from March through June, while sales tend to be weak from November through January. Thus, dealers stock heavy inventories during peak periods in order to maximize sales, and generally keep inventories at low levels during slow periods in order to minimize floorplan interest costs.

Dealer Orders Inventory from Manufacturer

The dealer places orders with the manufacturer to fill specific customer orders or to replace units that have been sold out of inventory. Occasionally, manufacturers initiate the process by attempting to induce dealers to take delivery of units the manufacturer wants to ship out of its supply of inventory. In this case, the manufacturer may offer some incentive to the dealer for taking delivery of units, such as paying part of the interest cost or providing free financing for a period of time.

Manufacturer Requests Approval from the Bank

The manufacturer normally contacts the floorplanning bank before filling a dealer's order. The purpose of this contact is to verify that there is enough credit in the floorplan line to cover the amount of the units to be shipped. If the total is within the maximum line amount, the bank gives the approval to ship the units. If, on the other hand, the new units would put the dealer over the maximum amount of the line, the bank may, at its discretion, refuse to pay for the units ordered. The dealer must then delay ordering the units or must seek approval from the bank to temporarily exceed the limits of the line.

Manufacturer Sends Approved Units to the Dealer and Bills the Bank

Once approval for shipment has been given by the bank, the manufacturer ships the units to the dealer and then sends the bill or draft on the bank for the total amount of the sale. In most cases, the actual ownership documents for individual units are sent directly to the dealer, though some banks hold these documents, depending on state law and bank policy.

Bank Sets Up Unit Under the Floorplan Line

The bank charges the dealer's floorplan line for units at the time the bill or draft is received from the manufacturer. Unit numbers are recorded on the bank's floorplan list along with the amount of the invoice for that particular unit.

Dealer Pays Off Units as Sold

Units remain on the inventory list until they are paid in full by the dealer. Dealers are required to pay off units immediately after they are sold. Failure to receive payment in full as units are sold is the primary risk banks experience in floorplan lending. If the dealer has sold and been paid by the purchaser but still owes the bank for the unit, the floorplan line is unsecured to the extent of that particular unit. Naturally, if the dealer were to do this with many units, the bank could face a very large loss. Indeed, banks have taken losses in the millions of dollars as the result of dealers selling inventory and failing to pay the bank.

Bank Conducts Monthly Inspection of All Units on Floorplan

Banks typically have someone inspect each dealer's inventory on a monthly basis. This task may be done by bank employees or by outside firms that provide such services for the bank. Inspectors go to the dealer's lot with a list of all units that are open on the bank's records. They examine each unit in inventory, checking off the units they actually see.

They also note anything unusual about the unit, such as damage or excessive mileage that could reduce the unit's value and expose the bank to loss. All units must be accounted for. If units are missing, the inspector determines whether they are sold, out on demonstration, or being traded to another dealer. Depending upon the bank's policies, the inspector may immediately require a check from the dealer to pay off all units that have been sold or cannot be accounted for satisfactorily.

The Bank's Perspective on Floorplan Financing

The bank's ability to extend wholesale lines can help its efforts to attract business from a given dealer. The more financial services the bank can provide to the dealer, the more value the relationship has to both parties. A bank that provides a floorplan line to a dealer generally is approached first when the dealer seeks to establish an indirect lending program or set up other bank accounts. In fact, dealers typically maintain their checking accounts and other cash management accounts with the bank that handles their floorplan. Often, the availability of these account relationships can help the bank sell its floorplan line to dealers whose current floorplan source—for example, a finance company—cannot provide additional services.

Floorplan lines of credit are typically priced in relation to the bank's prime commercial lending rate. The rate floats with changes in the bank's prime rate, sheltering the bank from the interest rate risk inherent in fixed rate lending. Loan yields on floorplan lines are generally not as attractive as other types of loans. However, they contribute to total dealer profitability and play a key role in ensuring that the bank is the dealer's primary source for other financial services.

There are also some significant challenges associated with dealer floorplan lines. One problem is their labor-intensive nature. A floorplan line can involve many transactions each day, the overall volume depending on the size of the dealership and the type of product financed. A car dealer with a $2 million floorplan line produces many more transactions daily than a dealer with a $500,000 line. Likewise, a sailboat dealer with the same $2 million line generates far fewer transactions, but each transaction involves larger amounts of money.

Automation of the wholesale accounting system can help reduce processing costs and improve efficiency. It can also enable the bank to handle larger lines and more dealers than a comparably staffed manual system.

What about the overall profitability of floorplan financing? Wholesale rates frequently are a major area of competition among banks. These rates are generally very close to the prime lending rate offered by the bank. Thus, bank managers need to examine the total profitability of the dealer account in order to determine if it is worthwhile to meet competitive pricing initiatives.

Inventory financing also presents some significant credit risks. Risk is best controlled by carefully selecting the dealers to whom the bank extends floorplan lines. Line requests should be subjected to a thorough credit analysis and the dealer's selling practices, reputation, and experience should be carefully weighed before a floorplan line is extended. Once a dealer is approved, the bank must continue to monitor the dealer's financial health, for it is in the face of strained business conditions, such as declining sales or operating losses, when dealers are most likely to resort to unacceptable and risky practices.

As noted earlier, collateral risk on a floorplan line is controlled by conducting regular inspections of the dealer's inventory. This vital step is an essential control point designed to quickly identify any practices that are not acceptable to the bank or that could expose the bank to credit losses.

The Dealer's Perspective on Floorplan Financing

Consumers shopping for goods, such as cars, boats, and appliances, often want to take immediate delivery of the item they select for purchase. If a dealer has the exact item the consumer wants in his inventory, a sale may be closed without delay. Therefore, dealers always attempt to have a representative display of inventory on hand. The availability of inventory financing lets them do this.

A floorplan line also allows the dealer to use its funds elsewhere in the business, rather than tying them up in inventory.

In fact, many dealers are not financially able to fund a representative supply of inventory without help from a floorplan line.

In addition, floorplan lines offer dealers a lot of flexibility. The line may be used as the dealer deems appropriate, as long as the total outstandings do not exceed the line limit. The dealer can vary the level of inventory based upon seasonal demand factors and according to the demand for various models and styles. This flexibility enables the dealer to optimize sales and improve cash flow. Dealers may also benefit by taking advantage of manufacturer incentives to buy units at a reduced price when they are offered.

A floorplan line is a debt obligation for the dealer. Interest must be paid on the outstanding balance used each month. Assuming a dealer has an average daily balance of $2 million on its floorplan account, and the floorplan rate is 9 percent, the monthly interest charges would be $14,795. Naturally, the dealer must cover this cost in the selling price of its inventory.

Dealers must also be prepared to reduce or curtail the amount owed to the bank for units that have been in inventory for extended periods of time. For example, the bank may allow the dealer to keep an automobile in inventory for up to 12 months without reducing the amount owed on the unit. However, after that time, it is prudent for the bank to require the dealer to reduce the amount owed on the unit since it is depreciating in value, which increases the bank's exposure. The bank may require a *curtailment* of 10 percent of the unit's original costs each month until the unit is sold or paid in full. For example:

$15,000	original unit cost
.10	10% curtailment factor
$ 1,500	monthly curtailment

Curtailments protect the bank from possibly being left with units that have depreciated in value and no longer are worth the amount owed on the floorplan line. They are also used to encourage dealers to sell older units, freeing up their lines for more popular units.

Banks may find it necessary to cancel a dealer's floorplan line or restrict the line based on a number of factors. Declining economic conditions or shifts in bank objectives or strategies occasionally lead banks to reduce wholesale lending. Cancellations most frequently affect smaller or financially weaker dealerships, which, by virtue of their size or financial condition, have fewer options available to them when lines are cancelled. Adding to the burden is the probability that cancellations usually occur during economic downturns, when competitors are less likely to be seeking new business. *Exhibit 5–5* shows the downward trends in domestic automobile outlets and the fluctuations in import outlets over the last 30 years.

The decline in the number of domestic automobile outlets and the rise in import outlets reflect changing buyer preferences over the period. However, it is important to note that many small dealers have disappeared in recent years and have been replaced by large multi-location dealer operations. These large dealers, sometimes referred to as "mega-dealers," are often very strong financially, and they offer new opportunities and challenges for lenders serving the indirect automobile market.

Leasing

Leasing programs directly compete with traditional direct and indirect lending programs. Though leasing is governed by discrete laws, it is so closely related to these traditional loan products—and such an important part of the automobile finance market—that a brief look at this product is essential to understanding the trends in the market.

Leasing is a financial arrangement in which one party owns the collateral (*lessor*) and rents it to the consumer (*lessee*) for a specific period of time. This type of financing became more popular among automobile buyers in the 1970s, and its availability and use has continued to spread.

Banks may attempt to develop leasing business on a direct or indirect basis. These programs are generally handled by a specialized unit within the bank due to the complexity of computing and documenting leasing transactions. However, the bank's branches and selected dealers may be relied upon to develop potential customers and service their requests.

Leasing programs are available predominantly on automobiles, though there are some programs available for equipment and other durable goods. Consumers who are indifferent about whether they own or rent a product, or who may be able to

EXHIBIT 5–5
Trends in Automobile Outlets

U.S.-CAR OUTLETS
1947 to 1986

Date		No. of Retail Outlets	Pct Gain or Loss from Previous Year
Jan. 1, 1947	.....	45,580	
Jan. 1, 1948	.....	46,092	+ 1.12
Jan. 1, 1949	.....	49,173	+ 6.66
Jan. 1, 1950	.....	46,821	− 4.78
Jan. 1, 1951	.....	47,543	+ 1.54
Jan. 1, 1952	.....	46,014	− 3.22
Jan. 1, 1953	.....	45,191	− 1.79
Jan. 1, 1954	.....	41,910	− 7.26
Jan. 1, 1955	.....	40,374	− 3.66
Jan. 1, 1956	.....	41,018	+ 1.60
Jan. 1, 1957	.....	37,982	− 7.40
Jan. 1, 1958	.....	37,188	− 2.09
Jan. 1, 1959	.....	35,077	− 5.68
Jan. 1, 1960	.....	33,658	− 4.05
Jan. 1, 1961	.....	32,482	− 3.49
Jan. 1, 1962	.....	31,331	− 3.54
Jan. 1, 1963	.....	30,853	− 1.53
Jan. 1, 1964	.....	30,827	− 0.08
Jan. 1, 1965	.....	30,691	− 0.44
Jan. 1, 1966	.....	30,278	− 1.35
Jan. 1, 1967	.....	28,422	− 6.14
Jan. 1, 1968	.....	27,784	− 2.24
Jan. 1, 1969	.....	27,486	− 1.07
Jan. 1, 1970	.....	27,071	− 1.51
Jan. 1, 1971	.....	26,126	− 3.49
Jan. 1, 1972	.....	25,621	− 1.93
Jan. 1, 1973	.....	25,441	− 0.70
Jan. 1, 1974	.....	25,349	− 0.36
Jan. 1, 1975	.....	24,980	− 1.46
Jan. 1, 1976	.....	24,453	− 2.11
Jan. 1, 1977	.....	24,268	− 0.76
Jan. 1, 1978	.....	24,147	− 0.50
Jan. 1, 1979	.....	24,051	− 0.40
Jan. 1, 1980	.....	23,379	− 2.79
Jan. 1, 1981	.....	21,772	− 6.87
Jan. 1, 1982*	.....	21,680	− 0.41
Jan. 1, 1983**	.....	20,799	− 4.06
Jan. 1, 1984	.....	20,841	+ 0.20
Jan. 1, 1985	.....	20,902	+ 0.29
Jan. 1, 1986	.....	20,673	− 1.10

*Jan. 1, 1982 and subsequent totals include Volkswagon
**Jan. 1, 1983 and subsequent totals include Renault

IMPORT OUTLETS
1957 to 1986

Jan. 1, 1957	....	2,930
Jan. 1, 1958	....	11,409
Jan. 1, 1959	....	14,031
Jan. 1, 1960	....	14,674
Jan. 1, 1961	....	13,135
Jan. 1, 1962	....	11,894
Jan. 1, 1963	....	7,138
Jan. 1, 1964	....	5,249
Jan. 1, 1965	....	5,856
Jan. 1, 1966	....	6,013
Jan. 1, 1967	....	6,588
Jan. 1, 1968	....	7,156
Jan. 1, 1969	....	7,869
Jan. 1, 1970	....	8,311
Jan. 1, 1971	....	9,860
Jan. 1, 1972	....	12,375
Jan. 1, 1973	....	13,332
Jan. 1, 1974	....	11,246
Jan. 1, 1975	....	11,489
Jan. 1, 1976	....	10,414
Jan. 1, 1977	....	11,387
Jan. 1, 1978	....	17,374
Jan. 1, 1979	....	17,114
Jan. 1, 1980	....	16,919
Jan. 1, 1981	....	16,681
Jan. 1, 1982	....	11.270**
Jan. 1, 1983	....	10,011***
Jan. 1, 1984	....	10,096
Jan. 1, 1985	....	12,427
Jan. 1, 1986	....	17,966*

**—VW counted as domestic in 1982 and subsequent years
***—Renault counted as domestic in 1983 and subsequent years

SOURCE: *Automotive News*

realize some of the other benefits that leasing plans offer, may be persuaded to lease rather than finance a product they need.

Some of the benefits consumers perceive in leasing are attributable to how leasing arrangements are structured. They require little money down, and the monthly payments do not have to cover the estimated value of the collateral at the end of the lease term—the *residual value*. Therefore, the monthly payments are usually lower than they are on installment loans. *Exhibit 5–6* illustrates these differences.

Despite the apparent benefits, leasing may be more expensive to consumers in the long run. In the example in *Exhibit 5–6*, the consumer who financed his car would have paid $29,988 (total of payments $25,150 plus a down payment of $4,838) and would own an asset worth an estimated $12,700—the residual value. The net investment would be $17,288. The lease customer would have paid $20,785.44 but would not own the asset at the end of the lease term. On the other hand, the lease customer would have had a substantially lower down payment and would pay $90.93 less per month.

Leasing programs often offer consumers added convenience benefits and greater flexibility in financial terms. Some leasing companies take the customer's order for a car, then locate, purchase, and deliver it to him. They also structure the lease to fit the consumer's particular needs. For example, consumers looking for the lowest monthly payment might be offered a five-year lease, while another person who likes to trade cars every two years would be set up on a two-year lease.

The attractiveness of leasing programs to lessors has centered on the potential profits and the growing level of consumer acceptance. Lessors have been able, in the past, to take advantage of favorable tax laws. Those laws allowed lessors to reduce their taxes by using accelerated depreciation, and then taking investment tax credits on the vehicles they leased. These tax features enhanced the yield from a lease portfolio, making it a very attractive product line.

Tax reform in 1986 reduced some of the tax advantages for lessors, and it is difficult to determine what effect these changes will have on lessors and retail customers. It remains true, however, that profits can only be achieved when consumer demand reaches a certain level.

EXHIBIT 5–6
Conventional Financing Versus Leasing for an Automobile

Conventional Financing		*Open-End Lease*	
Purchase price	$23,000	Capitalized cost	$23,000
Sales tax & registration	+1,190	Residual value	12,700
Down payment	−4,838	Amount liquidated over lease term	10,300
Amount financed	19,352	Monthly lease payment 48 months	$433.03
Monthly loan payment 48 months at 13.5% APR	$523.96	Initial payment—one month's rent	$433.03
Total payments	$25,150	Total payments	$20,785

NOTE: This example is based on Maryland state sales tax and registration information.

Summary

Indirect lending programs involve the use of dealers in the development and closing of loan requests from their customers. Dealers provide a number of loan processing services for the bank and are compensated for their services by sharing in the interest income on the loans generated.

Banks may profit from handling the dealer's retail loan needs and from providing other services to the dealer. Floorplanning is a particularly important credit service since it ties the dealer closely to the bank and produces an additional source of income. The bank may also provide dealers with checking and savings account services, investment services, capital and other loans, and credit card merchant accounts.

The indirect lending market, particularly the automobile segment, has changed in recent years due to the widescale use of interest subsidy programs by domestic auto manufacturers and the growing use of leasing programs. The former practice has diverted a significant share of domestic new car loans to the manufacturer's captive finance subsidiaries, while the latter has encouraged banks to expand their product lines to include this alternative form of financing.

Do questions

Questions for Review and Discussion

1. Among whom do agreements or contracts exist under an indirect loan arrangement?

2. In what way can a bank reduce its risk on an indirect loan? Define the various options.

3. Do dealers benefit financially from an indirect loan, other than being able to make the sale? Explain.

4. Do most banks offer identical credit terms on their direct and indirect loans? Why? Check with your loan department and compare your bank's direct and indirect automobile loan rates.

5. Give two reasons why an indirect loan to purchase a new car might not be the best loan alternative for a customer.

6. What is the connection between an indirect lending relationship and a floorplan financing plan? Describe generally the floorplanning process.

7. Get a list of dealers with whom your bank has an indirect loan relationship. Notice the different types and sizes of dealers and make some observations about the scope of the indirect lending program. If your bank does not offer indirect loans, talk to your consumer credit manager and ask him or her the reason.

8. Find out some facts about your bank's floorplan financing program, for example, how many accounts are active, what are the maximum credit limits, whether the bank uses outside services for inspections, and so on. Write a brief description of the program.

6 Open-End Credit Products

Open-end lines of credit are the fastest growing type of lending to consumers. Their growth has been spurred primarily by their high degree of acceptance by consumers and increased availability from lenders. Banks have been aided in their efforts to market more attractive credit products by recent legislative changes that have allowed the industry to offer borrowers a wide variety of open-end credit programs.

Retailer and gasoline company credit accounts and, soon after, the national credit cards were the first forms of open-end credit, and they rapidly gained acceptance. In recent years, banks have expanded their open-end product lines to include check overdraft lines, unsecured revolving lines, and home equity lines of credit. The newer programs have expanded both the borrowing power available to consumers and the versatility of the credit service provided by banks. Lines of credit, using access devices such as credit cards, checks, and automated teller machines (ATMs), give consumers the ability to use credit conveniently and privately.

Characteristics of Open-End Credit

Open-end credit accounts—also known as *revolving credit accounts*—are established with the intention that they will remain open as long as the customer handles the account in an acceptable manner, and the bank wishes to offer the product. This is in sharp contrast to closed-end loans, which are extended for a specific purpose and a predetermined period of time, with no provision for future borrowings.

Most open-end credit accounts have a specific *credit limit*, a maximum amount that can be outstanding at any time. The bank establishes the customer's credit limit at the time the account is opened. This limit may be increased in the future at the bank's option or if the customer requests an increase in his line.

The consumer has total freedom to use the line of credit, up to the maximum of the line. As he repays the account, the account holder replenishes the amount of credit available under the line. The amount of this available credit represents future borrowing power for the consumer. Once an open-end account is established, credit can be easily accessed at the time and place desired. No waiting is required for loan approvals, and no one needs to know the customer is borrowing money.

The Open-End Credit Process

Consumers may apply for an open-end credit account in the same manner in which they apply for a closed-end loan. They complete the bank's loan application form and wait for a credit decision. In many cases, applicants apply for a closed-end loan but are sold an open-end credit account by a consumer credit employee trained to sell the best loan for the customer and the bank.

Another common way in which consumers obtain an open-end credit account is to accept a preapproved credit offering. Preapproved credit offerings begin inside the bank. Lists of potential customers are obtained from a wide variety of sources specializing in list development. Names from selected lists are then run against credit bureau files to identify consumers who meet the bank's criteria. Consumers who pass this screening may then receive a preapproved credit offering. The consumer need only sign the acceptance form and return it to the bank to open the account.

Banks also offer open-end credit accounts on a prescreened basis. Many of these promotions closely resemble preapproved programs, but they give the bank the right to condition loan approval based on specified criteria. This usually means that the bank retains its right to verify the applicant's employment and income before making a final decision. Many consumers are understandably confused by the similarity between preapproved offerings and prescreened offerings. Indeed, marketers attempt to make the prescreened mailings resemble preapproved offers in order to increase the *response rate*, which is the number of consumers responding to the offer.

Once the appropriate legal documents are signed, the account is opened and the consumer receives access devices for the credit line. Usually, the access devices (see *Exhibit 6–1*) consist of a plastic credit card to use at merchant locations and automatic teller machines (ATMs), as well as special checks to write for cash advances. The types of access devices given to the customer and the restrictions placed upon their use are matters of bank policy, state law, and the type of account opened.

Once the line is established and the access devices have been delivered, the customer has control over how the credit is used, as long as he handles the account in a satisfactory manner and does not exceed the credit limit.

The bank is required by the Truth in Lending Act to send a monthly statement for all revolving credit accounts that have a balance at the end of the billing cycle or on which there has been any activity during the cycle. The statement provides required information about all activity on the account. The customer can pay the minimum payment due or any additional amount up to the balance on the account.

The popularity of open-end or revolving credit products and their increased availability in the market indicates that these products offer significant opportunities and challenges for both consumers and lenders.

The Bank's Perspective on Open-End Credit

Revolving credit accounts are attractive to banks because they: increase profits; broaden the bank's market area; have a high level of customer acceptance; represent a tie-in with technological developments; and offer some operational efficiencies.

The profitability of revolving loan products varies, depending upon state law, the type of product, competitive conditions, loan quality, loan volume and outstandings, and the efficiency of the operation. Banks have generally been able to market these products in such a way as to achieve desired profit levels.

The attractiveness of revolving loan products is enhanced by the fact that they generally can be marketed outside the bank's geographic market area. Credit cards, for example, are marketed nationally by some banks from states outside their home state. States such as Delaware and South Dakota have become havens

EXHIBIT 6–1
Credit Line Access Devices

for credit card-issuing subsidiaries of major banks from all over the country due to favorable usury limits, fee structures, and tax provisions in their laws. Unsecured lines of credit may also be offered beyond the bank's primary market area and state borders. This is particularly valuable when the bank is looking to open a new market or reach attractive market segments beyond those served by its branch and dealer network.

Secured lines of credit, particularly home equity line programs, are generally limited to the bank's primary market area. These loans are usually opened at bank branches and they require a network of appraisers and other support personnel in order to service the applications received. As banks expand their operations to other states, they will most likely offer these loans in a broader market area.

The high level of customer acceptance has been the driving force behind the expansion of revolving credit products. In fact, they have been the fastest growing category of consumer loans. If anything, the growth rate of open-end credit has probably been hampered until relatively recent times by the reluctance of many banks to offer these products, and the lack of provisions in state loan laws to permit many kinds of revolving loan products.

The flexible nature of open-end credit programs gives them a natural tie-in with the industry's efforts to expand its automated teller programs, merchant payment systems, and in-home banking products. Credit lines can be packaged with other consumer banking products to create unique product offerings that can be targeted to selected market segments. For example, some banks offer cash management accounts that tie together deposit, loan, and brokerage services for upscale customers. Banks can now deliver access to credit lines via ATMs and by telephone and electronic transfer networks.

Open-end credit products also offer banks significant operational efficiencies when compared to traditional direct and indirect loan programs. First, it is only necessary to go through the application and documentation process once. Second, applications are generally handled through the mail. This relieves the bank of the relatively high cost of conducting loan interviews, and provides some relief from the pressure to give fast credit decisions required on most closed-end loan requests. Third, open-end credit products lend themselves to a centralized approval process. Centralization is often helpful in handling high-volume products—such as credit cards—or products requiring specialized market knowledge—such as home equity loans, which require knowledge of appraisals, property reports, and similar specialized information. In these cases, centralization may improve productivity and ensure that only specialists handle the credit decisions.

Revolving credit products also pose some problems and challenges for the bank. Revolving credit products have historically been associated with higher levels of losses than traditional closed-end loan products. Several factors contribute to this adverse loss experience.

First, since these are relatively new products, there is a need to refine account controls. New control programs directed at fraud detection, periodic account reviews, and the handling of exceptions (delinquencies, deteriorating credit histories, overlimits, and so on) offer methods for improving loss experience.

Second, the aggressive manner in which many open-end credit products have been marketed has contributed to a higher level of credit risk. The "rule book" has sometimes been compromised as banks developed preapproved solicitations and expanded their market areas far beyond their traditional boundaries. Nevertheless, banks may be able to justify higher losses because of the higher gross yields available on some types of open-end credit accounts.

Third, credit reporting for open-end accounts is not consistently reliable. In fact, credit reporting on open-end accounts is frequently incomplete or even non-existent. Many banks are unable to report information about these accounts to credit bureaus, particularly for the newer equity line and unsecured line of credit programs, because of limitations in their operating systems. This gap in information is a concern since subsequent lenders might make decisions without full knowledge of a particular consumer's debt structure.

Fourth, the unsecured feature of most open-end products increases credit risk. Credit card and unsecured line of credit programs tend to rank lower on the typical customer's list of bills needing to be paid, especially when they encounter financial problems. This general tendency results in higher delinquencies and losses on unsecured lines. Home equity lines, due to their secured nature, do not present the same risk.

Fraud is a fifth major area of risk posed by revolving credit products, particularly credit card programs offered in major cities. Potential sources of fraud are lost and stolen credit cards, counterfeit cards, and dishonest merchants, cardholders, and bank employees. In recent years, credit card fraud has become a major business for organized crime and a favored activity of drug addicts.

One consumer used ten different identities to obtain fraudulent credit card accounts, bank loans, and even a commercial mortgage. The suspect used the names of some of his father's employees and business associates to apply for a variety of loans. He even obtained one loan using the name of a vice president of a major financial institution. Once the fraudulently requested cards were applied for, he would arrange to watch the mail and intercept the cards. Soon afterwards, he would notify the creditor to change the address on the account to a post office box he controlled. The suspect lived in a luxury apartment building for which he obtained the fraudulent mortgage and collected rent on six apartments. He was indicted for 86 criminal fraud, forged instrument, and grand larcency charges involving over $250,000 in credit.

In another case, drug addicts and employees of several merchants in one city were arrested for selling credit card names and account numbers to third parties. In some cases, the perpetrators obtained copies of credit purchase carbons out of trash cans—known as dumpster dipping—or storage slots near store cash registers. The account numbers and identifications were then used to purchase goods and services by mail or directly from merchants using the ploy: "I left my card at home."

In still another type of scheme, a person sells the account information to criminals, who then use the data to emboss counterfeit cards. Sometimes, addicts and card thieves use stolen cards to buy goods that they subsequently sell. The cost of fraud is difficult to pinpoint since much of it goes unreported. Clearly, though, the cost is in the millions of dollars.

In another notorious case, an organized crime ring stole credit cards in San Francisco and Los Angeles and then passed the cards to "shoppers" in Hong Kong or Singapore who went on shopping sprees lasting 30 to 45 days. The shoppers knew the store's *floor limits*—the amount that would be accepted on a charge without getting an authorization—and had all the necessary identification cards, such as driver's licenses, to make purchases. All their activities took place before the cards were added to stolen card lists. The crime ring also reportedly used postal employees, who were paid for their services, to steal cards in the mail and route them to the shoppers.

Fraud schemes are also known to be perpetrated by people posing as merchants. The usual situation goes like this: a fraudulent merchant asks a legitimate merchant to deposit drafts on his behalf. The fraudulent merchant may have all kinds of excuses why he cannot establish his own credit card merchant account with a bank; for example, he may claim to be newly in business or simply new to the area. The legitimate merchant, who usually earns a fee for processing the drafts, has an economic incentive to engage in this practice. Unfortunately, the perpetrator funnels a lot of fraudulent drafts through the legitimate merchant's account in a relatively short period of time, receives his money, and is gone before the fraud surfaces, leaving the gullible merchant "holding the bag."

The rapidly growing fraud menace is being addressed in a number of ways. First, VISA and MasterCard are sponsoring national efforts to reduce fraud through a variety of detection and prevention programs. Second, operational refinements are being made to improve the security surrounding credit card purchases. This involves a major commitment of resources to bring about technological changes, such as the use of *holograms* on cards and *point-of-sale* verification terminals, which verify every credit card transaction, thereby making fraudulent use more difficult. Third, credit approval and account opening procedures are being refined to detect fraudulent applications. Most national credit reporting agencies are developing more sophisticated systems for catching fake addresses, inaccurate social security numbers, and the use of a deceased person's name and credit file. Finally, efforts are being made to catch fraud soon after accounts have been opened by improving the timeliness of data dissemination on stolen cards and monitoring unusual activity levels on accounts. More timely data and spotting high activity can reduce fraud by stopping the perpetrator more quickly.

The Consumer's Perspective on Open-End Credit

Once a credit line is established, the consumer can use the available funds to purchase goods and services at the moment he makes a purchase decision. The availability of credit allows consumers to take advantage of unexpected opportunities, as well as to make planned purchases with relative ease. The wide acceptability among merchants of credit cards and access checks gives consumers a great deal of flexibility in making purchases.

Most people want to feel like they are in control, having an aversion to situations in which other people or events dictate to them. This critical psychological consideration explains the popularity of consumer items like the automobile and the videocassette recorder. A car gives consumers control over where, when, and how they travel, while a VCR gives them control over what they see on television and when they see it. Likewise, revolving credit products give consumers control over when, where, and for what purposes they use credit. This is a relatively new concept in consumer lending.

Revolving credit lines can meet a variety of family financial management needs. Most credit card programs enable consumers to purchase goods and services without interest cost if the balance is paid in full each month. Other revolving accounts may be used to meet short-term cash flow needs. For example, products such as *check overdraft lines* help consumers avoid the risk of an embarrassing and expensive overdraft.

In addition, high-limit credit lines can be used for virtually any purpose. Large lines are particularly attractive for borrowing needs that involve a series of expenditures, for example, college tuition and expenses and major home improvements. Large credit lines also allow consumers to reduce the number of bills they must pay and, in some cases, to reduce the amount of interest they pay monthly on their debts.

The flexibility of payments is attractive too since most open-end credit lines give the account holder the option of paying only the minimum monthly payment, paying more than the minimum—with the excess going to reduce the *principal balance*—or paying the balance in full. As he pays off the balance on a credit line, the consumer is, in effect, rebuilding his credit reserve. The available credit becomes immediately accessible and does not require any additional action on the customer's part.

Finally, open-end accounts, since they require a monthly billing statement, provide the consumer with a ready history of the activity on his account. This information can be helpful in his personal record-keeping efforts.

On the negative side, some customers are simply unable to properly control their use of revolving credit accounts. Lack of financial discipline can become a very serious problem when an individual has access to too much credit. Such customers often can be identified by looking at their credit reports. Typically, they have a large number of credit lines available, use most of the accounts, and are near or over the credit limits available to them. *Exhibit 6–2* shows sample credit information for a consumer in this situation. The customer has $14,500 in credit lines available, of which $11,492 has been borrowed. Two credit lines are over their limits, and three lines are very close to their limits. Though all of the accounts shown are current, the customer could easily go deeper in debt and may experience some payment problems in the future.

It is often necessary to rescue overextended customers by consolidating their loans into a well-secured closed-end loan. However, this approach has the effect of opening up all of the customer's available credit again unless steps are taken to close the revolving accounts. Although this is a difficult task, failure to

EXHIBIT 6–2
Sample Credit Bureau Data on an Overextended Customer

Creditor	*Status*	*Credit Limit*	*Balance*
State Bank	Current	$3,700	$3,256
Regional Bank	Current	1,500	1,556
Community Bank	Current	2,700	2,477
First Bank	Current	2,500	2,516
J.C. Penney	Current	400	112
Sears	Current	1,500	1,415
Wards	Current	500	0
Jewelry Store	Current	1,100	40
Department Store	Current	200	81
Retail Store	Current	400	39

limit a careless customer's access to credit could mean that more serious problems will surface in the future.

Types of Open-End Credit Products

The open-end credit product line is composed of credit cards, overdraft lines of credit, unsecured lines, and secured lines, primarily home equity accounts. Credit cards constitute the largest share of the market, though home equity lines are likely to be the fastest growing product over the next few years. Each product has a unique role in the overall consumer credit market.

Credit Cards

A wide variety of plastic cards resides in the hands of consumers today. These include retailer and nationwide bank cards, travel and entertainment cards, private brand cards, and debit cards. Each has its unique characteristics and markets.

Retailer Credit Cards

Retailers know they can increase the sale of merchandise by offering proprietary credit plans to their customers. The use of credit not only enables customers to purchase more goods, it also helps tie them more closely to the store that extended the credit.

Major retailers such as Sears, Roebuck and Co., J.C. Penney, and Montgomery Ward maintain large credit card customer bases, with Sears claiming the largest card base of any system—60 million cardholders. Many regional department store chains and specialty stores also maintain their own credit card programs. These retailers place a high value on building a customer franchise base, and they use their credit programs to increase customer loyalty and purchasing activity at their stores.

National Credit Cards

The two major national credit card systems—VISA and MasterCard—trace their roots to the 1950s, though they did not begin their major growth until the late 1960s. Mass marketing of both cards began in the mid-1960s as many banks, recognizing the significant potential of credit cards, rushed to gain some competitive advantage in what was to be a high-growth, high-profit new product.

The national credit card systems have continued to evolve as highly efficient systems capable of handling extremely high volumes of activity. Data furnished by MasterCard International and VISA U.S.A., Inc., reveal that in 1985 the two systems handled over 2 billion sales slips worth over $100 billion, and 64 million cash advance transactions worth over $15 billion.

It is particularly important to note the continued growth in the number of account holders, dollar volume, and dollar outstandings under these programs. While many in the industry now feel that the market is saturated, a very strong rate of growth was maintained in recent years.

The national credit card products have been segmented further with the introduction of prestige versions. MasterCard and VISA gold cards are targeted to reach the upscale market by offering product features like higher credit limits, travel services, and free travel accident insurance. Such features enhance the perceived value of the cards, which makes customers willing to pay higher annual fees. The premier cards are positioned to compete against travel and entertainment cards.

Travel and Entertainment Cards

Travel and entertainment (T&E) cards are differentiated by the unique manner in which they function. Most T&E cards are intended to be *transaction cards,* meaning they serve as an alternative to cash and personal checks. They may be used by the cardholder to purchase goods and services, which are then billed during the next billing cycle. The balance is due in full when billed and is not subject to any finance charges.

Cards that fall into the T&E category include American Express, Carte Blanche, and Diner's Club—all prestige cards—and cards issued by airlines and gasoline companies. The former group typically imposes significant membership fees, while the latter imposes no fees. Indeed, airline and gasoline company cards are often considered retailer cards since some allow unpaid balances to revolve. They rarely have a stated credit limit, though, as do most retailer credit card plans.

T&E cards are generally directed toward consumers in high socioeconomic groups. Their marketing themes, annual fees, and product features all tend to create an image of exclusiveness and high value. For example, Diner's Club, which is owned by Citicorp, offers such features as a club chauffeur program, club workout centers, and club meeting rooms in selected hotels, for an annual fee of $55.

Private Brand Credit Cards

Major firms like Citicorp and Sears now market their own private brand cards in direct competition with all other credit cards. Citicorp markets a regional card known as Choice in a number of states, while a banking subsidiary of Sears markets its Discover card nationwide. These programs represent an effort to optimize market share and profits by developing a variety of consumer market segments.

Debit Cards

Debit cards are closely associated with open-end credit products, and they are similar in appearance to credit cards. Some may be used to purchase goods and services in the same manner as a credit card. For example, VISA debit cards offered by some banks operate in this way. Others may only be used to access deposit accounts with the cardholder's own bank. A *point-of-sale* debit card transaction moves funds directly from a customer's deposit account with his bank to a merchant. When used in this way, the debit card is a convenient transaction device, not a credit device.

Many banks provide a direct link between their debit card programs and a line of credit. For example, if the customer has a checking account with the bank, he may be issued a debit card to access his checking account; he may also have a check overdraft line of credit with the account. Under this arrangement, if the customer attempts a debit card transaction that overdraws his checking account, the transaction would involve taking the money that remains in the checking account, then providing the additional funds from the line of credit.

Check Overdraft Programs

Check overdraft programs were one of the first forms of revolving credit offered by banks. These programs provide the bank's qualified checking account customers with a line of credit that can be used at their discretion. Overdraft lines offer customers protection against overdraft charges and help avoid the embarrassment and inconveniences associated with checks that are returned unpaid.

A customer with a checking account at the bank can apply for overdraft protection, and the bank, at its discretion, either grants or denies the line of credit based upon an analysis of the customer's creditworthiness. If approved, the customer is given a specific credit limit. The customer may access the line simply by writing a check in an amount greater than the balance in his checking account. The amount can equal up to the balance in the checking account combined with the amount of credit available under the line.

Although there are economic and psychological benefits to customers associated with these simple line of credit programs, as a source of loan business, they are relatively limited. One reason is that the credit limits on overdraft lines are generally small, ranging from $300 to $10,000, with most lines under $2,000. This limits their usage to small credit needs and short-term cash flow requirements. Furthermore, check overdraft loan programs experience relatively low usage levels, reflecting the fact that most consumers do not use them as a primary source of credit. Generally, dollar usage is less than 35 percent of the available credit, and fewer than half of the accounts have a balance during the month.

Unsecured Lines of Credit

The popularity of revolving credit programs spread rapidly and encouraged banks to develop and market accounts that would have greater value to customers as an alternative method of borrowing. Banks seeking to reach beyond their own customer base and attract highly desirable segments of the consumer market began to offer stand-alone unsecured lines of credit to a much broader base of borrowers. While some of these programs are marketed directly and exclusively to executive and professional customers, others are marketed as an alternative to closed-end loans and made available to any customer who meets the bank's borrowing requirements.

To enhance the value of these accounts as an alternative loan source, credit limits are generally high. For example, one large regional bank offers credit limits from $3,000 to $25,000 through its Delaware banking subsidiary. A similar program offered by a large west coast bank offers lending limits up to $100,000 for qualified customers. Obviously, high limits like these open up many additional borrowing uses. Customers who qualify can use the line to buy a car, make major home improvements, or handle other large borrowing needs.

Stand-alone unsecured line of credit programs typically experience a high amount of dollars in use, high average loan balances, and relatively low deliquency levels. The percentage of accounts in use is typically above 50 percent, while dollar usage is closer to the 60 percent level. These high usage levels reflect the value such products have as a source of credit for the consumer.

Secured Lines of Credit

Secured lines of credit were not offered by banks to any significant degree until the early 1980s. Home equity lines, in fact, were not permitted under most state laws until after the 1980 Consumer Credit Restraint Program. However, since their introduction, these loans have become one of the fastest growing products offered by financial institutions.

Most secured line of credit programs are based upon appreciating value collateral, primarily the borrower's residence. Some banks offer programs secured by savings accounts, which serve as stable value collateral. The limits on these lines tend to be lower and their popularity less widespread since they tie up the customer's cash assets without producing a real gain in buying power.

Some secured line of credit programs rely on fluctuating value collateral, primarily stocks and bonds. These programs require sophisticated operational support to continually monitor the value of the collateral. While lines secured by fluctuating value collateral are relatively limited at this time, they represent a market niche that could become increasingly attractive in the future.

Home Equity Lines of Credit

Home equity lines have become the most common form of secured line of credit programs. The size of the credit line depends upon the market value of the home and the consumer's ability to handle the debt repayment required by the line. Many banks offer programs that allow a customer to establish a credit line in an amount up to 80 percent of the equity in his home. For example:

$150,000	appraised value of residence
.80	80%
120,000	maximum advance limit
−50,000	amount owing on first mortgage
$ 70,000	maximum credit line

Obviously, credit lines of this size can accommodate virtually any type of borrowing need a customer might encounter. In fact, the line can serve as a replacement for any other consumer credit product.

Home equity line programs generally exhibit high credit limits, higher than average loan size, high levels of account and dollar usage, and low levels of delinquency and loss. Some banks report the percentage of accounts in use to be as high as 80 percent, with dollar usage close to 70 percent of the total amount committed. Additionally, the high average loan balance, in many cases over $20,000, reflects the value of home equity lines as a source of borrowed funds.

Home equity line accounts are the most exciting new consumer credit product since national credit cards appeared. They offer significant benefits to consumers and banks both. Consumers gain all the benefits of revolving credit products, plus access to substantial amounts of credit and some tax benefits. Banks can attract a base of consumers who have better than average credit characteristics, while securing the loans with sound collateral, optimizing profits, and achieving operational efficiencies associated with revolving accounts and large loan amounts.

Sources of Bank Income from Credit Card Programs

Banks derive income in a variety of ways from a credit card program, in contrast to most other types of loans, which almost totally depend upon interest and sometimes credit-related fees to achieve profitability.

Finance charge income accounts for the largest portion of income from a credit card program. According to the Federal Reserve's 1985 functional cost analysis, over 65 percent of all credit card income is in the form of finance charges.

Merchant discounts—fees charged to merchants for processing their credit card sales slips—are the second largest income source, accounting for approximately 23 percent of total income. These fees are designed to cover the cost of handling the account while generating a profit for the bank. The fee (or discount) charged varies from merchant to merchant and is based primarily upon the merchant's monthly sales volume and the average ticket price. A sample discount schedule is shown in *Exhibit 6–3*.

Merchants generating less than $1,000 in volume per month and having an average sales draft under $17 would be subject to a discount of 4 percent in the sample schedule shown in *Exhibit 6–3*; those generating $10,000 in monthly sales volume and an average sales draft of $80 would only be subject to a 2 percent discount.

Generally speaking, the discount rate declines as sales volume increases, reflecting the importance to the bank of successful merchants. The discount rate also declines as the average ticket size increases, the rationale being that less effort is involved in servicing an account that generates a $1,000 average ticket, in contrast to one that generates a $15 average ticket. For example, a retail drug store chain generates a much lower average ticket than a fashionable women's clothing store, with the result that many more transactions must be processed. However, the drug store may very well generate a higher monthly sales volume.

Annual fees and *transaction fees* account for approximately 10 percent of total credit card income. The recent emphasis in banking on increasing non-interest income led to the imposition

EXHIBIT 6–3
Sample Merchant Discount Rate Schedule

Monthly Bank Card Volume	*Average Sales Draft*				
	Under $17	*$17–$35*	*$35–$50*	*$50–$80*	*$80+*
Under $1,000	4.0%	3.75%	3.25%	3.0%	2.75%
$1,000–$2,999	3.75	3.5	3.0	2.75	2.5
$3,000–$9,999	3.5	3.25	2.75	2.5	2.25
$10,000–$49,999	3.25	3.0	2.5	2.25	2.0
$50,000 and up	3.0	2.5	2.25	2.0	2.0

of a wide variety of credit card fees. The most common fee is the annual fee, which allows banks to recoup some of the cost of servicing accounts, especially those of occasional users and convenience users (those who use the account and pay the balance in full each month, thereby avoiding finance charges).

Interchange fees are another possible source of income. These fees are charged by the national credit card companies and by member banks for using a credit card network. A bank receives fee income when cardholders with accounts at other banks purchase goods and services from its merchants; similarly, the bank is charged a fee when its own cardholders purchase goods and services from another bank's merchants. The interchange income and expense fees are netted out to determine whether the bank has earned income or incurred an expense in this category.

Other fees charged by banks include late charges, overlimit charges, and transaction fees. These fees are designed to offset specific actions by an account holder that result in an expense to the bank. The fees that may be permissibly charged on a credit card account are governed by state law.

Summary

The popularity of open-end or revolving credit products with consumers and bankers has continued to grow steadily throughout the 1970s and 1980s. This growth has been aided by new lending laws that enable banks to offer new products designed to more effectively and efficiently meet the borrowing public's wants and needs for credit.

Credit cards are the most widely used revolving credit products, while home equity line accounts have become one of the fastest growing products. These products, along with check overdraft and stand-alone unsecured line of credit accounts, have given banks a vehicle for reaching beyond their traditional markets to serve additional, attractive consumer market segments. They also provide consumers with alternatives to traditional closed-end credit products. Simply stated, open-end credit has changed the way in which consumers meet their borrowing needs as well as how lenders serve the market.

CONSUMER CREDIT AT WORK

The Home Equity Loan Market

The autumn of 1986 ushered in a frenzy of activity in the consumer credit market. Congress had recently approved tax legislation that would phase out the deduction for interest paid on most consumer loans. The interest deduction on loans secured by the borrower's residence was preserved, however. The media attention given this change in the income tax rules, combined with aggressive bank promotional campaigns that stressed the attractiveness of home equity lines of credit, set off a new wave of consumer interest.

Banks began to form their strategies as details of the new tax law emerged. Those already offering home equity loan programs considered more aggressive promotional efforts, while those banks that did not offer the product quickly developed plans to enter the market. Participants in the market—real estate appraisers, title search companies, and bank lending personnel—all began to gear up for the anticipated rush of activity.

In one large city, the opening round of competition began when one of the largest banks offered an introductory rate of 7.5 percent—the prime rate at the time—until the end of the year for all new home equity line customers. Other banks quickly followed by matching the rate, while some became even more aggressive, reducing rates as low as 5.9 percent or extending the introductory rate period from three to six months.

Round two of the competitive battle began when another large bank offered to pay all of the closing costs—typically $250 to $500—for customers opening a new account. The program was announced in expensive full-page newspaper advertisements, on the radio, and in other media. Previously, the closing costs were a barrier to many customers, preventing them from opening an equity line account or from moving an account to another bank. Once banks began absorbing closing costs, consumers could open a new equity line account or move an existing account without incurring additional expense.

The closing cost issue became the focal point for other marketing programs. One bank introduced a rebate program, promising to reimburse customers for closing costs up to the amount of interest paid on the account during its first year. Thus, if the closing costs were $300 and a customer paid at least $300 in interest on the account during the first year, he would receive a rebate for that amount. This creative twist was designed not only to encourage customers to open equity line accounts, but also to earn the rebate by using the accounts.

The rate war prompted one banker to state that he refused to become involved in "kamikaze pricing" and would hold to an introductory rate equal to the bank's 7.5 percent prime rate. Furthermore, he declined to offer free closing costs. Other bankers felt that, since customers could each have only one home equity line account, it was important to attract as many customers as possible. The long-term earnings potential on these accounts would, they reasoned, compensate for the short-term marketing costs associated with offering a low-cost introductory program.

In addition to the rate competition, many banks encouraged consumers to apply for equity line accounts by telephone or by completing a coupon included in a newspaper advertisement. Management trainees and other employees were brought in to help handle the crunch of applications, which seemed to be coming in from all directions.

A month or two after the tax revisions were enacted, many banks were overwhelmed with equity line applications. The workload was stretching the capacity of bank staffs to the breaking point, and some support organizations developed serious backlogs. Customer service became a major problem for many lenders, particularly those who had promised quick approvals.

Despite the problems, the results were very impressive and important. Consumers opened thousands of equity line accounts with millions of dollars in credit lines. These new accounts may have signalled a significant shift in the way many consumers will meet their future credit needs.

Questions for Review and Discussion

1. Why is the word "revolving" often used in reference to open-end credit products?

2. What constraints does a credit cardholder have in using his account? What freedoms?

3. Distinguish between a prescreened and a preapproved open-end credit offering. Why are banks making such offerings?

4. Why are some home equity accounts classified as open-end credit products? What primary advantages do home equity lines offer to banks in today's consumer credit environment? To customers?

5. What steps has your bank taken to counteract credit card fraud? Talk to your bank card manager to find out.

6. If your bank participates in one or both of the national credit card systems, find out some of the pertinent details like how many active accounts there are, what the bank's outstandings, earnings, and losses are, and how the bank markets its cards. Write a summary of your findings.

7. How are debit cards most frequently used today? What is their potential?

8. Briefly explain the various types of income a bank can derive from a credit card program.

PART III
THE CONSUMER LENDING PROCESS

The consumer lending process is composed of a series of logical steps, beginning with the generation of applications. Sometimes, the loan process is stopped short when an application must be declined, usually after the credit investigation reveals it to be a poor risk. Other times, the application sails through the investigative and decision-making stages and goes on to be approved, documented, closed, and booked.

Most loans are successfully repaid, and the bank realizes its investment. Unfortunately, though, some loans go into delinquency and default, and the lending process must accommodate this reality. Consequently, the collection and recovery operations of a bank must sometimes be activated during the lending process.

Despite the differences in individual bank procedures, it is useful to study the general processes involved in a consumer loan transaction. Related to the processes are the techniques—like loan structuring and selling, pricing, and profitability analysis—that, together with the bank's policies and procedures, define how a loan transaction works, beginning to end. Part III of *Consumer Lending* ties all the stages of the consumer lending process together into a logical, methodical whole.

7 Developing and Taking Loan Applications

One of the primary purposes of the consumer credit function is generating enough applications from consumers to meet the bank's objectives for loan volume, growth, and profitability. With the consumer credit product line continually expanding, this task has become quite complex. And, with consumer credit now being a more attractive asset for banks, this task has also become quite challenging.

Consumer credit managers are concerned not only with attracting applications from consumers who will meet the bank's credit requirements, but also with attracting applications in varying volumes for different credit products so as to diversify the portfolio and serve a variety of customer market segments. For example, as bank card profitability improved dramatically in the early 1980s, banks became aggressive in their attempts to generate credit card applications. At the same time, they tended to devote less effort to attracting applications from purchasers of domestic automobiles since captive finance companies offered rates far below those that banks could afford to offer.

This chapter looks at a variety of approaches used to generate loan applications for different consumer loan products. It also discusses different techniques used to take applications from consumers, and examines some of the problems that develop in the application process and ways of minimizing them. Note that the term "lender" is used in this chapter to mean the bank's consumer credit employee.

Objectives of the Application Generation Process

There are four primary objectives of the application generation process:

- obtain enough information to allow the bank to make the best possible credit decision
- ensure compliance with regulations
- initiate and develop the applicant's goodwill
- develop a flow of consumer applications to enable the bank to meet its consumer credit objectives.

The first objective—obtain sufficient information—is one that involves a number of trade-offs. It seems logical to state that the bank wants to get as much information about the loan applicant as possible. However, this desire must be tempered by the realities of the competitive market and the desire to keep the lending process as customer-oriented as possible. Balancing these divergent pressures presents a real challenge to consumer lenders.

The extent of information requested on loan applications varies widely. Application forms range from a brief solicitation for prescreened, open-end credit to a lengthy form used for direct loan applications. Generally speaking, lenders have learned to be comfortable with less information. The use of credit-scoring programs and the success of prescreened and preapproved solicitation programs have switched the emphasis from quantity to quality of information. Some credit variables simply do not prove to be as predictive of loan performance as others; thus, there seems little need to demand that the consumer supply extensive information if it is not necessary for sound credit decisions.

On the other hand, much of the information that has been eliminated in an effort to shorten loan applications—such as former residence and former employer and names of nearest relatives—is helpful to the collection department should a customer exhibit serious delinquency problems. Each bank's management must decide whether or not it is comfortable with this trade-off.

The second objective of the application generation process addresses the regulatory environment. A number of regulations are concerned with the manner in which applications are generated. The Truth in Lending Act governs disclosures made in advertising programs. The Equal Credit Opportunity Act is concerned with the types of information that can be asked on applications. And the Community Reinvestment Act is concerned with the extent to which the bank serves the legitimate borrowing needs of consumers residing in its primary market area. The bank must view its total loan application development program with an eye toward ensuring compliance with these laws and their implementing regulations.

As its third objective, the application process must initiate and develop the customer's goodwill. The programs used to generate applications must attract potential borrowers by offering something of value. Furthermore, they must create interest in the bank's products and motivate consumers to respond to the products being offered. As part of its effort to foster customer goodwill, the bank should be attentive to the convenience of the application process. If, for example, the bank does not take applications over the phone, but requires the applicant to make a trip to the bank to fill out an application form, it may lose some consumers who are looking for a more convenient loan source. Of course, there are probably many of them available.

Finally, in generating applications, the bank wants to develop a flow of credit requests that will help it meet its broader objectives, including portfolio diversification, product line mix, overall growth, and profitability. These considerations influence the advertising approaches used by the bank, the products to be promoted, and the commitment of resources to various credit programs.

Loan Interviewing

The loan interviewing or application stage culminates in obtaining a formal loan application. The objectives of the loan interview are to collect enough information to allow the bank to make the best possible loan decision and to initiate and develop the applicant's goodwill.

Even though the consumer is motivated to apply or shop for a loan, it is important that bank employees handle the application in an effective manner. This means that those involved in taking applications must develop their communication skills and have a thorough understanding of the bank's loan products and policies. A complete credit application contains a wealth of information about the consumer, as shown in *Exhibit 7–1*. This information is important to the lender in evaluating the credit request and recommending the best loan for the consumer. It may also be helpful in verifying the consumer's identity, handling delinquent accounts, and identifying cross-selling opportunities.

Applications are received in three basic ways: in-person, by telephone, and by mail. In-person and telephone applications involve personal contact between the consumer and a bank employee, while mail-in applications do not normally involve any personal contact.

Sometimes, it is difficult to fit taking loan applications into a busy work day. Occasionally, a low priority is assigned to consumer credit, resulting in loan generation taking a back seat to a bank employee's other duties. Or suppose an applicant comes in seeking a loan at peak banking hours, and no one has the time necessary to take the loan application in the desired manner. One common way of dealing with all these situations is to give the customer an application form and ask him to fill it out at home and return it to the bank. This approach may be acceptable to some customers, though it is far less personal and informative than a direct interview. It also does not enable the bank to control the application. Many customers leave under these circumstances, never to be heard from again.

In-Person Applications

Many lenders prefer to take applications face-to-face with consumers. They reason that doing so allows them the best opportunity to obtain complete information about the applicant. The lender can make certain that all necessary information is supplied on the application form and can take the opportunity to get a complete picture of the customer's situation.

Taking loan applications ideally involves the following techniques:

- create a comfortable environment
- smile and greet the customer
- determine the customer's name and use it
- set the customer at ease
- use a conversational approach
- practice active listening
- close by telling the customer exactly when he will be advised of a decision.

EXHIBIT 7–1
Consumer Loan Application

PLEASE READ THESE DIRECTIONS BEFORE COMPLETING THIS APPLICATION

☐ If you are applying for individual credit in your own name and are relying on your own income or assets and not the income or assets of another person as the basis for repayment of the credit requested, complete only Sections A and D. If the requested credit is to be secured also complete the first part of Section C and Section E.

☐ If you are applying for joint credit with another person, complete all Sections except E, providing information in B about the joint applicant. If the requested credit is to be secured, then complete Section E.

☐ If you are applying for individual credit, but are relying on income from alimony, child support, or separate maintenance or on the income or assets of another person as the basis for repayment of the credit requested, complete all Sections except E to the extent possible, providing information in B about the person on whose alimony, support, or maintenance payments or income or assets you are relying. If the requested credit is to be secured, then complete Section E.

Amount Requested	Proceeds of Credit to be Used For			Date
Number of Months	If eligible I wish to have Credit Life Insurance If eligible I wish to have Credit Accident and Health Insurance	☐ Joint	☐ Single ☐ Single	☐ No ☐ No

SECTION A — INFORMATION REGARDING APPLICANT

Full Name		Date of Birth	Telephone	
Present Address	City	State	Zip Code	How Long?
Previous Address	City	State	Zip Code	How Long?
Present Employer		How Long?	Telephone	
Employer's Address			Number of Dependents	Ages
Position or Title	Social Security Number		Present salary or commission $ per	
Previous Employer and Address				
Nearest Relative	Address			
Alimony, child support, or separate maintenance income need not be revealed if you do not wish to have it considered as a basis for repaying this obligation. Alimony, child support, separate maintenance received under: court order ☐ written agreement ☐ oral understanding ☐				
Other Income $ per	Source(s) of other income			

SECTION B — INFORMATION REGARDING JOINT APPLICANT OR OTHER PARTY (Use separate sheets, if necessary)

Full Name		Date of Birth	Telephone	
Present Address	City	State	Zip Code	How Long?
Previous Address	City	State	Zip Code	How Long?
Present Employer		How Long?	Telephone	
Employer's Address			Number of Dependents	Ages
Position or Title	Social Security Number		Present salary or commission $ per	
Previous Employer and Address				
Nearest Relative	Address			
Alimony, child support, or separate maintenance income need not be revealed if you do not wish to have it considered as a basis for repaying this obligation. Alimony, child support, separate maintenance received under: court order ☐ written agreement ☐ oral understanding ☐				
Other Income $ per	Source(s) of other income			

SECTION C — MARITAL STATUS (Do not complete if this is an application for individual unsecured credit.)

Applicant	☐ Married	☐ Separated	☐ Unmarried (including single, divorced and widowed)
Other Party	☐ Married	☐ Separated	☐ Unmarried (including single, divorced and widowed)

SECTION D — ASSET AND DEBT INFORMATION (If Section B has been completed, this Section should be completed giving information about both the Applicant and Joint Applicant or Other Person. Please mark Applicant related information with an "A". If Section B was not completed, only give information about the Applicant in this Section).

Presently Owe the Following Debts (including Credit Cards, Finance Companies, Credit Unions and Charge Accounts) Attach Sheets, If Necessary

Name of Creditor	Address	Balance Owing	Monthly Payment

AUTO	Year	Make	Model	Financed By	Balance Owing	Monthly Payment
HOME	☐ Own ☐ Rent	Purchase Price		Financed By	Balance Owing	Monthly Payment
BANK ACCTS.	Checking Account Number		Name of Bank	Savings Account Number	Name of Bank	

SECTION E — SECURED CREDIT (Complete only if credit is to be secured; briefly describe the property to be given as security.)

New or Used	Year	Make	Cash selling price including all taxes, accessories and equipment $
Body Type	Color	Current Loan Value	Less Down Payment
Serial Number			Trade$
Dealer Name			Cash $
Dealer Address			Total Down Payment $
			Unpaid Balance (Amount to be financed) $

PLEASE COMPLETE THIS SECTION AND SIGN

By signing below, the applicant and/or co-applicant: (1) authorize the Bank to obtain to the extent permitted by applicable law any information that it may require relative to this application from any source and (2) agree that this application shall remain the property of the Bank whether the loan is granted or not.

Any person making a false statement or report in connection with this application for the purpose of influencing in any way our action to make any advance, discount, commitment or loan, or any charge for extension of any of the same, may be subject to criminal penalties under Federal law.

(Signature of Applicant) (Date) (Signature of Co-Applicant) (Date)

FOR BANK USE ONLY

If you have a checking account at any bank in Maryland and wish to have it charged for your monthly payment, please ask for an authorization form from the branch manager or other authorized personel.

Approved ____________

____

Date ____________ Approved ____________

Form 339 (12-82)

EXHIBIT 7-1 continued

COMPLETE FOR HOME IMPROVEMENT LOANS ONLY

PROPERTY TO BE IMPROVED

LOAN INFORMATION

TOTAL COST $ ______
LESS DOWN PAYMENT $ ______
REQUIRED CREDIT $ ______ for ______ mos.

Address of property to be improved ______

Year Purchased ______ Price Paid $ ______

is owned [ ] Contract of Sale [ ] Rented [ ] ______ (Name of Titleholder, Purchaser or Renter)

______ Monthly Rental ______ Lease Expires ______ Month Day Year

PROCEEDS OF THIS LOAN WILL BE USED ON ABOVE PROPERTY AS DESCRIBED BELOW

Describe briefly Improvements Planned

Name and Address of Contractor(s)

PLEASE COMPLETE THIS SECTION IF AMOUNT REQUESTED IS MORE THAN $10,000 AND UNSECURED, OR IF APPLICANT AND/OR CO-APPLICANT IS SELF-EMPLOYED.

STATEMENT OF FINANCIAL CONDITION AS OF ______, 19 ____
FOR (check one): [ ] APPLICANT [ ] CO-APPLICANT [ ] JOINT

ASSETS (Do not include Assets of doubtful value)	In Dollars (Omit cents)	LIABILITIES	In Dollars (Omit Cents)
Cash on hand and in banks		Notes payable to banks — secured	
U.S. Gov't Marketable Securities — see Schedule A		Notes payable to banks — unsecured	
Non-Marketable Securities — see Schedule B		Due to brokers	
Securities held by broker in margin accounts		Amounts payable to others — secured	
Restricted or control stocks		Amounts payble to others — unsecured	
Partial interest in Real Estate Equities		Accounts and bills due	
see Schedule C		Unpaid income tax	
Real Estate Owned — see Schedule D		Other unpaid taxes and interest	
Loans Receivable		Real estate mortgages payable —	
Automobiles and other personal property		see Schedule D	
Cash value — life insurance		Other debts — itemize:	
Other assets — itemize:			
		TOTAL LIABILITIES	
		NET WORTH	
TOTAL ASSETS		TOTAL LIABILITIES AND NET WORTH	

SCHEDULE A — U.S. GOVERNMENT AND MARKETABLE SECURITIES

Number of Shares or Face Value (Bonds)	Description	In Name Of	Are These Pledged?	Market Value

SCHEDULE B — NON-MARKETABLE SECURITIES

Number of Shares	Description	In Name Of	Are These Pledged?	Source of Value	Value

SCHEDULE C — PARTIAL INTEREST IN REAL ESTATE EQUITIES

Address and Type of Property	Title In Name Of	% of Ownership	Date Acquired	Cost	Market Value	Mortgage Maturity	Mortgage Amount

SCHEDULE D — REAL ESTATE OWNED

Address and Type of Property	Title In Name Of	Date Acquired	Cost	Market Value	Mortgage Maturity	Mortgage Amount

Create a Comfortable Environment

Applications are best taken in a setting that gives the customer some feeling of privacy. The customer is asked a lot of personal questions, and he is understandably reluctant to share this information with customers in the teller lines or at neighboring desks. Privacy requires reasonable spacing, appropriate voice levels, and the projection of a feeling of confidentiality.

Smile and Greet the Customer

A smile projects many things to people. It can communicate friendliness, warmth, confidence, and caring. A smile can help convey a good first impression, not only of the employee but also of the bank. Bankers often impress this on tellers but forget to give it equal emphasis when training loan interviewers.

Determine the Customer's Name and Use It

Calling the customer by name helps create a personal touch, although it should be maintained at the proper level of formality for the situation. Some people want to be called by their first name, while others would prefer a more formal "Mr. Jones" or "Mrs. White." The safe rule is not to use a first name unless requested to do so or permission is granted.

Set the Customer at Ease

Although applicants do not consider the loan application meeting to be a social event, it is not always desirable to plunge right into the business of filling out the forms. Some general conversation is almost always helpful before beginning the more formal application steps. The loan interviewer should be well-organized and project the impression of competence. If he cannot find the application forms and otherwise appears hurried or disorganized, the interview is off to a bad start.

Empathy with the customer during the loan interview is also important at this point. Some customers are shy or restrained and need to be reassured, while others are cocky and demanding and need to be heard. Many customers fear rejection and are apprehensive. It is up to the loan interviewer to establish a relaxed, positive approach and thereby soothe these anxieties.

Use a Conversational Approach

Once the loan interviewer begins to take the application, the questioning should proceed in a smooth flow. The conversational approach is usually the most effective in meeting the objectives of gathering enough information to facilitate sound credit decision-making and developing the customer's goodwill.

The conversational approach involves asking questions and responding to the customer as if during a normal discussion. This is in contrast to an interrogative style in which the applicant feels like he has been placed under a bare white light and quizzed about his life. It is also preferable to a "fill-in-the-blanks" style often exhibited by inexperienced employees.

A central issue during the question-and-answer stage is who will actually fill in the application. Some banks prefer that the customer fill in the form and then have a loan interviewer review it for completeness and clarity. Other banks prefer to have the interviewer fill in the form and then have the customer review and sign it. The preferred method is a matter of individual bank choice, and many banks use both approaches, depending upon the situation.

Practice Active Listening

Listening is not an inborn trait; it is a developed skill. Tuning into what the customer is really saying involves paying close attention and providing appropriate feedback.

A good listener is generally skilled at asking questions. When a consumer is willing to talk freely, the interviewer may rely upon *unstructured questions*—those that do not limit the way someone can respond. The following are examples of unstructured questions:

- "Tell me something about your job."
- "What credit experience do you have?"

These questions allow customers a lot of latitude for their responses. Some customers give lengthy answers to unstructured questions, while others give only limited information. The interviewer may need to switch to *structured questions*—those that limit the way the customer can respond—if the customer is uncommunicative and does not divulge sufficient information to complete the application. The following are examples of structured questions:

- "Where do you work?"
- "How long have you worked for that company?"
- "Do you have any credit card accounts in your name?"

- "Have you ever had a loan with our bank?"
- "Do you want a home equity line of credit or an unsecured line?"

Occasionally it is necessary to use more skilled probing techniques with reluctant customers. There are four basic approaches that can be used to probe for essential information:

- *brief assertion of understanding*—This technique may be used to acknowledge that you are listening to the customer without interrupting what he is saying. In a face-to-face interview, this probing technique may take the form of body language, such as a quizzical look, a nod, raised eyebrows, or simply saying "uh-huh." These verbal and nonverbal messages tell the customer to keep on talking.
- *neutral phrases*—The use of a neutral phrase does not suggest agreement or disagreement, but rather encourages the customer to clarify a statement. Examples are: "What do you mean by that?" or "I'm not sure I know what you mean; could you elaborate a little?"
- *silence*—This is a powerful but somewhat risky approach. It may be used after the customer has made a comment that the interviewer feels needs more explanation. Silence should not last longer than ten seconds in a loan interview since it tends to produce anxiety, often making the rest of the interview more difficult.
- *echo*—This approach involves repeating something the customer has said in a manner that asks for more information. For example, in response to the statement, "I want a loan with the lowest rate possible," the interviewer might say, "The lowest rate possible?" The intent of echoing is to encourage the customer to elaborate, in this case, to say what he thinks the lowest rate possible is.

Once having developed questioning and probing skills, the loan interviewer should have little trouble conducting thorough, pleasant loan interviews. The interviewer should always remember to vary the types of questions and probes used in order to keep the interview as relaxed as possible.

Close By Telling the Customer Exactly When He Will Be Advised of a Decision

The customer should leave the interview knowing when the bank will contact him with a decision. The contact should be initiated by the bank, in preference to saying, "Get in touch sometime next week and we'll have an answer for you." It is far better to say, "Where can I reach you this afternoon with our decision?"

Telephone Applications

Taking applications over the telephone can be an efficient and effective approach for both the consumer and the bank employee. Telephone applications can take less time to handle than direct interviews, do not require the customer's physical presence, and can be fit into the day's schedule by arranging to call the customer back after hours or during slow traffic periods. Thus, there are some significant advantages to taking applications in this manner. It is also possible to set up a specific area in the bank to handle and service telephone applications, an approach used by many banks.

Some banks do not take applications over the telephone. This decision springs from concerns about the legal risks associated with handling telephone applications and the possibility of increased credit risk due to the lack of direct contact with the customer. These risks can be minimized by properly training lending personnel to take applications in a prescribed manner, giving the necessary legal disclosures, and using sound decision-making systems.

Mail-In Applications

Banks use a wide variety of approaches designed to generate mail-in loan applications. They range from passive techniques like displaying brochures in the lobby to aggressive preapproved loan campaigns. Mail-in applications have risen in importance as some banks have sought to offer enhanced convenience to consumers. Furthermore, mail-in applications allow a bank to reach beyond traditional market areas and tap attractive consumer markets in other states.

The two biggest concerns with mail-in applications are the absence of direct customer contact and missing information. Customer contact may or may not be important to the bank, but it clearly does not provide the opportunity to interview the consumer. This may result in less information being available for the decision.

Mail-in applications are generally less complex than in-person loan applications. Brevity and simplicity encourage consumers to complete the form. Still, many applications are returned only partially completed. Banks have different policies regarding how incomplete applications should be handled. Some banks return the application to the customer, while other banks require loan personnel to call the customer to obtain the missing information. A third approach is simply to reject the application, although this approach is the least customer-oriented. In a high-volume operation, however, it may be necessary.

Customer Relations Problems

Some applicants are more difficult to deal with than others. In this section, we will discuss how to identify and successfully handle some types of difficult customers.

The overbearing customer is easy to recognize by his attitude: he has a right to credit and is going to let you know it. He wants a credit decision on the spot and does not want to be bothered filling out an application. Be careful: fraud artists often use this approach.

It is essential to stick to the bank's requirements. Any sign of hesitation on the part of the loan employee will be interpreted as a willingness to compromise. Often, it is necessary to explain, in no uncertain terms, why procedures are in place and cannot be circumvented.

The shy customer is one who is easily intimidated by situations that are new to him. This type of customer does not offer a lot of information, so the loan interviewer may need to resort to structured questions and probing techniques to get the information needed for a loan decision.

Reticent customers need to be put at ease. More time should be spent making them comfortable with the process. It is usually helpful to explain the whole process in advance and to use positive terms. The easiest way to achieve a positive approach is to assume that the bank will be able to make the loan to the customer (this approach should actually be used with all customers).

Another customer relations problem to be leery of is the "present customer known" syndrome. Many lenders are tempted to compromise their application and credit investigation processes for customers they know. While this may seem reasonable, the lender runs the risk that something may have changed for the customer and he may not be quite as good a credit risk as he was in the past. In fact, we know that people lose their jobs, become overly indebted, develop personal problems—divorce, alcoholism, and so forth—and encounter other personal problems that change their behavior patterns on credit accounts. Therefore, it is always a good idea to follow the bank's lending process in full everytime the same customer requests a loan.

Lenders are often asked to make loans to consumers who are friends or employees of a good bank customer, that is, someone who has some leverage by virtue of a valuable or long-time account relationship with the bank. Occasionally, these people do not meet the bank's requirements; in fact, sometimes their credit is intolerably bad.

It is important to exercise good judgment in these situations. A reasonable customer understands that the bank cannot compromise its lending policies. In some cases, the bank customer may be willing to guarantee the loan, but lacking some way to properly protect the bank's interest, the loan should be declined if the borrower is not creditworthy.

Many lenders worry about a particular group of applicants: those who end up turning the bank down. Each day the bank approves many loans that never are made. In some cases, the applicant simply decides to postpone borrowing money; in other cases, the customer may have shopped around and found better rates or terms elsewhere. In still other cases, the applicant may have become dissatisfied with the manner in which the application was being handled. These situations are detrimental from the perspective of both cost and image. A lot of time and effort goes into processing a loan, and it is hard to let a good one get away.

Some banks have developed programs to determine why customers declined to pursue a loan request. This information can help the bank adjust its lending policies, identify procedural inefficiencies, and spot instances of poor customer service. The bank can then respond and thereby minimize the problem in the future.

Product Line Promotional Considerations

The bank's efforts to develop credit applications are bolstered by marketing and promotional programs. Consumer credit products are promoted in a variety of ways. The type of product has significant implications for the strategies and themes used.

Direct Loans

The location of a bank or branch office can have a great deal to do with its level of success in developing direct consumer loans. Banks or branches located in communities where a high percentage of consumers have heavy borrowing needs usually generate more consumer loans than those located in commercial market areas or sparsely populated rural markets.

Another major factor affecting the degree of success in generating direct consumer loans is the dedication and expertise of the lending staff. Some loan officers develop a loyal following of customers who not only rely on the officer for their borrowing needs but also refer many other prospective customers through word-of-mouth advertising. Such referrals are very helpful in building a direct consumer loan base.

Personal selling by all the bank's employees is a key element in direct loan production. Employees can be alert to possible borrowing needs expressed by consumers, or they may be able to identify needs through repeated contacts with a customer. They can also be aware of certain types of transactions that trigger an opportunity to sell a loan or to avoid having a customer pay off an existing loan. Examples of transactions that take place everyday in a bank's offices and that could open up an opportunity to make a loan include—

- withdrawals from savings accounts
- requests for certified checks or large money orders
- overdrafts
- making payments on loans
- asking for general information about loans
- responding to comments made in general conversation.

Indirect Loans

Application development through increased indirect loan business is the outcome of an ongoing sales effort directed toward dealers. Once the bank determines the types of indirect business it wishes to develop, a strategy for attracting dealers and maintaining existing ones can be developed. This strategy provides for targeted sales calls and continuous servicing of existing accounts.

The sales locations and product lines of dealers have a major impact on the types of loan applicants they attract, as well as the relative level of credit risk and potential volume of the loans generated. For example, a Mercedes dealer generates applications from high-income consumers, while a Chevrolet dealer draws customers from a much broader base of the consumer market. The Chevrolet dealer is likely to produce a higher volume of credit applications, while the Mercedes dealer would tend to produce a higher ratio of approved loan applicants.

Indirect dealers are highly price-sensitive and, as a result, are prone to moving loan business from one bank to another because of small price differences. While some loyalty may be given a floorplan bank, or a bank that has worked with the dealer over an extended period of time, it is still vital that the bank's services be priced competitively to generate new indirect loan applications.

Open-End Lines of Credit

To generate applications, open-end lines of credit are promoted in many of the same ways that direct loans are promoted. Indeed, many open-end products are sold to direct loan customers as altenatives to traditional closed-end products. For instance, home equity lines can be sold instead of closed-end second mortgages, and unsecured lines of credit can be extended to replace small closed-end loans.

Two aggressive promotional approaches have been used by many banks to push the growth of some open-end products. They are prescreened and preapproved direct mail programs.

Prescreening is a method of targeting a promotional campaign by identifying customers who probably meet the bank's requirements for a particular credit offering. The process used to prescreen potential open-end credit customers was discussed in Chapter 6.

Preapproved credit programs, which were also discussed in Chapter 6, are far more aggressive and potentially riskier than prescreened programs since an account must be opened for all applicants who return the offer properly signed. The process for handling a preapproved solicitation is virtually the same as that used for prescreened mailings; however, the credit criteria used in the screening process is usually much more stringent. The bank may require that the consumer have a longer credit history, more credit experience, and no derogatory credit information.

Prescreened and preapproved solicitation programs are both designed to increase the response rates (the percentage of consumers applying for the product offered) for direct mail campaigns. Since they help target mailings to consumers who probably meet the bank's credit requirements, and since they make it extremely convenient for consumers to open new credit accounts, they typically result in higher response rates and more effective promotional efforts.

Promotional Themes and Incentives

Banks must develop a sufficient flow of loan applications to enable them to meet their profit and growth objectives. To encourage consumers to apply for loan products, banks use a variety of promotional approaches. In this section, we will look at some of the more frequently used promotional themes and incentives.

Consumers are accustomed to discount sales used by retailers to move merchandise. Some banks have adopted this technique and periodically conduct a loan sale.

It almost goes without saying that consumers respond to price incentives, and automobile manufacturers have demonstrated the power of reduced rate financing to help sell new cars. Although banks are at a competitive disadvantage in the face of automobile manufacturers' interest subvention programs, they can still attract loan customers through realistic rate reduction incentives offered to car buyers.

Similarly, low introductory rates have been used to encourage consumers to open home equity line accounts. It is clear that affordable monthly payments attract loan applications, enabling the bank to make more loans.

It is important to note that not all consumers are interest rate-sensitive. Some are attracted more by affordable monthly payments, while others place a high value upon convenience, such as the kind offered by preapproved credit offerings. Moreover, good customer service is highly valued by many customers who are willing to pay a higher rate of interest to deal with a competent banker and someone they trust. Effective marketing enables banks to generate more loan applications than they otherwise might, but without sacrificing profitability.

Summary

Generating consumer loan applications in an increasingly competitive environment presents a major challenge to the banking industry. In recent years competition has encouraged banks to pursue different product line strategies and to develop new ways of promoting loan products. Banks have continued to sharpen their skills in order to attract loan applications from a broad cross section of consumers.

The application process varies, depending upon the type of product. Direct loan applications require that loan personnel develop their communication skills in order to obtain the necessary information; dealers control the application stage on indirect loans. Open-end products often involve applications generated by mail. These applications are typically much briefer in the interest of encouraging higher consumer response rates. At the same time, bank lenders have learned to emphasize the development of quality information in the application process, as opposed to just collecting large quantities of information.

Banks have become more aggressive in their efforts to develop loan applications. The use of innovative prescreening and preapproved credit offerings with targeted direct mail programs are designed to reach selected customer groups in a more effective manner. At the same time, many banks have benefitted from the increased emphasis upon improving the communication and selling skills of their employees. These skills help employees identify lending opportunities and lead to the development of more loan applications.

Questions for Review and Discussion

1. There has been a general shift among banks toward shorter loan applications. Why? Does less information necessarily compromise the decision-making process?

2. At the beginning of a loan interview, how might one go about setting a customer at ease?

3. Does your bank have a policy as to who fills out the loan application? Talk to a loan officer and find out how well the procedure works. Write a summary of your conclusions.

4. Give an example of a question asked in the structured format, and then alter it so the same question is expressed in the unstructured format.

5. In what way can a bank's lending personnel get involved in promoting consumer loans?

6. Give two examples of promotional incentives used by banks to sell direct loans.

7. Find an advertisement for loan services that a local bank—preferably your bank—has placed in a newspaper, and evaluate its contents. What is the promotional theme? Is it likely that the ad will be effective in bringing in loan business?

8. What role does the loan officer's personal experience and dedication play in the success of the bank's application generation process?

8 Credit Investigation

Once the lending process has been initiated, it proceeds to the credit investigation stage. The extent of the investigation depends upon the type of credit requested, the bank's loan policies, and the individual characteristics of each application.

Credit investigation practices have changed in recent years. Prior to 1960, it was common practice to conduct investigations using the mail to verify applicant information. As lending became more competitive, many banks abandoned references obtained by mail in favor of telephone references, which expedited loan processing. Since 1980, preapproved credit offerings have been made by banks that conducted investigations before even receiving an application.

Credit reporting agencies have been an important source of credit information since the early 1900s. These agencies provide a highly efficient means of exchanging information about the consumer's experience with and current usage of credit. Credit bureaus enabled banks to further improve the efficiency of the lending process because it was no longer necessary to directly contact each of the applicant's credit references. The bureaus also enabled lenders to uncover information concerning the applicant that may not have been disclosed in the application, but that could make a significant difference in the final decision.

The credit investigation process is structured in a manner that allows data to be gathered quickly and at the least possible expense. Lenders rely upon a variety of direct and indirect sources to verify applicant information. These include the bank's own account records, other creditors, credit reporting agencies, and employers.

The investigation provides verified data essential to the decision-making process. Sound credit investigations can help the bank make sound loans and avoid weak or marginal credit-risk consumers.

Objectives of the Investigation Process

There are three primary objectives of the credit investigation process:

- verify the accuracy and completeness of the data supplied on the application
- develop enough information to facilitate sound credit decision-making
- conduct the investigation in an efficient manner and at the least possible cost.

The credit investigation is made much easier if the loan interviewer is working with an application form that, when completed, provides all the information necessary to making a credit decision. The information to be verified should be clearly identified in the bank's loan policy. Some data are customarily accepted as given by the applicant, while other data are too important to the process of sound decision-making to be left unverified. Examples of data that are often accepted as given are—

- time at address
- number of dependents
- previous address
- previous job
- bank checking/savings reference.

Other data customarily verified by the credit investigator include—

- employer
- income amount/frequency
- other sources of income (source and amount)
- credit references
- home address
- value of collateral securing loan
- time on the job.

It is neither necessary nor desirable to investigate and verify every bit of data on the application. Experience has shown that most people are honest. Therefore, the investigator can focus on key data and not worry about trying to verify everything. If the investigator uncovers information that is inconsistent, inaccurate, or cannot be verified by a reliable source, he may increase the scope of his investigation. These incidents raise "red flags" that may or may not indicate a problem, but that do demand further investigation.

Credit decisions can only be sound if they are based upon factual information. Lenders must be able to rely on their raw material—the information obtained on the application and verified during the investigation. Data must be accurate and as complete as possible. Missing or inaccurate information can result in making loans that do not meet the bank's lending requirements. A sound investigation process develops information that will either substantiate the applicant's creditworthiness or indicate problems or factors that may represent an unacceptable level of risk.

Finally, the credit investigation process should obtain verified data quickly, but at the least possible cost. The following step-by-step approach may be used:

Step 1: application received and reviewed for any reasons that warrant its immediate rejection.

The object of this step is to eliminate from further processing any application that will not meet the bank's requirements for an obvious reason. For example, if the applicant requests a car loan with no down payment, and the bank's policy states that such loans may be made only with a 20 percent down payment, the application may be rejected without further delay or expense.

Step 2: check the bank's files to verify if the applicant has or had any accounts with the bank.

If the bank has had any unsatisfactory experience with the customer, the application may be declined at this point. On the other hand, if the customer has a satisfactory account relationship or no experience with the bank, the investigation can proceed to the next step.

Step 3: contact employers and other creditors for references.

Direct references are necessary for some items of information and may be obtained at this point. In many cases, employers and other creditors refuse to give direct references, forcing the investigator to rely on indirect sources. If adverse information is uncovered at this stage, such as finding out that the applicant has just quit his job, the application could be declined without further action.

Step 4: obtain report from credit reporting agency.
Credit reports contain information regarding the customer's accounts with creditors that furnish information to a particular credit bureau. Obtaining a credit report is often the final step in the investigation process, though some banks choose to take this action much earlier. In fact, some lenders limit their entire investigation to this one source. The cost of most reports is small and, with automated equipment, reports can be obtained in a matter of seconds. Thus, a bank may decide that merely obtaining credit reports is the most efficient, and least costly, process.

Once the investigation process is complete, the applicant's file is given to the loan officer or other decision-maker for the final credit decision. In some cases, approval of a loan might be conditioned on the consumer providing verification of certain data that could not be verified directly. For example, the lender may require that the applicant supply a recent pay stub to verify his income. The applicant may be asked to bring this form when he comes in to close the loan.

pay stub

Many banks establish time frames for completing the investigation process. These objectives are typically set at the product line level, in recognition of the unique character of each loan type. For example, a three-hour turnaround time, from receipt of an application to final credit decision, might be established for indirect loans, while a seven-day time frame might be used for equity line of credit applications. The longer time period takes into account the fact that external elements, such as appraisals and property reports, may be required in order to complete the investigation process.

What Should Be Investigated and How

The investigation is generally confined to six basic areas: the applicant's identity, credit history, income, employment, residence, and collateral. Generally, *direct verification*—checking information directly with the source—is preferable to *indirect verification*—checking information from a third party. However, when direct verification is not possible or when it cannot be done within a reasonable time frame, the credit investigator may rely on secondary sources. Additionally, if "red flags" surface, a more extensive investigation may be in order.

Applicant's Identity

Proper identification of the applicant is an essential part of the investigation process. Elements such as social security number, date of birth, and residence must be accurate to obtain valid credit reports and to ensure that information developed is complete and correct. Most identification problems arise, not because the applicant tried to misrepresent who he is, but because the bank did not obtain the correct identification information on the application.

Consumers occasionally obtain credit under a variety of names. One common example of this is a married woman who maintains credit in both her married and maiden names. Another example is inconsistency in the use of initials. For example, J. Donald Jones, Joseph D. Jones, and J.D. Jones may all be the same person. These situations can cause problems with verifications. Likewise, the use of generation designations—such as Sr. and Jr.—often causes considerable confusion in the investigation process. Some application forms specifically ask applicants to list all names in which they have obtained credit in an effort to catch those situations in which variations on a name have been used. No matter how this information is obtained, it is obvious that proper identification is essential to a complete investigation.

Social security numbers are commonly used to identify people. Some credit bureaus use this number to identify matches within their report files, and some banks use it as the customer's account number. Variations in social security numbers are usually flagged in credit bureau files. These variations might be simply typographical errors, or they might be evidence of fraudulent or criminal activity.

Credit History

Credit history is one of the most important decision-making variables. In compiling a credit history, the lender wants to know who the applicant has borrowed from, how long he has handled credit accounts, how he has paid his bills, and how much and to whom he currently owes money. This information may be obtained from four primary sources:

- the bank's own internal files
- directly from other financial institutions
- credit reporting agencies
- public records.

If the applicant had or now has an account relationship, the investigator should first refer to the bank's own files. The factual data obtained from the bank's files is the most current and least subject to error. Direct references from other lenders may also provide current and accurate credit information regarding their experiences with the consumer.

Credit reporting agencies are the largest providers of credit information to the banking industry. Upon a member company's request, they supply all the information they have regarding the consumer. Most communities are served by more than one credit reporting agency. These agencies vary in size from large national and regional firms—such as TRW Credit Services, The Credit Bureau, Inc., Trans Union Credit Information Services, Chilton Corporation, and the Pinger System—to small, locally operated credit bureaus. Reports obtained from competing credit bureaus can vary significantly, so it is essential that lenders evaluate the differences among the available credit bureaus, and periodically test each bureau to determine which one provides the best service. This may be done by obtaining a credit report on a customer from each bureau serving the bank's service area. The bank can thereby decide which bureau provides the most complete information regarding the consumer.

A common problem in attempting to investigate credit history is incomplete information. Due to variations in policies regarding the reporting of credit information, some lenders do not report their credit files to all credit bureaus in their area. Other lenders, such as credit unions, frequently do not report their loans to any bureaus, nor do they verify information directly. These situations pose problems for the credit investigator and also represent areas of risk exposure for banks. If the applicant does not disclose all his debts on the application, and if the undisclosed debts are not shown on the credit report, the risk on the loan might be higher than it appears.

Another recent problem has been the activities of so-called credit clinics which offer help to consumers with unsatisfactory credit records. These "clinics" often pressure lenders to change negative information on the consumer's report, either by threatening legal action or by offering some money on a previous loss. For example, the clinic may offer a settlement on an account that has been charged off as a loss as an inducement to get the bank to change the credit reference to a more favorable status.

Besides credit reporting agencies, another source of credit data is the public records. Items such as judgments, bankruptcies, and lien recordings may be available from credit reporting agencies, but, in some cases, are obtained directly from court house records. Because of the time and expense involved in checking court house records, this is generally done only on loans secured by real property or goods recorded via a financing statement.

There are a number of "red flags" commonly associated with credit report information. These include—

- all credit history is of recent origin
- no credit history
- heavy recent inquiries or applications for credit with other lenders
- all references with unknown or small companies
- all references are closed accounts
- undisclosed creditors.

When these characteristics appear, the investigator should use extra care in the verification process. The importance of these characteristics is weighed based upon their overall analysis of the application.

Income

As the principal indicator of the applicant's ability to repay the loan, income is a key variable in any credit evaluation process. The major elements of income that should be investigated are its source, reliability, frequency, and continuity over the term of the loan.

The reliability of the applicant's primary source of income is a key factor in evaluating creditworthiness. Therefore, it is desirable for lenders to have a "feel" for the stability of at least the major employers in their market area. The reliability of income is a composite measure of its source and the applicant's job history. Weakness in either area is cause for concern. For example, employees who have not been on the job long are usually riskier than those with a long employment history with a single company. Likewise, income that is subject to seasonal disruptions, such as in the construction industry, or that may not be guaranteed in the future, such as income from commissions and bonuses, introduce more uncertainty into the picture of the applicant's reliability of income.

Income may be verified directly by employers or indirectly by forms such as pay stubs, W-2 forms, tax returns, and legal documents. Direct references from employers are the best source of income vertification—they provide the most current information and may allow the investigator to verify other data, such as type of job and time on the job. Unfortunately, many employers do not provide direct verification, or they only verify that someone is employed. In these cases, lenders must rely on indirect sources to verify income.

A recent pay stub may be an acceptable alternative or additional support for direct verification. A pay stub gives the lender some insight into such data as payroll deductions and overtime income, thereby obtaining a clear picture of the applicant's net income. Care must be taken to ensure that the pay stub presented is valid and that the information is current. Old information may misrepresent the applicant's current status, and it is also possible for unscrupulous individuals to forge a pay stub.

Another source of information is a W-2 form, which offers a historical record regarding the applicant's annual income. An accurate W-2 form shows the name and address of the employer and the applicant, and the amount of income paid to the employee during the year covered by the form. It should be noted that a W-2 form can very easily be "dummied up" and that it is a historical record that should not necessarily be taken as proof of present income. Therefore, W-2s are regarded as a weak method of verification.

Tax returns, like W-2 forms, provide historical, not current, income information. However, they often contain a substantial amount of information about the applicant's financial behavior. Furthermore, tax returns are generally the only reliable way to verify income for self-employed people. Use of tax returns by consumer credit lenders is usually confined to large loan requests, applications from self-employed individuals, and requests for large, open-end lines of credit.

Legal documents such as divorce decrees, separation agreements, and public assistance notices are frequently necessary to verify non-wage income. Pension income may also be verified using documents supplied to recipients. It is important to review these documents carefully to determine both the amount of income and the benefit period or other limitations that may apply to these sources of income.

Employment

Employment is a key variable in assessing an applicant's stability. Major elements of employment that are frequently investigated include the type of job, time on the job, the employer's industry and stability, and the applicant's employment history.

The type of job held by the applicant gives some insight into the relative level of income, job mobility, continuity of income, and level of education. However, it should be noted that job titles alone can be misleading. For example, not all bank vice presidents are equal, and the term "teller" and "customer service representative" may refer to the same position. The point to remember is that it is the applicant's responsibilities and income that are important, not the job title.

Time on the job is also essential in analyzing the applicant's income stability. If the employer will not verify this information, the credit investigator may accept the information supplied by the applicant, assuming that the applicant's place of employment can be verified.

The final concern is the applicant's employment history. It may be desirable to verify previous employment when the applicant has been on his current job for a short time. A recent job change may indicate a positive change rather than a negative one. Thus, employment history may present trade-offs that require investigation and informed consideration. This factor becomes a major issue when the applicant is a "job hopper," with many different employers and gaps in employment.

Information obtained directly from the employer is the best source of employment verification. More information can be obtained from cooperative employers than from any indirect source. However, it has become increasingly difficult to obtain information directly from employers, forcing investigators to rely on indirect sources such as pay stubs, identification cards, or credit bureau reports.

"Red flags" that occasionally arise in the process of verifying employment include—

- home and business address the same
- home or business address a post office box
- variations in phone numbers
- questionable sources giving references
- telephone calls answered in an unusual manner.

Investigators should not use phone numbers supplied by the applicant to verify references. Rather, phone directories or operator assistance should be used before calling for employment and residence references. Variations in numbers may be an indication of a set-up verification in which a third party gives a phony reference. It is also possible that the company is out of business or that the applicant does not live or work where he indicated.

Most investigators are trained to obtain the identity of the person from whom they obtain a reference. This practice helps eliminate the problem of an unqualified or inappropriate source giving an important reference. When data are obtained from such a source, the investigator should dig more deeply into other areas of the loan request. For example, it is unusual for a secretary to be able to verify a manager's salary or for an employee to be able to verify the income of the owner of the business. While these people may be able to verify employment, it seems desirable to verify income using another source, such as a tax return.

Residence

Residence information is another variable that provides evidence regarding the stability of the applicant. The applicant's address may reveal a great deal of information about his lifestyle and financial condition. However, this information should serve only as a general indicator of stability rather than as a major determinant of credit risk. Care must be taken to avoid discriminatory practices such as redlining, in which residents of specific geographic areas are denied access to credit solely on the basis of their geographic area of residence.

The applicant's residence type—own/buying, renting, living with relatives, or other—is a measure of stability and may also give some indication of financial strength. Home ownership is associated with greater stability and financial strength, since the applicant has an asset that may be of significant value and is less likely to leave the area unexpectedly. Renting and other residence statuses, such as living with parents and military housing, do not provide the same level of stability, and, therefore, may be regarded as less desirable when evaluating credit risk. Despite the importance of this variable, the residence type is often accepted as given by the applicant, unless the place of residence is to be used to secure the loan.

Time at address is a measure of stability that should be analyzed in relation to the applicant's age and life cycle stage. Frequent changes in address are a significant negative factor, usually calling for further investigation. However, one would not expect young applicants to have long residency periods since they may have only recently established a household. Banks usually accept the information given by the applicant regarding time at address if the address can be verified.

Information regarding an applicant's previous address is usually requested, but is not often investigated. This information is helpful in obtaining accurate credit bureau reports, particularly when the customer is new to the area, and in evaluating stability. However, it may be expensive and difficult to verify.

Residence information may be verified directly with landlords or mortgage holders, through public records, or by telephone and criss-cross directories. Telephone and criss-cross directories are frequently used to verify place of residence. Although the information may not be current, it is usually satisfactory for the purpose of residence verification unless conflicting data surface elsewhere in the investigation. For example, if the credit bureau or another lender were to indicate a different address, the investigator might want to require a more direct form of verification.

Landlords and mortgage holders are the best sources for residence information if they are willing and able to provide the data on a timely basis. Many mortgage holders only give references in writing, making this type of verification rare on consumer loan requests, while many landlords refuse to provide any verification at all.

Collateral

The credit investigator is concerned with a number of issues when the loan will be secured. These include identification of the terms on any purchase-money loans, a determination of the value of the collateral, and identification of the owners of the collateral.

On *purchase-money secured loans*—loans in which the proceeds will be used to purchase the goods securing the loan—the lender must have factual information regarding the terms of sale in order to properly evaluate the collateral risk on the loan. A bill of sale, invoice, or purchase order should be obtained. These documents show the actual cash selling price, the amount and composition of any down payment, the amount financed, and a complete description of the collateral. This information is also essential to proper documentation of thc loan. Consumers should supply this information when they apply for a loan or when they come to the loan closing.

In analyzing the terms of a purchase, the investigator should look at the *cash selling price* of an item, which is the price that the consumer is actually paying, including the full price of the item plus any sales tax. The *down payment* represents the consumer's investment in the goods and is composed of actual cash paid toward the purchase of an item and the cash value of any trade-in. The amount of the down payment is then deducted from the cash selling price to determine the amount to be financed. The amount to be financed is a key concern to lenders.

The amount to be financed should be analyzed in relationship to the value of the collateral, using appropriate valuation sources. Simple reliance upon down payment requirements may result in excessive advances and increased risk for the lender. Therefore, the investigator should consult valuation guide books or take other steps necessary to determine the value of the proposed collateral.

Ownership of the collateral must be verified to ensure that the bank can obtain a lien and that it can be properly perfected. For collateral presently in the customer's possession, this can be done by examining the appropriate ownership document—deeds, titles, and the like. Ownership of goods to be purchased may be verified directly with the seller or by examining documents such as the bill of sale.

Other "Red Flags"

Credit investigators should always be alert to information that is negative or cannot be verified through normal channels. The identification of such problems should prompt greater care in the investigation process and perhaps a more extensive investigation. Many of these "red flags" were noted earlier in this chapter. Some other common warning signs follow.

Information Inconsistent With Applicant's Age

There is usually a strong correlation between an individual's age and life cycle stage and the characteristics that typically appear on a credit application. Indeed, lenders rely heavily on the fact that most people exhibit the same personal characteristics in the future as they have in the past, and that, as they grow older, they move toward greater stability, higher income, and the accumulation of assets.

Variations from these norms are not necessarily unacceptable or bad, but they may be cause for a closer investigation of the facts. They might also require an explanation by the consumer. For example, it is unusual when a 40-year-old applicant claims he has no credit, or when a 30-year-old person claims five different addresses in the last year. Such conditions warrant close investigation, such as insistence upon direct references.

Overly Pushy or Anxious Applicant

Many people have read books like *Winning Through Intimidation* that emphasize getting one's way by using manipulative, pushy behavior. The danger is that a credit investigator may, in fact, be intimidated and may compromise the investigation process, sometimes with disastrous results.

A similar dilemma is presented by customers who are intimidated by the bank and its lending process. Indeed, few customers actually relish applying for a loan, but most come through the process without difficulty. An overly anxious applicant can often be made comfortable by a skilled interviewer, while an excessively anxious customer may indeed have something to hide.

Gaps in Information

The credit investigator should provide the decision-maker with as complete a picture of the applicant as possible, given the time constraints on the application. Gaps in key information and the inability to obtain acceptable forms of verification should be communicated to the person responsible for the decision.

Summary

The credit investigation function is an important task in the lending process. Its primary objective is to verify the accuracy of data obtained on the credit application and to develop enough supporting information to allow lenders to make the best possible credit decision. Sound investigation procedures help the bank make good loans and reject applications that represent an unacceptable level of credit risk.

Investigations must be completed within the time frame appropriate for the type of loan product requested. The investigation process should flow in an efficient manner in order to obtain all necessary data at the least possible cost.

Finally, credit investigators always need to be alert to "red flags" that may arise in the process. These are signs of potential problems, and they require a more extensive investigative effort.

Questions for Review and Discussion

1. What are the four primary sources of credit information?
2. Assume an employer refuses to directly verify an applicant's income. What indirect sources can you turn to?
3. What areas are the subject of most credit investigations?
4. Why might a credit investigation begin by referring to bank files instead of credit reports or public records?
5. Name two drawbacks to the use of W-2 forms or tax returns to verify income data.
6. What data would you accept, without verification, from a loan applicant? Would it vary from one applicant to the next?
7. Pull the credit file of a customer whose loan has resulted in a charge-off. Can you find any "red flags" that, in retrospect, indicated the potential for a problem loan?

9 Credit Evaluation and Decision-Making

Proper credit evaluation and sound decision-making are essential to the success of any consumer credit operation. In this stage of the lending process, the lender analyzes the available data, using the bank's loan policies in combination with his understanding of the importance of various customer characteristics, to reach a decision consistent with the bank's definition of acceptable risk.

In this chapter, we will discuss the environment in which credit decisions are made and the various factors that must be taken into consideration before a decision can be reached. We will then examine the variables that lenders use to evaluate a credit application and examine how this analysis leads to the ultimate credit decision.

Our study will also include a look at the two primary approaches to decision-making—judgmental and credit-scoring systems. Next, we will discuss variable rate lending and the considerations that must be taken into account during the credit evaluation process. Finally, we will briefly explore how to handle a loan rejection.

Objectives of Credit Evaluation and Decision-Making

There are three primary objectives of the credit evaluation and decision-making stage:

- make the best loan for the customer and the bank
- ensure that the level of credit risk is acceptable
- ensure compliance with regulations and bank policy.

Making the best loan for the customer and the bank is a philosophy that emphasizes the importance of selling in the consumer lending process. It implies that the lender should not merely be an order taker who analyzes loan applications only on the basis requested by the customer. Rather, the lender is an active financial advisor who examines the customer's application and structures a loan that best meets both the customer's and the bank's needs.

An example is the customer who comes in for a home improvement loan for $5,000. The obvious choice would be to grant the customer a closed-end loan for 60 months, which would most likely serve the customer's current borrowing needs very well and would provide the bank with a profitable loan. However, a $20,000 equity line of credit might offer even greater benefits to both parties. The customer would benefit by: (1) having access to loan funds in the future without the need to reapply, (2) being able to do more extensive home improvements for the same monthly payment, and (3) receiving a lower rate and longer term on the loan. The bank would benefit by: (1) having a secured loan, (2) enjoying better operational efficiency, particularly on future borrowings, (3) developing a closer relationship with the customer, and (4) creating the opportunity to develop a larger loan at an acceptable rate of return.

It is essential that loans made by the bank's lenders be consistent with the level of credit risk desired. While it is difficult to be precise in defining the acceptable level of risk, consumer credit managers use several criteria to measure credit quality on an ongoing basis. These measures, including the tolerance levels of delinquency, loan losses, and rates of return on the portfolio, are post-credit decision tools for evaluating loan quality. Before loans are made, banks control the level of credit risk by developing lending policies that produce consistent decision-making, and ensure that customers meet certain minimum credit criteria.

Finally, decision-making must be within regulatory guidelines. Unfair discriminatory practices against protected groups are to be avoided. Within a logical and consistent framework, lenders should be able to establish a clear link between certain characteristics and the relative degree of risk that the loan will not be repaid in a satisfactory manner. At the same time, characteristics associated with a high probability of satisfactory repayment should also be identified. The lender must then weigh the pros and cons and come to the best possible credit decision, given the information at hand. The lender may not allow any criteria prohibited by the Equal Credit Opportunity Act or other regulations to enter into the decision-making process.

Decision-Making Parameters

Consumer lending is carried out in an environment far different from commercial lending. Perhaps the biggest difference between the two types of loans is that consumer loans are made based upon the law of probability, while commercial loans are made on a "no loss anticipated" basis. The consumer lender knows that some of his loans are going to result in losses, but seeks to limit delinquencies and charge-offs to an acceptable level.

Consumer lenders can say that a group of people who share certain characteristics will be more or less likely to default and cause a loss. They cannot say whether a particular person within that group will pay or default. The lenders' criteria do not specifically identify who will or will not pay, but rather whether an individual has the same characteristics as a group that is less likely to pay. If pricing is based on a 2 percent delinquency and .5 percent losses, a group of 9 out of 10 consumers who pay is not good enough. What is instead needed is a group in which 98 out of 100 will pay and only 5 out of every 1,000 customers result in a loss.

Consumer lenders also have less information to work with in considering a loan request. While commercial lenders analyze a company's historical financial performance, consumer lenders confine their analysis primarily to the customer's current financial condition, using tools that are far less precise than the sophisticated credit analysis methods used on business statements.

Consumer lenders rely heavily upon normal family life cycle trends and past customer behavior patterns to predict whether or not an applicant is likely to be a good or unsatisfactory credit risk. The behavioral sciences have found that human beings tend to follow certain behavior patterns throughout their lifetimes. Thus, consumer lenders make the assumption that, if a customer has been responsible about handling credit obligations in the past, his behavior will continue in the future. Likewise, individuals and families follow well-defined life cycle patterns.

General trends include rising income, greater stability, and credit needs associated with specific age and life cycle groups—all of which help lenders to make loans in conformity with the laws of probability.

However, it is equally clear that not all people follow normal life cycle trends. Divorce and separations cause some people to change behavior patterns. Mid-life crises lead some people to quit their jobs and change their lives dramatically. Such changes are virtually impossible for consumer lenders to predict or control, yet they are often the factors that cause an otherwise good loan to result in a loss.

Time requirements play a major role in the handling of consumer loan requests. Generally, a credit decision should be made the same day the application is received, if not within hours of its receipt. It is often not possible to conduct thorough investigations on consumer credit applications and remain competitive in the market. The entire loan process must be structured in the light of timing pressures.

Finally, consumer lenders rely on standardized loan policies to provide a sound framework for consistent and timely credit decision-making. It is vital, however, that loan policies not become so rigid that lenders are prevented from exercising judgment. A good decision-making system must provide a formal process for handling applications that are deserving of an exception to the standard credit policies. For example, if an applicant fails to pass the bank's credit-scoring program, but plans to fully secure a loan with his savings account, someone in the bank should be able to quickly approve an exception so that the loan can be made.

Credit Evaluation Systems

There are two basic systems used for consumer credit decision-making. They are judgmental and credit-scoring systems. Both approaches involve analyzing applicant variables to determine the probability that the applicant will turn out to be a good or bad credit risk. The underlying framework for both systems is the weighing of different applicant variables and the evaluation of trade-offs to reach a final credit decision.

The Judgmental Approach—The Six "C's" of Credit

The variables considered in the judgmental decision-making process are popularly known as the "C's" of credit. While experts may debate just how many "C's" there should be, the analysis here will focus on six "C's:"

- can we?
- character
- capacity
- capital
- collateral
- conditions.

Can We?

The first "C" is concerned with the question: "Is the loan within the bank's policy guidelines?" The lender must determine if the bank offers the type of loan product sought by the consumer. If the consumer wants to lease a car, and your bank does not offer this type of financing arrangement, there is little value in taking an application. The loan request must be for a purpose acceptable to the bank. Some banks prohibit loans for bill consolidations or to purchase motorcycles. Thus, if the applicant is pursuing a loan for either of these purposes, he should be referred to another financial institution.

In addition, the terms requested must comply with the bank's policies. If a customer asks for an automobile loan for 72 months and bank policy limits such loans to a maximum of 60 months, the customer must either accept the bank's terms or pursue the loan elsewhere.

Finally, the customer should be within the bank's market area. Customers living outside this area may be declined for that reason. In some cases, banks restrict loans only to customers of the bank. Under this policy, the lender must verify that the applicant is a bank customer before going through the time and effort of taking a loan application.

It is usually possible to eliminate loan requests that will not be in conformity with the bank's policies before taking an application or conducting an investigation. Such actions are appropriate and can save the consumer and the bank a lot of time.

Character

This variable addresses the question: "What type of person are we dealing with and what are his primary behavior patterns as they relate to key variables?" Specifically, the lender needs to look at the applicant's stability, credit history, and personal characteristics for clues as to how he can be expected to handle the loan requested. Character is regarded by many lenders to be the most important factor in granting a loan, but it is also one that is difficult to measure precisely.

Stability is measured by the individual's time on the job, time at a residence, type of employment, and time within the community. Since time factors are closely related to the applicant's age, it is essential to analyze an applicant's stability with the age factor in mind. Consider the following applicant characteristics:

Applicant 1: Age—22; time on present job—1 year; prior employment—college; time at address—1 year; time within community—22 years; occupation—salesperson.

One would not expect someone 22 years old and recently graduated from college to exhibit long-term stability; thus, to the lender, this variable should be somewhat less important than other variables. On the positive side, the applicant is a college graduate, is from the local community, and has maintained the same job since graduating from college.

Applicant 2: Age—40; time on present job—2 years; prior employment—9 years; time at address—1 year, buying home; time within community—14 years; occupation—manager.

By age 40, one would expect the applicant to demonstrate some stability, though some of the variables may be of short duration. In this case, the fact that the applicant's time at the present address is short is offset by the fact that the applicant is buying a home. Present job time is also short. The importance of this factor may be determined by considering the current employment history along with prior job history. If the applicant remained in the same industry, there may be evidence that he has moved to a higher paying or higher level job. This would certainly offset the relatively short employment history.

Applicant 3: Age—33; time on present job—6 months; prior employment—1 year; time at address—4 months, renting; time within community—6 months; occupation—salesperson.

This applicant should certainly have more stability established than is shown by these variables. Indeed, the lack of stability is a major negative factor. This is not to say that this negative will not be offset by other positive variables, resulting in loan approval.

Stability is important because consumer loans are made for extended periods of time. The lender wants to be reasonably sure that the customer will continue to be employed during the term of the loan, will continue to have regular income to service the debt, and can be found if problems develop. Job changing, career instability, such as moving from one occupation to another, and frequent changes in residence are all indicators of potential problems. Renting is also considered to be less stable than home buying or ownership. While all renters are not high credit risks, the factor requires additional consideration.

Another primary measure of character is the applicant's credit history. A thorough analysis of credit history should take into account the following characteristics:

- credit ratings
- types of credit the borrower has used
- sources of credit
- dates accounts are opened and closed
- level of debt
- credit usage patterns.

Exhibit 9–1 shows the credit history for a loan applicant. We will use this credit report to examine the applicant's credit history as it relates to each characteristic.

This credit report contains a variety of credit ratings. Ratings such as "CURR ACCT," an open or closed account in good standing, and "PAID SATIS," a closed account paid satisfactorily, are considered positive. However, the customer also has several accounts that have not been paid satisfactorily. These include: Maryland Bank—"CUR WAS 90," Sears—"CUR WAS 60," Lord & Taylor—"CUR WAS 30," and Woodward and Lothrop—"CUR WAS 150." These ratings indicate that the customer has been slow in paying some creditors. Thus, the credit ratings provide a real mixed picture of this customer. While some lenders would decline this applicant based upon the nega-

EXHIBIT 9–1
Sample Credit Report

Report Date: July 1987

Creditor	*Status*	*Status Date*	*Date Opened*	*Account Type*	*Credit Line or Loan Amount*	*Balance*
Chase	Curr Acct	3-84	4-80	Revolving	$ 2,000	
Union Trust	Paid Satis	3-83	2-79	Auto	10,900	
Union Trust	Paid Satis	5-86	7-83	Auto	11,200	
Sovran Bank	Curr Acct	6-86	3-83	Credit Card	2,000	
United Virginia	Curr Acct	6-86	4-84	Revolving	2,600	$ 2,570
Maryland Bank	Cur Was 90	10-84	4-84	Revolving	2,000	
Beneficial Bank	Curr Acct	6-86	3-82	Revolving	16,000	12,500
Union Trust	Curr Acct	6-86	7-84	Revolving	7,500	
Sears	Cur Was 60	3-86	9-81	Revolving	1,300	
Bloomingdales	Curr Acct	6-86	1-79	Revolving	800	
Lord and Taylor	Cur Was 30	4-86	3-80	Revolving	200	
Woodward & Lothrop	Cur Was 150	7-85	10Y	Revolving	2,500	2,400
Hechts	Curr Acct	6-86	10Y	Revolving	800	
Hutzlers	Curr Acct	6-82	10Y	Revolving	300	
Citicorp/Choice	Curr Acct	8-81	10Y	Revolving	700	
HFC	Paid Satis	9-82	6-79	Note	4,900	
I Magnin	Curr Acct	7-86	11-77	Revolving	100	
Diners Club	Paid Satis	10-81	6-79	Revolving	Unknown	
Bank of NY	Inquiry	6-30-86				
Bank Ohio	Inquiry	10-24-85				
Union Trust	Inquiry	7-1-86				

tive ratings, it seems appropriate to examine the report in more detail.

The report shows that most of the applicant's credit is in the form of revolving credit accounts (14 of 18 accounts are revolving accounts). Two accounts are installment automobile loans, and one is an installment loan from Household Finance. The final account is Diners Club, which is a travel and entertainment card calling for payments in full each month. This tells us that the customer has had experience with a variety of types of credit.

The applicant has borrowed from a variety of sources, including banks, retailers, and finance companies. There is a bias among some lenders regarding applicants who borrow from finance companies since such companies frequently attract only high-risk customers. However, this factor should be viewed in the context of the individual application.

The dates that accounts are opened and closed are important to a proper evaluation of each credit reference. The dates help to identify recent credit activity and the length of credit experience. Recent credit activity can be identified by looking down the "DATE OPENED" column and noting any loans opened within the past year. Assuming the sample credit report was taken in June 1987, this customer would not have any loans in this category. However, should an applicant have a lot of recent credit activity, it could be an indication that he is *pyramiding* his debts—taking on a significant amount of debt in a short period of time. The danger in this situation is that the customer may be unable to adjust his finances to properly handle the new debt requirements. Indeed, a high percentage of loans that are charged off deteriorate in the first year after the loan is made.

The length of credit history should also be evaluated in the context of the applicant's age. Young customers do not have long credit histories, while customers 30 years old and older should show at least 5 years of credit history. The applicant whose credit report is shown in the exhibit has a credit history running back more than 10 years.

The dates of references are also important to the lender. The credit report indicates the date that a specific reference was given. For example, in evaluating the delinquent ratings on the sample credit report, it is important to note that the delinquency on the Maryland Bank account is from 10–84, and Woodward & Lothrop from 7–85, while the more recent delinquencies are on retailer accounts, which now have zero balances. This indicates that the customer has not had any significant credit problems in the most recent year.

Level of debt has become an increasingly important measure due to the increased usage of open-end credit. For example, our sample customer has $17,470 in credit account balances as of the date of the report. But, the customer also has access to credit lines with an available balance of $21,330, which is the difference between the available amount and any current balance due on accounts that are shown as still being open. Thus, the customer could increase his debts to $38,800 without requesting any new credit.

Another consideration is the total amount of debt in relation to the customer's income. It is possible for consumers to accumulate very high debts and still meet the bank's debt-to-income standards. This has occurred as a result of maturities on loans being stretched out to keep monthly payments at a level consumers find attractive. The result is that monthly payments may be low, while aggregate loan amounts can be substantial.

The final item on the credit report that should be analyzed is the applicant's credit usage patterns, in particular the use of revolving credit accounts. This is analyzed by looking at the total amount of open-end credit lines available and the amount owed on those accounts. In our example, the customer is a heavy user of three credit lines—United Virginia, Beneficial, and Woodward & Lothrop—while most of the other lines are not used at all.

The customer usage patterns can have an impact upon the final credit decision. For example, if a heavy user of revolving credit applies for a loan to consolidate his revolving accounts, the lender must be concerned with protecting the bank's interest in the event the customer begins using the accounts again after the new loan is made. *Exhibit 9–2* is an example of a credit report on a heavy user of revolving credit.

Note that this credit report shows that the customer has established many open-end credit accounts and that virtually every account is up to or over the credit limit established by the lender. This is a sign that the customer is so entrenched in making purchases using credit cards that it would be very difficult for him to change his behavior pattern. If offered another line of credit, this person would most likely accept the offer and use it fully.

Credit reports are, therefore, an essential tool in helping the lender develop a general opinion of the applicant's character. This is easy when all of the information is positive and there is no evidence of any problems. However, most lenders will be confronted with credit reports that contain a mixture of good and bad references, and perhaps a few "red flags." The lender's ability to correctly interpret these "gray area" loans can determine whether or not an acceptable lending record is achieved over time.

Character may also be evaluated based upon such variables as type of job and personal reputation. Personal reputation undoubtedly comes into play when the applicant is known to the lender. However, care must be exercised in making credit decisions based upon such personal knowledge. In some cases, the lender may know that the applicant is related to a family that has a history of bad credit with the bank, or that the applicant is an alcoholic who is constantly getting into trouble with the law.

EXHIBIT 9–2
Sample Credit Report for a Heavy Revolving Credit User

Report Date: August 1985

Creditor	*Status*	*Status Date*	*Date Opened*	*Account Type*	*Credit Line or Loan Amount*	*Balance*
Equitable Bank	Curr Acct	7-85	11-84	Revolving	$2,000	$1,885
Dominion Bank	Curr Acct	7-85	5-84	Revolving	2,000	1,953
Citibank VISA	Curr Acct	6-85	9-84	Revolving	1,500	1,443
JC Penney	Curr Acct	7-85	10Y	Revolving	1,700	1,496
JC Penney	Curr Acct	7-85	10Y	Revolving	1,300	1,139
Sears	Curr Acct	7-85	10Y	Revolving	3,100	3,073
Wards	Curr Acct	6-85	10Y	Revolving	3,000	1,947
Citicorp/Choice	Curr Acct	7-85	6-84	Revolving	1,000	986
Security Pacific	Curr Acct	7-85	6-84	Note	4,100	2,843
Finance America	Curr Acct	6-85	3-83	Note	1,600	277
Spiegel	Curr Acct	7-85	10Y	Revolving	1,900	1,507
Firestone	Curr Acct	6-85	6-83	Revolving	900	884
GECC	Curr Acct	7-85	4-84	Revolving	1,000	1,029
Beneficial Bank	Curr Acct	7-85	5-78	Revolving	3,200	3,356

Such intangible information must be evaluated along with more objective tangible credit criteria in order to avoid making an inappropriate credit decision.

Many studies have demonstrated a correlation between job type and credit experience. Some credit-scoring programs assign points based on the type of job (see *Exhibit 9–3*), and many lenders consider this factor as part of their judgmental system.

Job rankings arise out of the fact that certain occupations are associated with higher income levels, greater employment security, and higher levels of job mobility, while others are associated with inconsistent employment, high failure rates, and short job tenures. Many lenders using judgmental systems also have their own list of problem occupations. This list may be influenced by recent experiences or local economic conditions.

Capacity

This variable addresses the question: "Does the applicant have the ability to repay the loan and handle the proposed new level of debt?"

EXHIBIT 9–3
Sample Credit Scoring of Job Type

Occupation	*Points*
Professional & official	27
Foreman & operative	26
Technical & managers	14
Clerical & sales	12
Service worker	5
Farm worker	3
Craftsman & non-farm labor	0
Proprietor	−3

There are two parts to measuring capacity. One is determining the customer's income; the other is evaluating the customer's financial obligations. Although it might seem easy to determine each of these factors, there are many factors that make an assessment difficult.

Determining the customer's income begins with the issue of which income to consider. This is a matter of bank policy and credit regulation. The Equal Credit Opportunity Act requires lenders to count income from part-time jobs and public assistance in addition to income from the applicant's primary job. In addition, if the applicant wishes, the bank must take into account any income from alimony, child support, and separate maintenance payments. To assure consistency, the eligible types of income should be specified in the bank's policy. Income from investments and less predictable and consistent sources, such as commissions and bonuses, must be treated carefully.

A common, but less clear-cut, issue is which income to include when evaluating the capacity of joint or multiple applicants. For example, if two people, who are not married to each other, apply for a loan, should the incomes and debts be combined to evaluate capacity, or should the lender look only at the primary applicant's income? When the bank's policy calls for the lender to count both incomes for married applicants, then the lender may also combine the incomes of unmarried joint applicants. This issue becomes even more complex when the joint applicants do not live at the same address. It is not uncommon to have couples who are engaged to be married to apply for joint credit accounts, or for unmarried couples who live together to apply for joint accounts. Thus, the bank should structure its lending policies to recognize the realities of the social environment as well as the legal environment. The bank's attorney should carefully review these issues and develop a consistent credit evaluation policy.

Age is a factor when the applicant will reach retirement age during the term of the loan. Retirement can mean a change in the level of income and life-style, and this should be taken into account when evaluating future capacity to handle the debt. The lender will need to determine the post-retirement level of income before reaching a decision on applicants in this category.

The other part of the capacity equation is measuring the applicant's obligations. Many lenders have made the mistake of reviewing an application from a high-income consumer and leaping to the conclusion that, because the income is high, the customer must be able to afford a loan. Often overlooked is the fact that, as income rises, so might a customer's expenses. People tend to spend what they make, and, while the amount available for discretionary spending tends to increase with income, such is not always the case.

Evaluation of financial obligations is sometimes confined to the customer's contractual obligations. Using this approach, the lender totals the required minimum monthly debt payments, and then relates that amount to the customer's income to determine the debt-to-income ratio. An example is presented as *Exhibit 9–4*.

The ratio of 26.5 percent should then be compared to the bank's policy to determine whether or not the proposed loan falls within the acceptable debt-to-income ratio. *Exhibit 9–5* shows the amount of debt that borrowers could have at various income levels based upon a 30 percent and 35 percent debt-to-income ratio.

The debt-to-income table can be used to help structure a loan that a customer can afford. Assuming an applicant had a gross annual income of $36,000, he could afford $1,050 in monthly debt payments at the 35 percent debt-to-income ratio level. Assuming the customer currently had the following debt structure, he would not meet the bank's requirements:

EXHIBIT 9–4
Sample Debt-to-Income Ratio Calculation

Debt	*Minimum Required Monthly Payment*
Mortgage payment	$500
Auto loan	295
VISA	50
MasterCard	65
New loan request	150
Total monthly debt	$1,060
Gross monthly income	$4,000
Debt-to-income ratio	26.5%

Mortgage—$400
Auto loan—250
Finance company loan—175
VISA—75
MasterCard—50
Store account—50
Bank loan—200
New loan: home improvements—150

Monthly Payments: $1,350

However, if the lender were to restructure the applicant's debts, and consolidate some existing loans with the new loan, the applicant could meet the bank's requirements:

Mortgage—$400
Auto loan—250
0
0
0
0
0
New loan: second mortgage—325

Monthly payments: $975

This illustrates how a lender may be able to structure the best loan for the customer and the bank. The loan request, resulting in $1,350 in monthly payments, would end in a rejection. The

EXHIBIT 9–5
Sample Debt-to-Income Table

Gross Income	Maximum Debt Service 35%	Maximum Debt Service 30%	Gross Annual Income	Maximum Monthly Debt Service 35%	Maximum Monthly Debt Service 30%
10,000	292	250	41,000	1196	1025
11,000	321	275	42,000	1225	1050
12,000	350	300	43,000	1254	1075
13,000	379	325	44,000	1283	1100
14,000	408	350	45,000	1312	1125
15,000	438	375	46,000	1342	1150
16,000	467	400	47,000	1370	1175
17,000	496	425	48,000	1400	1200
18,000	525	450	49,000	1429	1225
19,000	554	475	50,000	1458	1250
20,000	583	500	55,000	1604	1375
21,000	613	525	60,000	1750	1500
22,000	642	550	65,000	1896	1625
23,000	671	575	70,000	2041	1750
24,000	700	600	75,000	2188	1875
25,000	729	625	80,000	2333	2000
26,000	758	650	85,000	2479	2125
27,000	788	675	90,000	2625	2250
28,000	817	700	95,000	2770	2375
29,000	846	725	100,000	2917	2500
30,000	875	750	105,000	3063	2625
31,000	904	775	110,000	3208	2750
32,000	933	800	120,000	3500	3000
33,000	963	825	130,000	3791	3250
34,000	992	850	140,000	4083	3500
35,000	1021	875	150,000	4375	3750
36,000	1050	900	160,000	4667	4000
37,000	1079	925	170,000	4958	4250
38,000	1108	950	180,000	5250	4500
39,000	1138	975	190,000	5542	4750
40,000	1167	1000	200,000	5833	5000

proposed debt structure, which includes paying off five existing loan balances, would result in $975 in monthly payments, thus qualifying the customer for a loan.

Some banks have developed more elaborate systems for measuring capacity. These systems recognize that people have different life-styles and different expense patterns, which can affect their ability to assume debt. Factors such as the number and age of dependents, hobbies, geographic location, and general life-style all have an impact on cash flowing through the family budget. However, measurement of varying expenses can be a difficult and time-consuming exercise. The problem of inconsistency in calculation can also occur, increasing the risk of illegal discrimination.

An example of this approach to measuring capacity follows. The customer is asked to complete the schedule that follows to assist the bank in its credit evaluation.

Expense Category	Monthly Amount
Rent or mortgage	______
Food	______
Gas & electric	______
Clothing	______
Transportation	______
Telephone	______
Insurance	______
Auto loan	______
Other loans	______
Entertainment	______
Miscellaneous	______
Total monthly expenses	______
Total monthly income	______
Difference	______

The total amount of all expenses is then compared to the applicant's income to determine if it is sufficient to cover all of the itemized expenses. This provides a full cash flow analysis for the applicant. The problem with this approach, however, is that it is impossible to verify most of the information on the schedule, and the customer's estimations could be way off. Accumulating this information can also be time-consuming, which is contrary to the emphasis on convenience and fast decision-making.

No matter which approach is used, it is essential that the bank develop a measure of capacity and use it consistently. It is clear that consumers get into trouble handling their debts when either their income declines or their level of debt increases beyond a certain point.

Capital

Capital is concerned with answering the question: "Is there backup capacity for the customer to pay the bank if adverse situations develop?"

Backup capacity comes from the individual's personal assets. The value of personal assets is often very difficult to determine without formal appraisals or reference to valuation guidebooks for tangible goods. The consumer's *net worth*—the amount by which the value of assets exceeds the amount owed on those assets—is of equal interest to the lender. This information is generally shown on a personal financial statement as shown in *Exhibit 9–6*.

Assets may be divided into several groups in order to examine their value as backup capacity. *Liquid assets* are a measure of the consumer's ability to meet short-term cash needs, while *tangible assets*, such as a home, may provide more protection against serious financial problems.

Liquid assets are assets that may easily and quickly be converted to cash, such as cash on hand and in banks; stocks, bonds, and similar investments; and the cash value of life insurance. These represent an individual's first line of defense against unexpected financial emergencies. They help the consumer meet short-term declines in income or increases in expenses such as medical emergencies, funeral expenses, and accidents that cause a loss of income.

Equity in a home comprises a substantial portion of most consumers' net worth. *Equity* is the difference between the market value of the home and the amount owed on mortgages on the property. From the lender's viewpoint, this equity can represent a significant source of backup capacity.

The equity in a home can give consumers access to borrowing power that can increase their liquidity. Given the wide availability of second mortgage and home equity loans, consumers may be able to borrow to meet financial needs. But, liquidity is not guaranteed. Consumers with credit problems may not be able to borrow when they need money since lenders generally do not make loans to financially troubled consumers. In addition, selling a home is not always an easy task, and homes often do not sell for the fair market value. The result is that home equity is usually viewed as valuable backup capital in a worst case environment—when the bank has taken or is about to take a loss on a loan. Home equity has a far more positive connotation when it is viewed as primary collateral for a second mortgage or home equity line of credit account.

Automobiles, boats, recreational vehicles, and other assets may also provide backup capacity for a loan. The value of these

EXHIBIT 9–6
Sample Personal Financial Statement

PERSONAL FINANCIAL STATEMENT
(Type or Print)

SECTION A – INDIVIDUAL INFORMATION				SECTION B – OTHER PARTY INFORMATION			
Name	Franklin Stone			Name			
Address	2209 Dabney Road			Address			
City, State & Zip	Ames, Iowa 56129			City, State & Zip			
Position/Occupation	Self-Employed			Position/Occupation			
Business Name	Franklin Stone, Inc			Business Name			
Business Address	same as above			Business Address			
City, State & Zip				City, State & Zip			
Res. Phone	630-8644	Bus. Phone	630-9129	Res. Phone		Bus. Phone	
Soc. Sec. No.	589-XX-XXXX	Date of Birth	10/26/48	Soc. Sec. No.		Date of Birth	

SECTION C – STATEMENT OF FINANCIAL CONDITION AS OF December 31, 19 85

ASSETS		LIABILITIES	
Cash on hand and in Banks (Schedule 1)	5,700	Notes payable to banks - secured (Schedule 6)	5,000
U.S. Gov't. & Marketable Securities (Schedule 2)	9,600	Notes payable to banks - unsecured (Schedule 6)	
Cash Value of Life Insurance (Schedule 5)	2,000	Due to brokers	
SUBTOTAL LIQUID ASSETS	$17,300	Loans against Life Insurance (Schedule 5)	
		Notes payable to others - secured (Schedule 6)	
Non-Marketable Securities (Schedule 3)		Notes payable to others - unsecured (Schedule 6)	
Securities held by broker in margin accounts		Accounts and bills due	2,700
Accounts Receivable – good		Accrued taxes and interest	
Notes Receivable – good		Other unpaid taxes	
Real Estate owned (Schedule 4)	120,000	Real estate mortgages payable (Schedule 4)	45,000
Real Estate Mortgages owned		Other debts - itemize:	
Partial interest in Real Estate Equities (Schedule 4)			
Automobiles and other personal property (Schedule 7)	3,000		
Interest in Business Owned	50,000	TOTAL LIABILITIES	$ 52,700
Other assets – itemize:			
		NET WORTH	$137,600
TOTAL ASSETS	$190,300	TOTAL LIABILITIES & NET WORTH	$190,300

SECTION D – SOURCE OF INCOME FOR YEAR ENDED December 31, 1985			SECTION E – GENERAL INFORMATION
Alimony, child support, or separate maintenance income need not be revealed if you do not wish to have it considered as a basis for repaying this obligation.			Are you obligated to pay alimony, child support or separate maintenance payments? If so, describe. No.
Salary		$	Are any assets pledged other than as described on schedules? If so, describe. No
Bonus and commissions		$	
Dividends		$ 1200.00	Are you a partner or officer in any other venture? If so, describe. No
Real Estate income		$	
Other Income	Business	37,609.00	Are you a defendant in any suits or legal actions? No
			Have you ever taken bankruptcy? Explain: No
TOTAL		$ 38,809.00	

SECTION F – CONTINGENT LIABILITIES NONE		SECTION G – MARITAL STATUS
As endorser or comaker	$	THIS SECTION IS OPTIONAL IF YOU ARE REQUESTING INDIVIDUAL UNSECURED CREDIT FOR PERSONAL OR HOUSEHOLD USE.
On leases or contracts	$	Applicant: ☐ Married ☐ Separated
Legal claims	$	☒ Unmarried (including single, divorced, and widowed)
Provision for Federal Income Taxes	$	Other Party: ☐ Married ☐ Separated
Other special debt	$	☐ Unmarried (including single, divorced, and widowed)

Form 1386 (12/82) Rev.

Most banks don't require a PFS
Bank of Mortgage or Equity loan (FANNIE MAE)

assets depends upon their age, model, market demand, condition, and the amount of any existing debt that they are securing. If the consumer has equity built up in these assets, they can provide additional protection for other lenders. It should be noted that equity in automobiles, boats, and similar assets can deteriorate significantly in the event it is necessary to repossess or foreclose on the collateral since assets, except for homes, usually depreciate over time. As a result, the proceeds from the sale of assets may not even bring enough to cover the first lien, much less provide equity to cover a second lien.

Assets such as art collections, antiques, and the like are rarely of value as backup capacity. The problems of appraising, obtaining a lien, repossessing, and selling such assets make it difficult, if not impossible, to view these assets as providing tangible net worth.

The personal financial statement also provides insight regarding the consumer's debt structure. As already noted, a clear picture of a consumer's equity position is obtained by looking at his assets in relation to the debts that they secure. Another frequently used measure of a consumer's financial condition is the level of debt in relation to net worth, known as *leverage*. Young customers are generally in a highly leveraged position—that is, their debts are nearly equal to or exceed their assets, and their net worth is small or nonexistent. Net worth should increase over time if the consumer is practicing sound financial management. In some extreme cases, debts may actually exceed the value of the consumer's assets, making the customer insolvent. This condition is frequently observed in individuals who find it necessary or desirable to declare bankruptcy.

The importance of capital in evaluating consumer credit requests has been increasing in recent years. This is due to the increased use of open-end credit programs. The ongoing availability of an open-end line exposes the bank to loss over a much longer period of time than the normal closed-end loan. Therefore, in analyzing requests for large open-end lines of credit, and when reconfirming a line of credit as part of a periodic review, lenders are placing more emphasis upon the evaluation of capital. Some banks require consumers to submit financial statements at regular intervals so they can identify any adverse trends or marketing opportunities.

Another reason for the increased use of analytical tools to evaluate capital is the increasing size of some consumer loans.

Closed-end loans for boats, airplanes, and second mortgages range up to $200,000 and more. As the size of loans increases, the level and extent of required credit analysis also increase. Backup capacity becomes a critical issue, and the size of the loans dictates that more time be spent analyzing the proposed credit extension.

Collateral

The issue of collateral raises the question: "Is there a readily available secondary source of repayment on the loan?" The analysis of collateral differs from the analysis of capital in that it evaluates a specific asset that is actually pledged to secure the loan.

The primary source of repayment is always the customer's regular income. But, when something happens to diminish the customer's ability to repay loans from his regular income, the bank may look to some form of collateral to provide the funds necessary to pay off the loan balance. This is not to say that it is necessary or even possible to take collateral on every loan. Sound unsecured lending is a part of virtually every successful consumer credit program. The lender places reliance upon the other elements of the "C's" of credit, particularly the customer's character and capacity, when lending on an unsecured basis.

Collateral provides protection to the bank to the extent that it can be sold for more than it costs to be repossessed. More often than not, the forced sale of collateral results in a loss or *deficiency balance*—in other words, money is still owed the bank after the collateral has been repossessed and sold and the proceeds applied to the account. Therefore, it is sound practice not to make a loan simply because it appears that the bank will have a good collateral position. All too often, the bank may still take a loss or incur very high expenses in trying to collect loans from borrowers who should not have been granted a loan in the first place. Collateral does not replace character, credit, or the ability to handle the debt level. The evaluation of collateral includes—

- the value of the collateral
- the behavior pattern of the collateral's value—depreciating, appreciating, stable, or fluctuating
- the ease of collateral possession
- the marketability of the collateral
- ownership of the collateral.

Collateral becomes more important as the size of the loan or credit line increases. Lending personnel should know how to evaluate various types of collateral, and the bank's loan policies should provide precise guidelines for acceptable and unacceptable collateral. Ideally, collateral should be viewed as a means of strengthening a loan; it should not be a substitute for the bank's other credit requirements. This philosophy is evident in the growing use of 100 percent automobile finance programs. Less emphasis is placed upon equity and collateral and more upon the customer's character and ability to pay.

Conditions

This variable addresses the question: "Are there any relevant outside influences?" Outside influences might include changes in the economy, social environment, government regulation, or condition of the bank itself, all of which may influence the bank's lending policies, in general, or the loan request, in particular. Consider the following examples:

- You receive an application from an individual who works for a firm that has recently announced it is going to close its local plant.
- You receive an application from an individual who is an alien resident who has a temporary visa.
- Your bank is experiencing severe earnings problems and is reducing the consumer credit staff.
- The latest economic forecast calls for rising interest rates, growing unemployment, and an increase in the inflation rate.
- Your bank recently became the target of a women's activist group, which is charging that the bank has discriminated against women in employment and in the granting of credit. You are currently considering an application from a member of the protest group.
- Several local industries are expecting to lay off portions of their work forces due to seasonal declines in sales. You are considering applications from a number of consumers who are employed by those firms.

In cases such as these, outside factors may have an effect on the ultimate credit decision. Often, only individual credit requests are affected; in other cases, the bank may alter its lending policy so that all customers are affected equally. The latter situation was prevalent in 1980 when many banks tightened their credit criteria in response to the squeeze on profit margins resulting from the dramatic rise in the bank's cost of funds.

Changes in the external environment are normally reflected in changes to the bank's lending policies. New government regulations become an immediate part of lending policy, while changes in the social environment tend to take a little longer to be reflected in lending practices. Economic trends affect banks in widely different ways. Small banks are much more susceptible to economic problems in their primary market area than are larger banks, which operate in more diverse market areas. As a result, small banks may need to make more frequent changes in their lending policies in response to fluctuating local conditions. In any case, it is essential that each bank monitor the external environment so that changing conditions can be responded to effectively.

Decision Models

In a judgmental system, the final credit decision rests upon an analysis of each of the six "C's." Strengths and weaknesses are weighed against each other to form an overall opinion of the loan. *Exhibits 9–7* and *9–8* demonstrate the way in which tradeoffs may be evaluated and decisions made. In *Exhibit 9–7*, the matrix is filled in by indicating a "+" for all positive customer characteristics, a "−" for all negative characteristics, and a "0" for all nominal characteristics. This analysis can help the lender weigh each characteristic and arrive at a more objective decision. It should not be assumed, however, that if the customer ends up with more pluses than minuses that the loan should be made since some variables are more important than others.

Another approach is known as the *teeter totter system* of analysis, as shown in *Exhibit 9–8*. This approach attempts to balance the pluses and minuses on a fulcrum and establish ranges of acceptable, unacceptable, and marginal loans. The teeter totter approach illustrates the kind of thought process lenders go through to reach a final credit decision. In a judgmental system, lenders further condition the decision based upon their experience and their "feel" for the customer and the loan requested. The art of lending lies in being able to balance all of the variables

EXHIBIT 9–7
Decision-Making Matrix

Can We? Policy	Character	Capacity	Capital	Collateral	Conditions
+	+	+	+	+	−
	−	+	−	+	
	−			−	
	+				

and, using experience as a guide, make the best possible credit decision.

The Credit-Scoring Approach

Credit-scoring systems are an attempt to quantify—that is, reduce to hard numbers—the pluses and minuses of the judgmental system. Variables are numerically weighted to predict the probability that the customer will repay the loan in a satisfactory manner. Credit-scoring systems are an attempt to make lending a science, using sophisticated mathematical analysis to help define the level of risk on a given application.

Scoring systems are developed using the same logic used in any judgmental system. Many credit variables are analyzed in an attempt to identify which combination of variables is most predictive of the level of credit risk. The list is usually reduced to a group of from 6 to 12 variables, which are assigned point values based upon the bank's previous experience with a large base of customers. Characteristics that exemplify "good" accounts are assigned a high number of points, while characteristics of "bad" accounts are given a lower value. The result is a decision-making system similar to the one in *Exhibit 9–9.*

The lender first tabulates the applicant's score for each personal characteristic. Assuming the applicant's total score exceeds a predetermined minimum requirement, the lender then proceeds to the next step, which may be to obtain a credit

EXHIBIT 9–8
Teeter Totter Analysis System

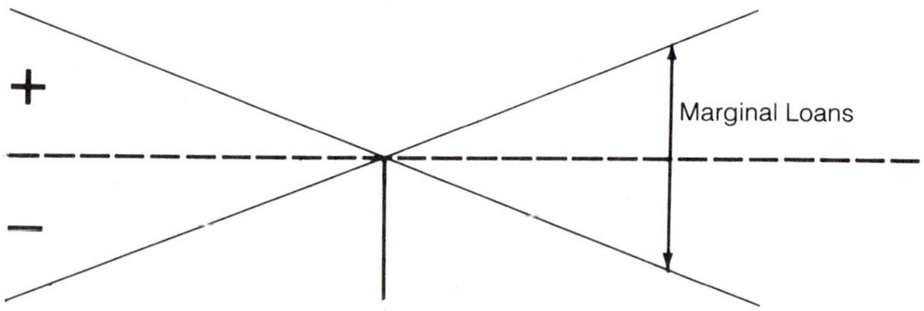

bureau report or credit references. Elements on the credit report are scored and added to the total to arrive at a grand total. If the applicant does not achieve the minimum score requirement, the loan may be rejected at this point, eliminating the need to spend time and money conducting a thorough credit investigation. If the customer meets the scoring requirement, the lender may then proceed with such time-consuming steps as an in-depth credit investigation and calculation of debt-to-income ratios.

Among the advantages of credit scoring are the following:

- *Increased management control.* An effective credit-scoring system ensures consistent decision-making. All loans that comply with the bank's loan policy and meet the scoring requirements will be made, while loans not meeting those requirements will be rejected. Furthermore, credit requirements can be raised or lowered simply by adjusting the minimum acceptable score.
- *Reduced loan processing costs.* Consideration of a loan can be concluded at any point where the applicant fails to meet minimum requirements. Thus, it is possible to eliminate the need to pull credit reports or conduct investigations on loans that are below cutoff scores.
- *More legally defensible system.* Empirically derived, statistically sound credit-scoring systems are recognized by the Equal Credit Opportunity Act. They provide more consistent decision-making and help control the variables that are used in

EXHIBIT 9–9
Hypothetical Credit-Scoring System

Applicant Characteristics	*Points*
Home Phone	
Yes	36
No	0
Housing Status	
Own or buying	34
Rent	15
Other	5
Applicant Occupation	
Professional & official	27
Foreman & operative	26
Technical & managers	14
Clerical & sales	12
Service worker	5
Farm worker	3
Craftsman & non-farm labor	0
Proprietor	−3
Finance Company Reference	
Yes	−12
No	0
Applicant Age	
30 or less	6
30+ to 40	8
40+ to 50	11
Over 50	16
Time on Job	
Under 1 year	0
1 to 5 years	8
5+ to 10 years	12
Over 10 years	20
Total Score	______
Credit References	
All references good—3 or more	20
At least 2 good references & no negatives	15
No references	0
Some minor derogatory references	−5
Major derogatory information—judgments, repossessions, bankruptcy	−15
Credit Inquiries	
None	8
1 to 3 in last 6 months	2
More than 3	−5
Grand Total	______

arriving at a final decision. Consequently, there is no opportunity to unfairly discriminate based upon a prohibited variable.

- *Easier training of new lenders.* Banks with large lending staffs often have a hard time maintaining a high level of lending skills. Credit scoring makes it far easier to train new lenders and to get consistent decisions. Credit scoring shifts the role of the lender from being one who evaluates the relative level of credit risk to that of a marketer, responsible for structuring loans and selling other bank services.
- *Facilitated data gathering.* Good system design allows the bank to constantly monitor the loan portfolio to ensure that the system is functioning properly. Management is better able to monitor trends in the ranges of credit risk for the entire portfolio or, if desired, the portfolio can be subdivided into smaller units, such as branch offices or marine loans.

Credit scoring is not for every bank, however. Many banks are simply too small to justify the expense of establishing and using an empirically derived, statistically sound system to be developed. In many cases, the bank is fully satisfied with its judgmental system and, as long as the results are in line with management's portfolio objectives, there is little need to change. Other banks, particularly large branch banking systems, have much to gain by using credit scoring. In fact, some banks have managed to automate the process to the point where it is possible for customers to sit down at a computer terminal, type in their applications, and have the system score the request and give a conditional approval on the spot. This use of credit scoring shows just how far the "lending is a science" philosophy has developed.

Evaluating Variable Rate Debt

Prior to 1980, the overwhelming majority of consumer loans had fixed rates. However, since that time, many banks have placed increased emphasis upon the development of variable rate portfolios. Variable rate loans can have a positive effect on maintaining the bank's interest margins, but they can also have a negative impact on the level of credit risk on some accounts. For example, for a consumer with an adjustable rate mortgage and several other variable rate loans, a rise in the interest rate translates into higher monthly payments, quite possibly driving up the monthly debt-to-income ratio from an acceptable level to a precarious one. Thus, in a rising interest rate environment, the consumer may be squeezed without taking on any additional debt.

On the other hand, if rate increases are passed on in the form of extended payment schedules, the result is *negative amortization,* a situation in which the minimum monthly payment is not sufficient to cover the interest due. The shortfall may be added to the consumer's balance to be paid later. If this were to continue for very long, the consumer could lose any equity position that he may have had in collateral securing the loan, thereby increasing the level of credit risk and damaging the bank's position.

Variable rate lending has introduced new considerations into the credit evaluation process. In analyzing credit, it is important to know if the applicant has any variable rate loans and, if so, how changes in the interest rate will affect the applicant's ability to repay debt. In response to this situation, many banks have changed their formulas for calculating capacity to allow for an increase in the level of monthly payments on variable rate loans. For example, if a customer had variable rate loan payments of $300, the bank may figure in an increase of 15 percent—$45—before calculating the debt-to-income ratio. This approach provides an extra measure of protection and caution in the decision-making process.

Declining a Loan

Not all loan applicants end up with an approved loan. The percentage of loan requests resulting in adverse action range widely from bank to bank and from loan product to loan product. On average, 20 to 50 percent of all loan applications are rejected. These decisions must be properly documented to ensure compliance with the provisions of the Fair Credit Reporting Act and the Equal Credit Opportunity Act.

The loan officer has two primary objectives in informing the customer of an adverse loan decision: maintaining the customer's goodwill and complying with all regulations regarding adverse action. One way of preserving goodwill is to offer financial counseling. If the consumer is aware of what factors the lender considers in evaluating creditworthiness, he may be able to take positive steps that will enable him to qualify for credit in the future. For example, many loans are rejected because a borrower has overextended himself on existing credit accounts and simply does not have the income to support additional debt. The lender may be able to suggest ways that the consumer can get his debts under control and reduce the level of monthly payments to an acceptable level.

Although many consumers know in advance that they will not qualify for a loan, this does not stop them from applying. What they may not know is how to correct the problem. This lack of knowledge gives the lending officer a chance to provide some valuable counseling and to send the consumer away with a positive impression of the bank.

The second objective, ensuring regulatory compliance, is an equally important consideration when dealing with rejected loan applications. Consumers must receive notice of an adverse action within 30 days from the time the application was made. These notices must be prepared in accordance with the Equal Credit Opportunity Act and accurately reflect the reasons for the adverse decision.

Summary

The credit evaluation and decision-making process requires lenders to evaluate the relative importance of many variables in order to arrive at a final decision that will best serve the needs of the customer and the bank. Credit analysis involves weighing trade-offs and balancing key decision variables to determine which variables are most important in any given situation.

Consumer loans may be analyzed in a judgmental system using the six "C's" of credit—can we?, character, capacity, capital, collateral, and conditions. Judgmental and credit-scoring systems are used to evaluate the information that was gathered on the application and verified by the credit investigation, thus enabling the lender to reach a final credit decision.

Credit analysis has become more complex and taken on added importance in recent years. New products, higher average loan amounts, expanded use of lines of credit, and the introduction of variable rate loans have introduced new considerations into the decision-making process.

Questions for Review and Discussion

1. How does the law of probability enter into the consumer credit decision-making process?

2. What principle of human behavior helps the credit decision-maker in making assumptions about an applicant's future creditworthiness?

3. What elements of the applicant's "character" are judged during the credit evaluation process?

4. Name the six "C's" of credit and give an example of what information the credit analyst examines regarding each.

5. What is your bank's debt-to-income ratio, if it has one, for personal, unsecured loans? Ask your consumer credit manager if it is standard for the bank's market area or whether it is on the liberal or conservative side. Finally, is it rigidly applied or relatively flexible, depending on other facts indicative of the applicant's capacity?

6. What effect do the borrower's personal assets have on the evaluation of his creditworthiness?

7. Name several assets that have value as backup capacity for a loan. Name several with little real value as backup capacity.

8. Does your bank use a credit-scoring or a judgmental approach to credit evaluation; or are both used, each for different types of credit? If your bank uses a credit-scoring system, was it developed internally? If it uses a judgmental system, who has final authority for the decisions?

10 Credit Math, Loan Pricing, and Profitability

Managing a profitable consumer credit operation has become more challenging in recent years due to the deregulation of banking. Deregulation has led to greater uncertainties in the market, affecting the price and behavior pattern of deposit costs and the rates and manner of pricing loan products. To meet the challenge of these new uncertainties, consumer lenders have changed their traditional product lines and have become more astute managers of their operations.

In this chapter, we will first examine the basic elements of credit math—the various types of interest rates that are associated with consumer credit and some of the methods that are used to compute finance charges and monthly loan payments. We will then discuss the factors that affect how consumer credit products are priced, including the role that regulators, competitors, general economic conditions, and the bank's unique objectives play in setting loan pricing decisions. Attention will then be directed toward understanding the cost factors involved in consumer credit operations and the measurement of loan profitability. Finally, we will examine the role of fixed and variable rate pricing programs and how these programs are structured.

Credit Math

Computing the terms of a loan has been made much easier thanks to the availability of rate books and computers. Essentially, lenders need only understand how to use these resources in order to answer consumers' questions about the cost of borrowing money and the relative costs of one type of loan over another. Banks have expanded their use of computer technology to provide better service to customers and more support for the bank's selling effort. However, there are basic elements of credit math that all lenders should understand, including the dfiferent types of rates quoted in the market and the relationship of the various elements that make up the terms of the loan.

Types of Rates

Six types of rates are frequently referred to by consumer lenders:

- annual percentage rate (APR)
- simple interest rate
- add-on rate
- discount rate
- fixed rate
- variable rate.

The first four rates represent a method of calculating the interest on a loan, while the last two represent the behavior pattern of the loan rate during the term of the loan.

The Truth in Lending Act requires that the APR be disclosed for consumer loans. The act provides detailed and precise formulas that must be used to calculate the APR under a wide variety of loan terms. The *APR* is the finance charge on a loan expressed as an annualized percentage. It is important to understand that the annual percentage rate can be different from the interest rate on the loan if the loan includes certain fees that are considered by the Truth in Lending Act to be part of the finance charge. For example, if the bank charges points, loan fees, or similar charges, the simple interest rate on a loan might be 12 percent, but the APR could be 12.25 percent because the fees must be added to the interest charge before calculating the APR.

Simple interest is a method of computing and quoting interest rates based upon applying an interest rate to the average daily loan balance outstanding on the loan during a specific period of time. The rate is generally expressed as an annual rate; however, it is also commonly shown as a daily periodic rate on open-end credit accounts. For example, if the APR is 12 percent, the daily periodic rate is .032876 percent—that is, the annual rate divided by 365 days. (In this case, the APR and the simple interest rate are the same, since there are no fees.) The average daily balance is determined by adding the balance for each day in the billing cycle and then dividing by the number of days in the cycle. This number is multiplied by the number of days the loan was outstanding and then by the daily periodic rate to yield the finance charge for any given period. For example:

$1,294.89 average daily loan balance × 29 days = 37,551.81
$37,551.81 × .032876% (daily periodic rate) = $12.35 finance charge

Prior to the Truth in Lending Act, *add-on interest* was the most commonly used method of calculating and disclosing installment loan interest rates. The add-on interest is calculated by simply applying a rate to the original principal amount of the loan and multiplying it by the loan period in years. For example:

Principal	$2,000
10% add-on rate	200
24-month term	× 2
Total interest	400
Total of note	$2,400

Add-on rates result in higher APRs than do simple interest rate loans at comparable rates because they disregard that the principal will be reduced during the term of the loan as payments are made. Comparisons are shown in *Exhibit 10–1.*

Add-on rates are often not quoted because they do not allow the consumer to make meaningful comparisons with other rates. However, they are still frequently used in indirect lending programs to quote bank retention or buy rates. Therefore, those engaged in this type of lending should fully understand how these rates work.

Discount rates, like add-on rates, were commonly used before the Truth in Lending Act. The terms of a loan using a discount rate is determined as follows:

$2,000	Amount of note
− 200	Interest at 10% for 1 year
$1,800	Principal amount given to borrower

The use of discount rates for loan disclosures is prohibited by the Truth in Lending Act on all loans covered by the act. Discount rates may still be used in commercial transactions, so it is important that lenders be aware of their existence so that they may intelligently discuss them with consumers.

EXHIBIT 10–1
Comparison of Annual Percentage Rates and Add-On Rate

	Annual Percentage Rate				
Add-on rate	*12 Mos.*	*24 Mos.*	*36 Mos.*	*60 Mos.*	*120 Mos.*
6.00%	10.89%	11.12%	11.08%	10.84%	10.21%
9.00%	16.21%	16.42%	16.24%	15.71%	14.50%
12.00%	21.45%	21.57%	21.20%	20.31%	18.48%

With fixed rate loans, the interest rate does not change during the entire term of the loan. The use of a fixed interest rate on a closed-end loan means that the customer will have a fixed monthly payment for as long as the account is repaid in a satisfactory manner. If the customer makes payments after scheduled due dates, he may end up paying more finance charges. Minor adjustments may be required in the final monthly payment to reflect early or late payments received on simple interest loans. On open-end credit accounts, a fixed rate means that the creditor cannot change the rate without the customer agreeing to accept the new rate. Consumers in most states may avoid rate increases on fixed rate, open-end accounts simply by not using the account after receiving notification of a rate change.

The interest rate charged on variable rate loans is tied to a preselected index rate, such as the prime rate or the 90-day Treasury bill rate. As the index changes, either up or down, so does the rate on variable loans. Increases may be passed on to the consumer in the form of higher monthly payments or they may result in an increase in the number of payments required to pay off the loan. Decreases may result in lower monthly payments, fewer monthly payments, or a smaller final payment.

Calculation of Loan Terms

Lenders are rarely called upon to manually calculate the terms of a loan. Rate books, payment charts, and sophisticated computer programs allow lenders to quickly and accurately determine all of the terms for a given loan.

Basically, three elements must be known to calculate the interest charges and monthly payment on a loan: (1) *principal*—the total amount of money that will be loaned to the borrower, including any fees or insurance premiums that are to be financed, (2) *rate*—the interest rate applicable to the type of loan requested, and (3) *time*—the proposed term of the loan or time the money will be used.

The interest on the loan is calculated by multiplying: Principal × Rate × Time = Interest. For example, the calculation of interest on a 30-day single payment loan in the amount of $1,000 at a rate of 12 percent simple interest, would be as follows:

$$\$1{,}000 \times .12 = \$120 \times \frac{30}{360} = \$10 \text{ interest}$$

Thus, at the end of 30 days, the customer would pay back a total of $1,010.

The rate chart presented as *Exhibit 10–2* may be used to calculate the terms of an installment loan bearing a 15 percent APR and a term of 36 months.

To determine the various elements of a $4,500 loan for 36 months, simply look at the line in *Exhibit 10–3* for a loan amount of $4,500. To determine the finance charge simply subtract the loan amount from the total note: $5,615.64 − $4,500 = $1,115.64. The monthly payment on the loan is $155.99 ($5,615.64/36).

Adding insurance coverage to the amount of the loan increases the amount financed, thus increasing the monthly payment and the finance charges, since the bank is lending the customer more money to pay for the insurance premium. These charges are reflected in *Exhibit 10–3*, which contains both a single credit life and accident and health option. Adding the insurance coverage, therefore, increases the finance charge by $73.24 (from $1,115.64 to $1,188.88), the note amount by $370.44 (from $5,615.64 to $5,986.08), and the monthly payment by $10.29 (from $155.99 to $166.28).

Selling insurance not only generates additional interest income, since the premiums are financed, it also increases non-interest income, since the bank usually receives a commission on any insurance sold.

The term of the loan can have a significant impact on the monthly payment. *Exhibit 10–4* shows the effect that increasing the term of the loan has on the monthly payment and interest

EXHIBIT 10–2
Sample Rate Chart

15,000 APR			SINGLE LIFE ONLY WITH LIFE + A/N 36 MONTHS		
(1) UNPAID BALANCE	(2) LIFE PREM LIFE + A/H	(3) DISA.PREN LIFE + A/H	(4) FIN. CHG. LIFE + A/H	(5) TOTAL NOTE LIFE + A/H	(6) PAYMENT LIFE + A/H
1	0.02	0.05	0.01	1.00	0.03
2	0.04	0.09	0.39	2.52	0.07
3	0.06	0.14	0.76	3.96	0.11
4	0.08	0.18	0.78	5.04	0.14
5	0.10	0.23	1.15	6.48	0.18
6	0.12	0.28	1.52	7.92	0.22
7	0.14	0.32	1.54	9.00	0.25
8	0.16	0.37	1.91	10.44	0.29
9	0.18	0.41	2.29	11.88	0.33
10	0.20	0.46	2.30	12.96	0.36
20	0.40	0.92	4.96	26.28	0.73
30	0.60	1.38	7.62	39.60	1.10
40	0.81	1.84	10.27	52.92	1.47
50	1.01	2.29	12.94	66.24	1.84
60	1.21	2.75	15.60	79.56	2.21
70	1.41	3.21	18.26	92.56	2.58
80	1.61	3.67	20.92	106.20	2.93
90	1.81	4.13	23.58	119.52	3.32
100	2.01	4.59	26.24	132.84	3.69
200	4.03	9.18	52.83	266.04	7.39
300	6.04	13.77	79.07	398.58	11.08
400	8.06	18.36	105.66	532.08	14.78
500	10.07	22.95	131.90	664.92	18.47
600	12.09	27.54	158.49	798.12	22.17
700	14.10	32.13	184.73	930.96	25.86
800	16.12	36.72	211.32	1,064.16	29.56
900	18.13	41.31	237.56	1,197.00	33.25

income on a $4,500 loan at 15 percent APR, with life and disability insurance.

p 203

The importance of the monthly payment in selling consumer loans should not be underestimated. In fact, many consumers make their borrowing decision based more upon the affordability of the monthly payment than upon the interest rate on the loan. The size of the monthly payment is also an extremely important variable in evaluating credit risk and measuring the customer's ability to repay the loan. Thus, structuring the loan

EXHIBIT 10–3
Loan Charges

Advance	*Life Ins.*	*A&H Ins.*	*Fin. Chg.*	*Note*	*Mo. Pmt.*
$4000.00	$80.59	$183.59	$1056.98	$5321.16	$147.81
500.00	10.07	22.95	131.90	664.92	18.47
$4500.00	$90.66	$206.54	$1188.88	$5986.08	$166.28

term and the monthly payment to fit the borrower's capacity are critical elements for both the lender and the customer.

Maturities on closed-end loans are generally set by the bank's policy based upon the type of collateral securing the loan. Open-end accounts, on the other hand, generally have no set maturity. Instead, the bank establishes a monthly payment based upon a specified percentage of the outstanding balance being repaid each month. Credit card programs may require the borrower to repay a minimum of 5 percent of the outstanding balance per month, while home equity lines may require a minimum payment of 2 percent or less of the outstanding balance per month. The actual percentages used are a matter of product design and bank policy. The lower the percentage, the longer the maturity and the greater the finance charges paid, as shown in *Exhibit 10–5*.

Competitive pressures since the 1960s have led to a reduction in the outstanding balance that must be repaid each month. This has allowed consumers to take on more debt for the same monthly payment, while increasing bank income by slowing the liquidation rate of outstanding balances.

Loan Pricing

Loan pricing is affected by four major factors:

- the legal environment
- the competitive environment
- general economic conditions
- the bank's objectives, strategies, and financial condition.

EXHIBIT 10–4
Effect of Loan Term on Monthly Payments

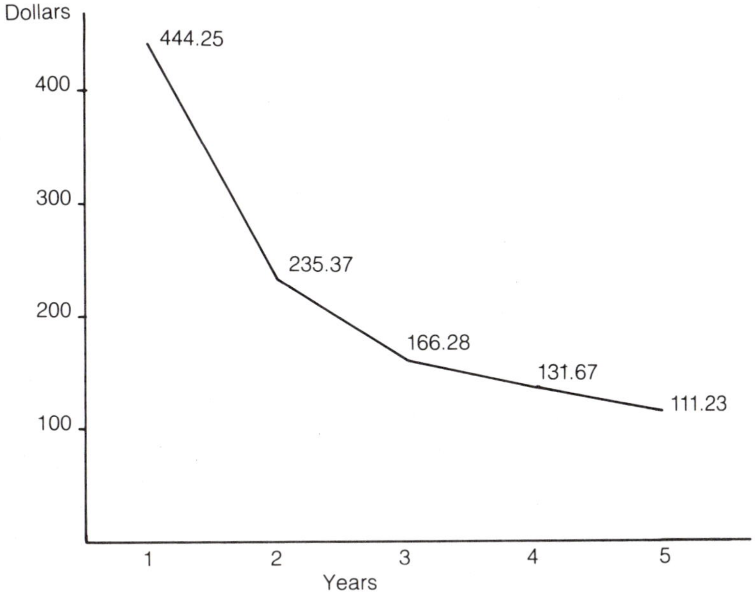

The legal environment has a significant impact on the prices that lenders can charge. State laws govern the rates and fees lenders can charge for consumer loans. Consequently, there is considerable variability among states, ranging from the extremely low rates allowed by the state of Arkansas (5 percent over the Federal Reserve discount rate) to the virtually uncapped rates allowed in Delaware. Broadly speaking, the rate structures provided by a state's lending laws have much to do with the kind of loan products offered by banks, the availability of credit, and the level of credit risk that banks are willing to accept.

Federal law does not currently restrict the rates that may be charged on consumer credit. However, the federal government periodically threatens to impose a national maximum rate on selected consumer credit products. Credit card programs have come under attack in the past, particularly when the spread between the rate charged on fixed rate credit card programs and

EXHIBIT 10–5
Relationship of Minimum Payment to Maturity

Percent of balance payable monthly	*Approximate maturity*
5%	20 months
4%	25 months
3%	33 months
2%	50 months
1.5%	67 months
1%	100 months

the rates for variable rate money market instruments widens. Legislative "jawboning" often leads some members of the industry to change their policies or rates, and also serves to heighten awareness of the issue among consumers. This combination encourages normal market forces to respond to any pricing inequities that may exist in the short term. Banks and other financial institutions generally resist rate restrictions, reasoning that they constrict the funds available for consumer credit.

Competition for consumer credit has increased in recent years as new participants have entered the market and as banks have expanded their lending operations beyond their traditional target market areas. Lenders must closely monitor their competitors' rates to stay in a position to attract the level of business desired.

Closed-end credit rates typically change more frequently than open-end rates and, therefore, require closer monitoring. Information about competitor rates and products is easily obtained by following media advertisements. Ads not only give information about the competition's prices, they also give a clear indication of the kinds of loan products the competition is trying to sell. Competitor information can also be obtained simply by "shopping" the competition. A designated shopper calls major competitors and requests information about loans and loan pricing. This allows the bank to assess not only the rates offered by the competition, but also the quality of their service.

Another approach to evaluating the competition's products and prices is to question dealer personnel. Keep in mind, though, that dealers are quick to let the bank know when competitors reduce rates and slower to let them know about rate increases.

Information about open-end credit rates can be obtained by monitoring advertisements and "shopping" competitors. It is difficult to determine exactly which competitors are competing for open-end credit business in a given market area due to the use of direct mail campaigns and affinity group programs. Therefore, the bank needs a good information system to identify when such programs are in process.

It is impossible to continually monitor all competitors. Emphasis should be directed to competitors that are the price leaders by virtue of their share of the market or their aggressiveness in marketing products. Major banks, finance companies, and thrifts are the normal targets of monitoring efforts.

General economic conditions also have a bearing on pricing decisions. *Money market rates*, the level of demand for credit, and overall economic conditions in the bank's market areas are all reflected in the bank's pricing of its consumer loan products.

Fluctuations in money market rates are reflected quickly in the bank's cost of funds. Thus, as the cost of deposits and other bank liabilities rise and fall, they have immediate implications for the cost of consumer credit. Rising money market rates mean that the costs of funding the loan portfolio go up. The bank may react by raising rates (this occurs automatically with variable rate loans) or it may elect to hold rates at the current level. Raising rates on new loans helps preserve profit margins; holding rates at the current level narrows short-term profit margins, but may result in a higher market share if competitors raise their rates. Declines in money market rates, particularly the Federal Reserve's discount rate, generally result in price reductions, which tends to stimulate demand for consumer credit and increase the level of activity in credit markets.

The relative level of demand for consumer credit influences pricing decisions. Several indices are monitored to assess the level of demand. Measures of retail sales, consumer buying intentions, consumer confidence, and direct measures of lending activity itself indicate the relative strength of demand. All things being equal, loan prices tend to rise or hold firm when demand is strong; they decline when demand softens.

In pricing its loan products, it is important that the bank understand the elasticity of demand. *Elasticity* is a measure of the relationship between the level of rates and demand for loans. Elastic demand is portrayed in *Exhibit 10–6*.

When total consumer credit demand is elastic, it does not change significantly in response to a change in price. However, when demand for a particular bank's loans is inelastic, its loan volume will change significantly if its interest rates are higher or lower than those of its competitors (see *Exhibit 10–7*). For example, a bank that charges its indirect dealers a higher rate than competitors will probably find volume dropping and profits declining as well.

If demand is elastic, changes in price tend to result in higher profits if rates are raised, and lower profits if rates are lowered. If demand is inelastic, the inverse is true—lowering rates increases demand and profits, while raising rates decreases demand and profits.

Loan products with inelastic demand patterns require closer monitoring and more active price changing than do products with more elastic demand patterns. For example, credit cards exhibited a highly elastic demand pattern through 1986. Although credit card interest rates remained relatively high, demand grew vigorously. This indicates that the product had high value to consumers and that price was a secondary issue. Undoubtedly, this will change as credit card loans mature in their product life cycle and as the effects of tax reform become apparent.

Economic conditions in the bank's market area also influence loan pricing to some extent. Weak economic conditions, as evidenced by high unemployment, low retail sales, and similar factors, may result in some rate reductions as a response to low demand. However, since loan demand is generally elastic, economic conditions do not have much effect on loan prices.

Finally, the bank's objectives and strategies have an impact on its loan pricing patterns. Since objectives and strategies are generally set at the product line level, pricing tends to vary from product to product. If the bank has set aggressive growth plans for a product, it will tend to price at the low end of the available rate range. If growth goals are modest, and if other goals are more important for a given product line—increased prof-

EXHIBIT 10–6
Elastic Demand

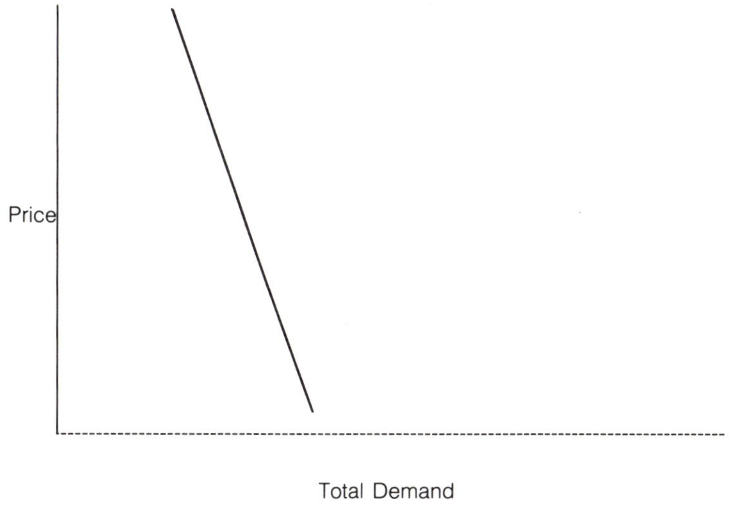

itability, for example—rates will be set more toward the middle to upper end of the competitive price range.

Each bank's financial condition has some impact on its loan pricing. In an increasingly competitive, deregulated environment, financial institutions that can deliver loan products at the lowest cost have a significant advantage over their competitors. This is not to say that loan rates can be set simply by looking at the bank's cost structure and adding the desired profit margin. Rather, the lowest cost providers will be better able to price their loan products at the lower end of the prevailing rate scale and still achieve desired profit margins.

Pricing Patterns

Loan pricing is no longer regarded as simply an issue of rates. All of the following are elements of contemporary loan pricing:

- annual percentage rate
- monthly payment
- application fees

EXHIBIT 10–7
Inelastic Demand

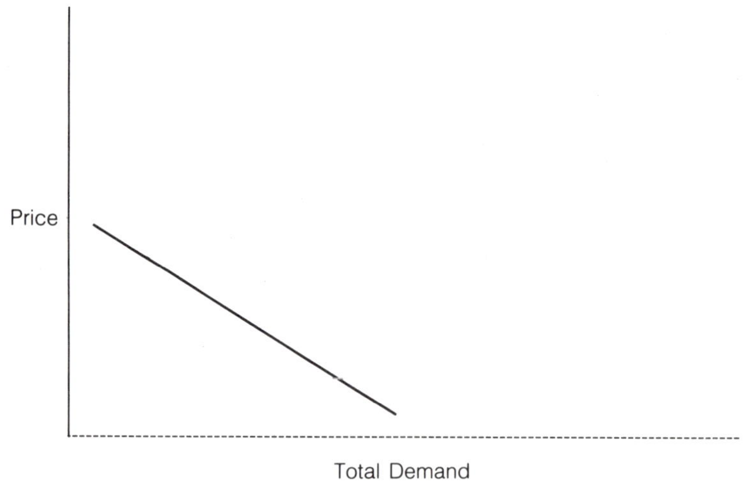

- miscellaneous loan fees, such as late charges, overlimit fees, returned check charges, and credit report fees
- annual account fees
- credit insurance rates.

Each of these elements represents an opportunity for the bank to increase its income and provide a basis for competing in the marketplace.

Although pricing of loan products varies significantly from market to market, there are some common practices. For example, most competitors vary loan rates based upon the type of loan and the collateral securing the loan (see *Exhibit 10–8*). This schedule reflects the relative level of risk associated with various types of collateral. Rates may also be varied for given products based upon the term of the loan, the customer's credit strength, and the size of the loan. For example:

- *Variations based upon loan term*

New automobile loans—48 months: 10.25%; 60 months: 10.50%

- *Variations based upon size of loan*

EXHIBIT 10–8
Sample Pricing Schedule

Loan Type	*Fixed Rate*	*Variable Rate*
New Auto:		
Up to 48 months	13.00%	11.00% (P + 1.5)
Up to 60 months	13.25%	10.50% (P + 1)
Used Auto:		
Up to 42 months	14.75%	12.00% (P + 2.5)
New Recreational Vehicles:		
Up to 48 months	14.00%	11.50% (P + 2)
Up to 60 months	14.25%	11.50% (P + 2)
Up to 120 months	N/A	11.50% (P + 2)
Used Recreational Vehicles:		
Up to 42 months	15.50%	12.50% (P + 3)
Boats (New or Used):		
Up to 10 years	13.00%	11.00% (P + 1.5) $25M or more 11.50% (P + 2) Less than $25M
Up to 15 years	13.25% $25M min.	N/A
Unsecured Loans:		
$1,500 to $2,500	17.50%	N/A
$2,501 and over	16.50%	13.50% (P + 4)
Second Mortgage	N/A	11.50% (P + 2)
Revolving Credit:		
Check Command	18.00%	N/A
Equity Line	N/A	11.50% (P + 2)
Personal Line Unsecured	N/A	13.50% (P + 4)
Secured with savings	N/A	9.50% (P) $5M/more 10.50% (P + 1) $5M

Boats—$5,000–$24,999: 12.00%; $25,000 and Up: 11.50%
Unsecured loans—Up to $3,499: 18.00%; $3,500 and Up: 16.00%

- *Variations based upon level of credit risk*

Credit score—180–200: 11.50%; 201–225: 11.25%; 226–250: 11.00%

These examples illustrate the concept that: (1) risk increases as the term of the loan increases, therefore resulting in a higher rate, (2) good customers are rewarded with lower rates, and (3) larger loans offer some efficiencies that may be reflected in lower rates.

Loan Cost Factors

Consumer credit managers must have a sound understanding of the cost factors affecting their portfolio and the behavior pattern of these costs.

Federal Reserve Functional Cost Analysis

The Federal Reserve publishes an annual functional cost analysis for most bank products. It identifies four primary cost categories for consumer loans:

- acquisition costs
- maintenance and liquidation costs
- loan loss rate
- cost of funds.

Acquisition costs include all of those expenses that are incurred in generating loan applications, processing them through to the final decision, and either documenting the approved loans or processing adverse action documentation. These expenses include: advertising and sales promotion expenses, personnel costs for handling loan applications at all stages of the lending process, related legal expenses, credit-scoring program expenses, miscellaneous supply costs, and communications costs.

Acquisition costs have risen steadily over time. Banks have responded to this trend by placing greater emphasis upon improving operating efficiency and on directing loan business to more cost-efficient products, such as open-end credit products, that eliminate the need to go through the full application and documentation process each time the consumer needs to borrow. Operational efficiencies have also been achieved by automating portions of the lending process and developing larger size loans. Automated application tracking systems, credit scoring, and automated document preparation are examples of practices that help control costs and also improve performance.

Maintenance and liquidation costs include those expenses related to servicing loan accounts once the loan has been made. This includes the cost of: coupon books and billing statements, processing payments through the bank's accounting system, and servicing, collecting, and recovering loans. A major portion is personnel expenses, computer hardware and software expenses, and related communication costs, including the maintenance of the data base and the preparation of reports.

Maintenance and liquidation costs were the first to receive attention when banks began to automate. This effort has now extended from the accounting department into such areas as the central file department, customer service, and, finally, to the collection and recovery departments. Still, this cost category has experienced a gradually rising cost pattern.

The *loan loss rate* is a cost factor that represents the bank's loss experience on all of its consumer credit products over time. Loans that are charged to loss represent an expense because they are assets that will not be recovered by the bank.

This factor varies widely from bank to bank, but it usually follows a fairly consistent pattern and range within a given bank. Loan losses tend to fluctuate with general economic conditions, the extent of risk taken by the bank, and the mix of consumer loans in the overall portfolio.

The final factor—the *cost of funds*—is the most important of all of the cost elements. This factor represents the price that the bank must pay for the money it loans to consumers. Banks have little money of their own to lend. They must attract deposits and borrow money to provide the funds needed for their lending activities. Increased competition in the financial services industry has had a significant impact on the cost of funds. Consumer credit managers are now confronted with greater risk due to the more volatile behavior pattern in the bank's cost of funds. Fluctuations in this expense can result in loans becoming unprofitable or their profit margins being eroded. It is important to note that consumer credit managers do not have control over this cost factor, while they do have some control over the other expenses.

The cost of funds follows a fluctuating behavior pattern over time, affecting not only loan pricing, but also the bank's product strategy, credit policies, and, in some cases, growth objectives. Because cost of funds is the largest single item of expense on most loans, it is essential that the bank plan for fluctuations in this category.

The pattern in acquisition costs, maintenance and liquidation expenses, loan loss rate, and cost of funds in recent years is shown in *Exhibit 10–9*. These numbers will be examined in greater detail when loan profitability is considered later in this chapter.

Average Versus Marginal Cost Analysis

From an economics perspective, there are two primary methods of analyzing loan costs—either on an average or marginal basis.

EXHIBIT 10–9
Functional Cost Analysis Trends

Banks Over $200M in Deposits

Cost Factor	*1972*	*1976*	*1981*	*1985*
Acquisition	$34.21	$56.72	$97.54	$85.67
Maintenance & liquidation	$ 2.55	$ 3.17	$ 5.17	$ 5.67
Loan loss rate	.41%	.55%	.65%	.30%
Cost of funds	3.50%	4.60%	9.13%	7.42%

SOURCE: Federal Reserve Functional Cost Analysis.

The average cost approach breaks the consumer credit department's total expenses down based upon the number of items in the loan portfolio. In many cases, it is possible for a bank to reduce its average costs simply by putting more accounts on the books. This is particularly true if the bank does not incur a significant amount of fixed costs as it adds to its account base, but rather only incurs variable costs associated with making the additional loan. However, if the bank must add to its staff, buy office equipment, and incur other fixed costs in order to handle additional volume, this may increase the average cost.

The variable costs associated with each additional loan are also known as *marginal costs*. Economic theory states that the loan should be made as long as the income from the loan exceeds the marginal cost of making and servicing the loan. Thus, if it will cost $100 to make the next loan, the loan should be made if it will produce at least $101 in interest income. While the theory seems relatively simple in concept, it is far more difficult to implement in practice. However, the concept does point out a weakness in making pricing and policy decisions solely on the basis of average cost numbers.

Loan Profitability

Banks are profit-making institutions. As such, one of their primary goals is to generate an acceptable level of profit for their shareholders. In recent years, banks have become more skilled at evaluating profitability, not only of their entire portfolio, but also of individual products and accounts. Profitability at the individual account level will be considered first, to be followed by an examination of how income is recognized and how loan yields are calculated.

Using data from the functional cost analysis, the profitability of individual accounts can be evaluated and applied to establishing reasonable loan pricing and policies. *Exhibit 10–10* shows the effect that the term of the loan has on loan profitability, using 1985 cost data.

From *Exhibit 10–11*, it is apparent that the net income varies in relation to a change in term. Although the acquisition costs do not change as the term of the loan increases, the maintenance cost increases since more payments must be processed. The cost of funds also increases because the loan is outstanding for a longer period of time. The loan loss rate is based upon the size and type of loan, so it does not change in this case. Clearly, it is advantageous from a profitability standpoint to extend the term of this loan. The 12-month loan is barely profitable, while the 36-month loan produces much higher income. Increasing the size or rate on a loan also has a significant positive effect (see *Exhibit 10–11*). For example, a 150 basis point increase or one and one-half percent increase (from 11.5 percent to 13 percent) in the rate results in a shift in income of $354.24 over the term of the loan.

A functional cost analysis can also provide guidance in determining minimum loan rates and terms for the bank to break even on a loan assuming a specified cost of funds (see *Exhibit 10–12*). If, for example, the cost of funds is 7.42 percent, then to break even on a 9 percent 4-year loan, the bank needs to lend no less than $9,726. This is a handy tool for setting the bank's overall policy regarding minimum loan size, pricing, and term combinations.

Income from individual accounts may also be analyzed by running a loan amortization schedule like the one shown in *Exhibit 10–13*. The amortization schedule shows how each payment is distributed between interest and principal, together with the remaining balance on the loan. The actual loan amortization depends upon the method used to compute interest on the loan. There are three primary methods of recognizing interest earned on consumer loans: (1) simple interest, (2) actuarial interest, and (3) Rule of 78s.

EXHIBIT 10–10
Profitability Analysis

$3,000 Loan—18% APR

	12-month loan	36-month loan
Acquisition cost	$ 85.67	$ 85.67
Maintenance cost	68.04	204.12
Cost of funds	120.58	343.17
Loan loss rate	4.88	13.87
Total costs	$279.17	$646.83
Finance charge	$300.48	$904.46
Net income	$ 21.31	$257.63

Simple interest calculations are used on all open-end credit accounts, all variable rate loans, and many closed-end loans. A simple interest loan is calculated based upon when payments are actually received. For example, if an account has a balance of $10,000 at a rate of 13 percent—therefore accruing interest at a rate of $3.56 per day—and payments were applied on different dates of the month, the amount of interest would vary. Sample figures are shown in *Exhibit 10–14*.

Thus, on a simple interest loan, the customer can reduce his interest costs when he pays early, but the bank will realize higher interest income when he pays late. The customer may also reduce his interest costs on a simple interest loan by paying more than the minimum monthly payment since this will result in a greater reduction in the unpaid balance.

Actuarial and Rule of 78s interest methods work differently. These approaches, used only on closed-end loans and in states that permit their use, assume that a payment has been made every 30 days, whether it has been or not. Further, when computing interest due, they do not take into account any excess amount paid on the account by the borrower. Earned interest is calculated using rebate tables. A Rule of 78s rebate schedule is shown in *Exhibit 10–15*.

If the customer has a 36-month loan, and wants to pay the loan off at the end of 12 months, he would receive a refund of 45.05 percent of the original interest precomputed for the loan.

EXHIBIT 10–11
Profitability Analysis—Rate Increase

	$10,000 loan for 48 months/11.50%	*$10,000 loan for 48 months/13%*
Acquistion cost	$ 85.67	$ 85.67
Maintenance cost	272.16	272.16
Cost of funds	1514.92	1514.92
Loan loss rate	61.25	61.25
Total cost	$1934.00	$1934.00
Finance charge	$2523.20	$2877.44
Net Income	$ 589.20	$ 943.44
Monthly payment	$ 260.90	$ 268.28

Thus, on a $3,000 loan at 18 percent, with a total of $904.20 in finance charges, the bank would earn $496.86, and the customer would receive a credit for unearned income in the amount of $407.34. The customer receives no benefit from paying early or for paying more than the minimum monthly payment on these loans. If, on the other hand, a customer made all 36 payments on their due date, he would pay exactly the same amount of interest, regardless of whether he had a simple interest or Rule of 78s loan.

The refund methods under the Rule of 78s and actuarial approaches have been widely criticized by consumers and consumer advocates for many years. Some states prohibit both approaches, and many lenders have voluntarily switched to the simple interest method to avoid customer relations problems and to receive interest on delinquent amounts.

Product Line Profitability

Each consumer credit product has unique profitability characteristics. These characteristics reflect varying levels of risk, differing cost structures, and variations in the interest rates. It is possible and desirable to construct a profitability analysis for consumer credit products, as in *Exhibit 10–16*. Credit cards have high gross yields and other income sources to offset high operating and loan loss expenses. Auto loans have much lower yields, but also offer lower operating expenses and loan losses. Second

EXHIBIT 10–12
Break-Even Loan Size

Based on a 7.42% Cost of Funds

	Annual Percentage Rates (Monthly Payments Presumed)						
Maturity in Years	*7.50%*	*8.00%*	*11.00%*	*12.75%*	*14.50%*	*16.25%*	*18.00%*
1	**	20,263	8,202	5,383	4,000	3,180	2,636
2	**	13,873	5,817	3,843	2,861	2,275	1,884
3	**	11,267	4,871	3,237	2,415	1,920	1,589
4	**	9,726	4,328	2,886	2,156	1,715	1,419
5	**	8,658	3,937	2,643	1,979	1,574	1,302
6	49,376	7,853	3,647	2,460	1,844	1,467	1,211
7	37,676	7,212	3,413	2,312	1,736	1,382	1,143
8	30,382	6,686	3,219	2,190	1,646	1,311	1,084
9	25,423	6,243	3,053	2,084	1,570	1,251	1,035
10	21,845	5,863	2,908	1,993	1,503	1,199	992

mortgage loans offer even lower operating expenses and losses to go with a yield that is somewhat higher than that for auto loans.

Indirect loans present some unique profitability considerations because the bank generally must pay a dealer a percentage of the finance charge. In addition to serving as a financial inducement, it also compensates the dealer for handling the application and loan closing. Two examples of dealer earnings on typical retail contracts follow.

Example 1	
Amount financed	$15,079.90
Bank buy rate	10.00%
Customer rate	16.00%
Total finance charge	$4,005.86
Bank interest retention	$2,437.34
Dealer reserve	$1,568.52
Term—36 months	
Example 2	
Amount financed	$8,873.07
Bank buy rate	9.50%
Customer rate	12.50%
Total finance charge	$2,447.73
Bank interest retention	$1,827.09
Dealer reserve	$ 620.64
Term—48 months	

EXHIBIT 10–13
Loan Amortization Schedule

Rate %	Payment $	
7.00	207.92	10,500.00
Term: Years	Months	Periods
5		60

Prepared by Financial Publishing Company, Boston

Payment Number	Payment on Interest	Payment on Principal	Balance of Loan
1	61.25	146.67	10,353.33
2	60.39	147.53	10,205.80
3	59.53	148.39	10,057.41
4	58.67	149.25	9,908.16
5	57.80	150.12	9,758.04
6	56.92	151.00	9,607.04
7	56.04	151.88	9,455.16
8	55.16	152.76	9,302.40
9	54.26	153.66	9,148.74
10	53.37	154.55	8,994.19
11	52.47	155.45	8,838,74
12	51.56	156.36	8,682.38
13	50.65	157.27	8,525.11
14	49.73	158.19	8,366.92
15	48.81	159.11	8,207.81
16	47.88	160.04	8,047.77
17	46.95	160.97	7,886.80
18	46.01	161.91	7,724.89
19	45.06	162.86	7,562.03
20	44.11	163.81	7,398.22
21	43.16	164.76	7,233.46
22	42.20	165.72	7,067.74
23	41.23	166.69	6,901.05
24	40.26	167.66	6,733.39
25	39.28	168.64	6,564.75
26	38.29	169.63	6,395.12
27	37.30	170.62	6,224.50
28	36.31	171.61	6,052.89
29	35.31	172.61	5,880.28
30	34.30	173.62	5,706.66
31	33.29	174.63	5,532.03
32	32.27	175.65	5,356.38
33	31.25	176.67	5,179.71
34	30.21	177.71	5,002.00
35	29.18	178.74	4,823.26
36	28.14	179.78	4,643.48

The dealer can also increase the income on a retail transaction by selling credit life, accident and health insurance, and warranty policies. Referring to Example 2, if the dealer sold all of these policies, the income would increase as follows:

EXHIBIT 10–14
Interest Accrual on Simple Interest Loans

Date payment received	*Number of days balance open*	*Interest*
5 days before due date	25	$ 89.00
On due date	30	$106.80
5 days after due date	35	$124.60

	Premium	Dealer Income	
Life premium	$255.41	$ 85.14	(33% commission
A&H premium	651.07	217.02	(33% commission)
Warranty policy	885.00	435.00	($450 cost)
		$ 737.16	fee income
		620.64	dealer reserve
		$1,357.80	total income

Fixed Rate Versus Variable Rate Lending

Until 1981, virtually all consumer loans were made on a fixed rate basis. However, fixed rate loan portfolios, particularly those that are at the low end of the rate scale, expose lenders to a high level of interest rate risk. In response, most financial institutions added variable rate loans to their consumer credit portfolios during the 1980s. They are now a permanent part of consumer credit pricing.

Fixed rate loans allow the lender to pass on to loan customers any changes in the cost of funds. However, as shown in *Exhibit 10–17*, this has a limited effect on the total portfolio yield in the short-run. In the event of rising rates, profit margins narrow or disappear. On the other hand, fixed rate portfolios can be very attractive when the cost of funds are declining since profit margins widen.

Variable rate portfolios have a behavior pattern that is different from that of a fixed rate portfolio, as shown in *Exhibit 10–18*. The variable rate feature virtually eliminates the effects of interest rate risks, though it may increase credit and collateral risk.

EXHIBIT 10–15
Rule of 78s Rebate Schedule

ORIG.	NUMBER OF MONTHS LOAN HAS RUN																							
TERM	**1**	**2**	**3**	**4**	**5**	**6**	**7**	**8**	**9**	**10**	**11**	**12**	**13**	**14**	**15**	**16**	**17**	**18**	**19**	**20**	**21**	**22**	**23**	**24**
1																								
2	33.33																							
3	50.00	16.67																						
4	60.00	30.00	10.00																					
5	66.67	40.00	20.00	6.67																				
6	71.43	47.62	28.57	14.29	4.76																			
7	75.00	53.57	35.71	21.43	10.71	3.57																		
8	77.78	58.33	41.67	27.78	16.67	8.33	2.78																	
9	80.00	62.22	46.67	33.33	22.22	13.33	6.67	2.22																
10	81.82	65.45	50.91	38.18	27.27	18.18	10.91	5.45	1.82															
11	83.33	68.18	54.55	42.42	31.82	22.73	15.15	9.09	4.55	1.52														
12	84.62	70.51	57.69	46.15	35.90	26.92	19.23	12.82	7.69	3.85	1.28													
13	85.71	72.53	60.44	49.45	39.56	30.77	23.08	16.48	10.99	6.59	3.30	1.10												
14	86.67	74.29	62.86	52.38	42.86	34.29	26.67	20.00	14.29	9.52	5.71	2.86	.95											
15	87.50	75.83	65.00	55.00	45.83	37.50	30.00	23.33	17.50	12.50	8.33	5.00	2.50	.83										
16	88.24	77.21	66.91	57.35	48.53	40.44	33.09	26.47	20.59	15.44	11.03	7.35	4.41	2.21	.74									
17	88.89	78.43	68.63	59.48	50.98	43.14	35.95	29.41	23.53	18.30	13.73	9.80	6.54	3.92	1.96	.65								
18	89.47	79.53	70.18	61.40	53.22	45.61	38.60	32.16	26.32	21.05	16.37	12.28	8.77	5.85	3.51	1.75	.58							
19	90.00	80.53	71.58	63.16	55.26	47.89	41.05	34.74	28.95	23.68	18.95	14.74	11.05	7.89	5.26	3.16	1.58	.53						
20	90.48	81.43	72.86	64.76	57.14	50.00	43.33	37.14	31.43	26.19	21.43	17.14	13.33	10.00	7.14	4.76	2.86	1.43	.48					
21	90.91	82.25	74.03	66.23	58.87	51.95	45.45	39.39	33.77	28.57	23.81	19.48	15.58	12.12	9.09	6.49	4.33	2.60	1.30	.43				
22	91.30	83.00	75.10	67.59	60.47	53.75	47.43	41.50	35.97	30.83	26.09	21.74	17.79	14.23	11.07	8.30	5.93	3.95	2.37	1.19	.40			
23	91.67	83.70	76.09	68.84	61.96	55.43	49.28	43.48	38.04	32.97	28.26	23.91	19.93	16.30	13.04	10.14	7.61	5.43	3.62	2.17	1.09	.36		
24	92.00	84.33	77.00	70.00	63.33	57.00	51.00	45.33	40.00	35.00	30.33	26.00	22.00	18.33	15.00	12.00	9.33	7.00	5.00	3.33	2.00	1.00	.33	
25	92.31	84.92	77.85	71.08	64.62	58.46	52.62	47.08	41.85	36.92	32.31	28.00	24.00	20.31	16.92	13.85	11.08	8.62	6.46	4.62	3.08	1.85	.92	.31
26	92.59	85.47	78.63	72.08	65.81	59.83	54.13	48.72	43.59	38.75	34.19	29.91	25.93	22.22	18.80	15.67	12.82	10.26	7.98	5.98	4.27	2.85	1.71	.85
27	92.86	85.98	79.37	73.02	66.93	61.11	55.56	50.26	45.24	40.48	35.98	31.75	27.78	24.07	20.63	17.46	14.55	11.90	9.52	7.41	5.56	3.97	2.65	1.59
28	93.10	86.45	80.05	73.89	67.98	62.32	56.90	51.72	46.80	42.12	37.68	33.50	29.56	25.86	22.41	19.21	16.26	13.55	11.08	8.87	6.90	5.17	3.69	2.46
29	93.33	86.90	80.69	74.71	68.97	63.45	58.16	53.10	48.28	43.68	39.31	35.17	31.26	27.59	24.14	20.92	17.93	15.17	12.64	10.34	8.28	6.44	4.83	3.45
30	93.55	87.31	81.29	75.48	69.89	64.52	59.35	54.41	49.68	45.16	40.86	36.77	32.90	29.25	25.81	22.58	19.57	16.77	14.19	11.83	9.68	7.74	6.02	4.52

Most consumer credit portfolios contain a blend of fixed and variable rate loans. Fixed rates tend to be concentrated in high gross yield products, such as credit card and check overdraft programs, and in traditional markets such as automobile loans. Variable rates are increasingly used on open-end credit accounts, boat loans, and second mortgage loans. These blended portfolios appear to offer a sound middle ground in the effort to optimize profits.

Variable Rate Program Structure

There are many considerations that go into establishing a variable rate loan program. These include—

- selecting an index rate
- determining pricing policy and strategy
- determining frequency of pricing changes
- using rate floors and caps
- evaluating the effect on credit and collateral risk.

Many banks have elected to use the prime rate or a U.S. Treasury bill rate as their index. An *external index*—one that is not controlled by the bank—is easier to defend against criticism

EXHIBIT 10–16
Product Line Profitability Structures

	Bank Card	*Auto Loans*	*Second Mortgage*
Portfolio Yield	17.00%	12.50%	13.00%
Cost of Funds	− 7.50	− 7.50	− 7.50
Net Yield	9.50	5.00	5.50
Other Income	+ 4.00	+ .25	+ .25
Operating Expenses	− 5.00	− 3.00	− 2.00
Loan Losses	− 3.00	− .50	− .15
Net Pretax Yield	5.50%	1.75%	3.60%

than an *internal index*—one that is controlled by the bank. Ideally, the index should follow the behavior pattern of the bank's cost of funds. However, as customer acceptance and understanding of the index are important, a readily available and understandable index should be chosen.

One strategy for marketing variable rates has been to offer them side-by-side with fixed rates, with the variable rate loan priced somewhat below that of the comparable fixed rate loan. This provides an incentive to the customer to take the variable rate, with its lower monthly payment, rather than choosing the fixed rate loan. The gap between the fixed and variable rate tends to grow as rates rise and narrow as rates fall.

Many variable rate loan programs call for monthly changes in the rate, although some banks have used less frequent adjustment periods in an attempt to position their product differently in the market. Less frequent adjustments can help bank yields when rates are declining, but hurt them when rates are rising.

The use of floors and ceilings are an effort to balance interest rate risk considerations with credit and collateral considerations. For example, a *rate cap* protects the consumer from higher monthly payments or negative amortization, while limiting somewhat the bank's ability to pass on the total interest rate risk to the consumer. *Rate floors*, on the other hand, protect the bank yield during periods of falling prices and help to preserve a targeted gross yield objective.

EXHIBIT 10–17
Fixed Rate Loan Portfolio—Yield Characteristics

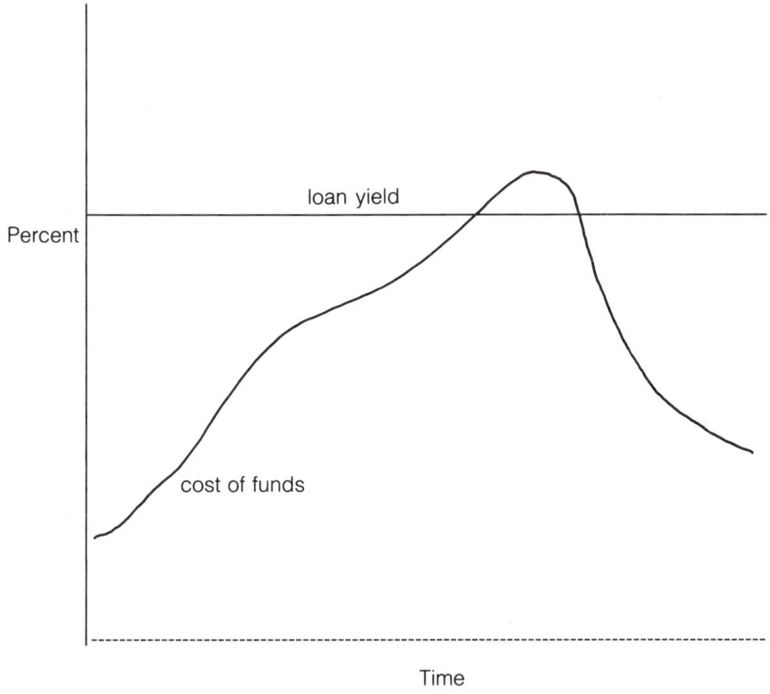

Summary

The profitability of consumer loans is affected by the bank's pricing policies and practices and the cost structure of its operation. Consumer credit costs fall into four categories—acquisition expenses, maintenance and liquidation costs, loan losses, and the cost of funds. The cost of funds is the largest single expense and is also the one that consumer credit managers have the least control over.

Loan pricing is affected by the legal environment, competition, general economic conditions, and the bank's objectives, strategies, and financial condition. While price has a bearing on the bank's loan volume, it is also a feature that can be matched or beaten by competitors in a very short period of time. Thus, it is difficult to achieve a pricing advantage for very long.

EXHIBIT 10–18
Variable Rate Loan Portfolio—Yield Characteristics

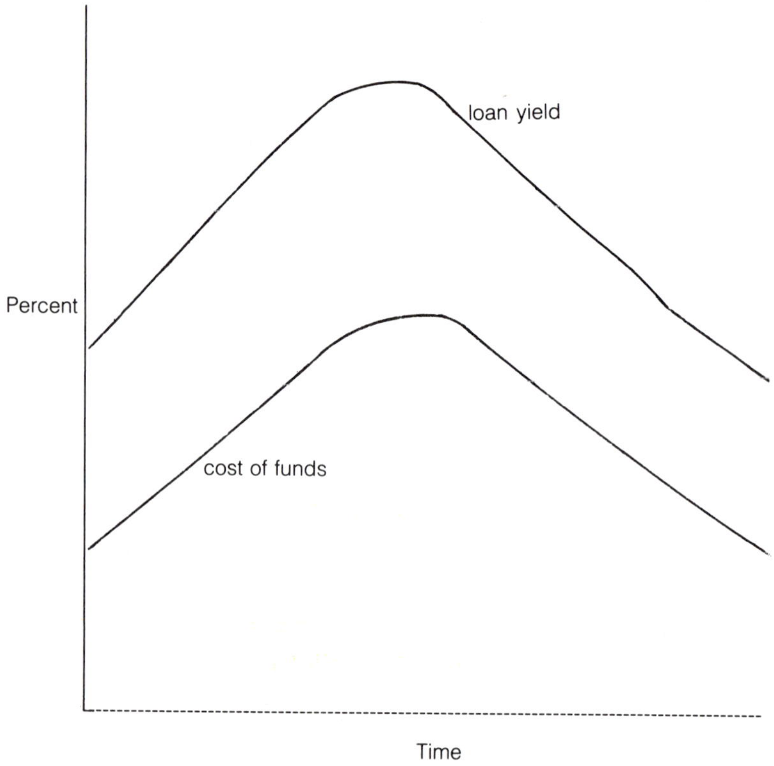

Individual account profitability is affected by the method used to rebate interest or recognize income on the loans, the term of the loan, its rate, whether or not other services, such as credit insurance, are included, and any fees that may be charged on the loan. Lenders should be aware of how each of these factors affect profitability, and they should understand the basics of calculating loan terms.

Questions for Review and Discussion

1. How do most consumer lenders compute the terms of a loan today? What methods does your bank use?

2. Why is the annual percentage rate sometimes different from the interest rate on a loan?

3. *Define principal*, *rate*, and *time*. What results when you multiply these three factors?

4. Why is the amount of the monthly payment on a consumer loan such an important variable when structuring a loan? In what way can it be adjusted to lower the payment without lowering the principal or rate?

5. When pricing the bank's loans, how might one gather information about rates offered by competitors?

6. Explain the principle of elasticity as it pertains to the demand for loans.

7. Does your bank use the Federal Reserve's Functional Cost Analysis in its loan pricing strategy? Talk to your consumer credit manager and ask what other analytical techniques are used to set loan prices.

8. Why did consumer variable rate lending come into being? What particular profitability problem does it address?

11 Loan Structuring and Selling

Selling bank products and services has received more attention in the 1980s. No longer is the banking environment heavily regulated, in which products all looked alike, and there was little innovative product development, limited pricing flexibility, and few promotional programs. Competitive advantage was based primarily upon locational convenience and the quality of service. Today, as a result of competition, traditional order-taking practices have given way to the development of a sales culture.

In this chapter, we will examine the implications of creating a sales culture for consumer loans. First, some broad objectives will be introduced, followed by an examination of how to effectively apply selling techniques to achieve those objectives. We will then consider approaches to structuring loan products and cross-selling other bank services to loan customers. Attention will be focused on the selling process and the employee sales skills needed to succeed in the consumer credit market.

Before beginning, however, let us distinguish between the terms "selling" and "cross-selling." Selling is an approach used by astute bankers who actively decipher a customer's needs and then use that knowledge to offer a particular bank product or service that fulfills those needs. Selling by bankers often involves financial counseling; it always involves an interest in and sensitivity to the real needs of the client. A selling approach, furthermore, usually results in higher loan volumes at greater profitability for the bank, as opposed to the outcome of traditional order-taking.

Cross-selling is a form of selling in which a banker suggests related products and services that might be of interest to a customer. Cross-selling opportunities are especially abundant during the lending process. In servicing a customer's request for a loan, the banker discovers information that helps him make appropriate suggestions for other products and services, in addition to the loan, that suit the customer's needs. Effective cross-selling results in expanded account relationships with customers, enhanced customer loyalty, and higher bank profits.

Objectives of Loan Structuring and Selling Strategies

There are five broad objectives that should be considered when developing the bank's strategy regarding loan structuring and selling:

- make the best loan for the customer and the bank
- sell loans, and not just take orders
- optimize bank earnings by selling other bank products
- optimize customer retention
- minimize credit and interest rate risk.

The concept of making the best loan for the customer and the bank embodies most of these objectives. The consumer is looking for a loan product that meets his specific needs, is priced fairly (not necessarily the lowest rate in town), and can be obtained in a convenient and friendly manner. The bank wants to earn an acceptable yield on its investment, limit its risk to an acceptable level, and build strong customer relationships.

For both parties to realize their objectives, there must be some trade-offs. For example, if the customer is charged a very high interest rate on a loan, the bank will realize higher earnings, but at the risk of losing the customer in the future. Likewise, consumers are often willing to pay higher prices for products and services that they perceive as having added value. Convenience stores are a good example. Many consumers patronize these stores knowing that they may buy the same goods for less at the grocery store. However, their convenient locations and store hours offset any price disadvantage they may have.

A bank that sets an objective of making the best loan for the customer and the bank may wish to individually structure each loan sold to a consumer. The opposite approach is simply to fill customer orders. The problem with the latter approach is that it presumes the customer has full knowledge of the different loan products that are available to him and that he knows the best way to manage his financial affairs. Quite often, these assumptions are false. Professional lenders, on the other hand, are up-to-date on what loan products are available in the market and are skilled in matching the customer's needs with the appropriate product.

Selling the best loan does not mean the bank should not promote individual loan products. The bank may still need to advertise credit cards, home equity lines, automobile loans, and other products in order to develop a flow of loan applications. These product promotions may generate new customers, who, in turn, are promising candidates for cross-selling other services.

Optimizing bank earnings involves a long-term, rather than a short-term, perspective. This is often easier said than done, since bank managers are usually under pressure to achieve short-term growth and profit objectives. Maximizing profits in the long term may involve pricing loans below current market levels to achieve other objectives, such as an increased market share that will eventually produce greater profits. An example of this strategy is the aggressive marketing of home equity lines of credit following passage of new tax legislation favorable to this product in 1986. Many banks offered introductory rates to induce consumers to open an equity line account. While these introductory rates produced low yields in the short run, they attracted new accounts that will perhaps generate significant income over the following years as rates return to normal.

One of the most important assets any bank has is its base of retail customers. Some bankers prefer to think of their customers as clients who are receiving "professional" service from the bank. These clients not only represent a current source of income, but also a potential market for the bank's other retail services. Developing and maintaining the customer base are critical to the success of any retail business. Customer retention is enhanced by consistently delivering high-quality service and selling products that meet the client's tangible and intangible needs. Products and services that have ego-enhancing benefits can go a long way to strengthen the account relationship. VISA gold cards, affinity group credit programs, and quality service help meet this need.

A loan officer must also be able to properly structure a loan. For example, knowing when to sell a bill consolidation loan can reduce the customer's monthly payments, thereby improving his cash flow and enabling the customer to meet other financial needs without strain. In other instances, an equity line of credit may be preferable to an unsecured home improvement loan. It reduces the bank's risk, while potentially offering the customer lower interest rates, longer maturities, and reduced monthly payments.

Loan Structuring by Product Line

The opportunity to cross-sell and structure loans varies depending upon the type of loan being requested by the borrower. The bank has more opportunities to do these two things when it has direct contact with the customer. However, direct mail and telemarketing programs can also be used to cross-sell services.

Direct Loans

As previously noted, the direct lending environment provides the best opportunity to structure the most appropriate loan and to cross-sell other bank services. Assuming that the bank employee has developed basic selling skills, he should be able to identify some products that offer attractive benefits to the consumer and to present these benefits using an effective sales approach. Direct contact allows the salesperson to better obtain information and respond to concerns raised by the customer. These advantages are clearly removed when applications are received by mail or through third parties such as dealers.

The credit application can provide a wealth of information that can help identify potential product sales. *Exhibit 11–1* presents sample customer characteristics and a list of potential products that could be sold.

Loan structuring should take into account the following:

- pricing—fixed or variable rate
- type of loan—open-end or closed-end
- amount of the loan advance
- term of the loan
- collateral
- control of loan proceeds
- credit insurance protection.

Many banks have elected to offer fixed and variable rates on at least some of their loan products. In most cases, the customer will be able to choose which pricing approach is preferable. In

EXHIBIT 11–1
Cross-Selling Opportunities

Customer characteristic	*Product cross-sold*
Has only a checking account	Overdraft line of credit
Has no checking or savings accounts	Checking and savings programs
Has dependents in their mid-teens	Guaranteed student loans
Is a homeowner	Equity line of credit
Invests in stocks	Discount brokerage service
Has no credit cards	VISA or MasterCard
Has four dependents	Credit life and disability insurance

general, consumers are more likely to opt for variable rates during periods of relatively high market rates, while preferring fixed rates when market rates are low. When both a fixed and variable rate loan product are offered, the consumer usually elects to take the one that offers the lowest monthly payment at the time. For example, the following options may be available to a consumer purchasing a new car:

Loan Amount	Rate	Term	Monthly Payment
$10,000 w/life	13% Fixed	60 months	$234.44
$10,000 w/life	12% Variable	60 months	$229.20

Assuming that the bank is indifferent about which option the customer selects, the lender would simply present both options to the consumer and allow him to make a choice between taking the fixed rate loan with a monthly payment that is $5.24 higher, or selecting the variable rate to gain the lower monthly payment (while also taking some interest rate risk). The greater the difference between the monthly payments, the more attractive the variable rate loan will appear.

The bank may elect not to give the consumer a pricing option for all loan types. This may be controlled simply as a matter of lending policy. For example, the bank may not want to offer fixed rates on loans with a maturity of over five years.

The type of loans to offer to a consumer is a matter of growing importance to the bank. In part, the decision should be based upon the loan products the bank wishes to promote and the customer's unique needs. Consider the following:

Example 1

An applicant has requested a $5,000 unsecured line of credit to be used to consolidate a number of accounts open with other banks. The lender notes that the customer now has three open lines of credit and that all of them are used up to the limit. The customer has a good credit history, but the lender is concerned that the customer would reopen all of the other accounts and then be unable to handle the added debt burden.

Many lenders are reluctant to grant an additional open-end line of credit under these circumstances, and some banks even have policies prohibiting loans to consumers who have more than two or three lines of credit. The lender may be able to structure a closed-end loan that would deny the borrower access to further debt without reapplying for additional money. This requires paying off and closing the revolving accounts to give the bank more control over the borrower's future credit usage.

Example 2

An applicant has requested a $2,500 loan to pay the tuition for her daughter's first semester of college. Her credit history is excellent, she is a homeowner, and she has the ability to handle a significant level of debt.

This situation is one that fits well with open-end loan programs. To meet the expense of future semesters, the borrower will probably need to incur additional debt. Rather than filling the customer's order, it would be desirable to sell her a home equity line of credit that would meet both her current and future borrowing needs, *tie* her to the bank, and *reduce* the bank's cost. It would also be desirable to counsel her regarding special tuition loan opportunities, such as the Guaranteed Student Loan Program, which could help meet her needs at the lowest possible cost.

The size of the loan advance or credit limit is closely related to profitability. Selling a customer a higher loan advance can make the difference between a profitable and an unprofitable loan. Many banks encourage their lenders to look for ways to sell a larger size loan. One practice is to set minimum loan sizes high enough to make each loan profitable. For example, a bank might set a minimum loan size of $2,000 or more for closed-end loans, while smaller loan requests are directed toward open-end products where they can be handled more cost efficiently. *Exhibit 11–2* shows the effect of increasing loan size on interest income, underscoring the importance of convincing the customer to borrow more money whenever appropriate.

If the lender can offer some tangible benefits, the customer may agree to a larger loan. Some benefits include a reduction in overall monthly debt payments, reduced interest rates on at least some of the debts, a lower monthly payment as the size and term of the loan increase, or tax advantages associated with certain types of loans.

The term of the loan also is a vital consideration in structuring a closed-end loan. The term has a direct impact on the monthly payment, which is a key concern of many consumers. Some lenders would argue that the amount of the monthly payment is as important, or more important, than the APR in being able to sell a loan. Small differences in interest rates have little effect on monthly payments, while stretching out the loan term can dramatically lower payments. These characteristics are demonstrated in *Exhibit 11–3*.

The exhibit demonstrates the potential to compete against a competitor's low interest rates by resorting to longer maturities, a strategy adopted by many finance companies. The lower monthly payment brings the loan within the reach of a broader segment of the market, while allowing lenders to present some options to price-sensitive customers. For example, many banks attempt to compete against manufacturer interest subvention programs by emphasizing the monthly payment reductions available at standard rates. As shown in *Exhibit 11–3*, the monthly payment on a $15,000 loan can be lowered from $435.56 to $317.96 when the loan is financed at 9.9 percent for 60 months instead of 2.9 percent for 36 months. This difference enables banks to compete against these manufacturer-subsidized programs since many consumers cannot afford the higher monthly payments required under the manufacturer's plans.

Consumers can also be sold on a higher rate loan if it can be demonstrated that such a loan will cost only slightly more per month, and that the bank is providing a service that is worth this insignificant difference. Notice the very small difference that a 1 percent change in the rate makes. On a $2,000, 12-month loan, the payment at a 16 percent interest rate is only $.95 more than at 15 percent. Most borrowers are willing to accept such a small difference in the monthly payment when other considerations—

EXHIBIT 11–2
Loan Size Relative to Interest Income

Advance	Term	Rate	Interest Income
$1,000	12 months	18%	$100.16
$2,000	12 months	18%	200.32
$3,500	12 months	18%	350.36
$2,000	36 months	15%	495.88
$3,500	36 months	15%	867.52
$5,000	36 months	15%	1,239.52
$5,000	60 months	12%	1,673.20
$7,500	60 months	12%	2,509.80
$10,000	60 months	12%	3,346.40

such as the ease of making application, the speed of credit decision, and the convenience of branch offices to handle loan closings—are brought to mind by the lender. The following are examples of these benefits.

Example 1
Ms. Brown wants to borrow $2,000 for home improvements. She currently has the following debts:

Loan	*Monthly Payment*	*Balance*	*Rate*	*Term*
Car	$250	$2,800	13%	36 months
VISA	50	1,000	19%	revolving
Bank loan	75	500	18%	24 months
Department store	15	200	21%	revolving
	$390	$4,500		

Option A: One option would be to give her a $2,000, 24-month loan at 16 percent as follows:

New loan	$ 98	$2,000	16%	24 months
Total	$488	$6,500		

Option B: An alternative would be to consolidate all the existing loans with the new loan as follows:

Consolidated loan	$222	$6,500	14%	36 months

Option B benefits the customer by—

- reducing her monthly debt payment by $266 (from $488 to $222)
- reducing the rate on most of her open loans
- giving her a lower rate on the new money than if she were to make a smaller separate loan.

EXHIBIT 11–3
Term, Rate, and Monthly Payment Comparisons

Advance	*Term*	*Rate*	*Monthly Payment*
$2,000	12 mos.	15%	$180.51
$2,000	12 mos.	16%	181.46
$2,000	36 mos.	16%	70.31
$5,000	30 mos.	13%	196.10
$5,000	60 mos.	13%	113.76
$5,000	60 mos.	14%	116.34
$15,000	36 mos.	2.9%	435.56
$15,000	60 mos.	9.9%	317.96
$15,000	72 mos.	10.5%	281.69

Option B benefits the bank by—

- creating a new loan of $6,500, rather than $2,000
- enhancing the relationship with the customer.

Example 2

Mr. and Mrs. Johnson are trading in their car for a new one and need to borrow an additional $8,500, plus pay off their current balance of $1,500. They currently owe the following debts:

Loan	*Monthly Payment*	*Balance*	*Rate*	*Term*
Second Mtg.	$175	$ 9,000	12.5%	120 mos.
Boat	350	17,500	13.0%	120 mos.
Car	125	1,500	9.5%	48 mos.
VISA	20	400	18.0%	revolving
MasterCard	45	900	18.0%	revolving
Department store	15	300	21.0%	revolving
Department store	25	500	16.0%	revolving
Total	$755	$30,100		

Option A: One option would be to lend the Johnsons $10,000 to finance the car purchase and pay off the remaining balance on the loan. A 60-month, 10 percent loan would result in a monthly payment of $842 as follows:

	Monthly Payments	*Balance*	
Current debts	$755	$30,100	
Minus trade-in	125	1,500	
	630	28,600	
Plus new loan	212	10,000	@ 10% for 60 months
Total	$842	$38,600	

Option B: An alternative is to consolidate all loans except the boat loan with the new loan request. An 11 percent, 10-year second mortgage loan of $21,100 results in a total monthly payment of $640 as follows:

New Second Mtg.	$290	$21,100	@ 11% for 120 months
Boat	350	17,500	
Total	$640	$38,600	

Option B benefits the customers by:

- reducing the monthly payment for debts by $202 (from $842 to $640)
- reducing the interest rate on a significant portion of debt
- simplifying their financial management by reducing the number of open credit accounts.

These examples show the potential for loan structuring that is possible with many consumer loan accounts. Options that provide significant benefits for the customer and the bank without compromising credit quality should certainly be presented to consumers for their consideration. It should be noted that any loan structuring effort should strengthen the bank's position, never weaken it.

The credit limit established for an open-end credit account has a significant effect on the value of the account to the consumer. Higher line limits encourage greater use of the account and allow the customer to use the line for different purposes than would be possible for a smaller line. For example, a $1,000 check overdraft line of credit places significant limitations on how and for what purposes the customer uses the line. Larger borrowing needs are automatically eliminated, as the line is restricted to small borrowing needs and short-term cash flow requirements. A $25,000 equity line of credit, on the other hand, allows the customer to meet all but a few borrowing needs without continually applying for a loan.

Likewise, a credit card with a $3,000 credit limit may be preferred by a consumer over another card with a $1,000 limit. The larger line can be used to purchase higher ticket items and could also alleviate a consumer's concern about going over the limit and being embarrassed at a checkout counter.

The close relationship between the size of the line and the level of account usage is reflected in the lending practices of marketing-oriented banks. Many banks set low to moderate initial credit limits, then follow up by steadily increasing the size of the credit limit available to good customers. For example, a bank may decide to increase the credit limits on all of its good check overdraft or credit card customers by 15 percent. This is accomplished by calculating the new limits and advising the consumer of his new limit. No action is required on the customer's part. This approach can be viewed as a form of loan structuring since the bank is attempting to increase the value of the account to the customer while increasing the level of account usage and ultimately increasing portfolio profitability.

The availability of collateral is important to loan structuring. Normally, the greater the security that an item of collateral offers the bank, the lower the interest rate the bank may offer the consumer. Thus, stable and appreciating value collateral usually qualify the customer for lower rates than depreciating or fluctuating value collateral.

For example, selling the consumer a real estate-secured loan rather than an unsecured loan not only provides the bank with a much stronger position, but also it gives the consumer access to higher loan amounts, lower rates, and longer terms. Thus, both parties may benefit from such a structuring effort.

Care should always be exercised when considering the value of collateral on a loan. Collateral should not be used to justify selling a larger loan to a customer who does not have a sound credit history. However, the prudent lender should request collateral to help strengthen the many loans that fall into the "gray area" between obvious approval and obvious rejection.

Control over the loan proceeds is an important benefit of direct lending. This feature allows the lender to structure the loan with the assurance that the loan proceeds will be used as intended. This control is particularly important when the lender is making a marginal loan or a bill consolidation loan. On a direct loan, the lender may require that certain obligations be paid off directly by the bank. Individual checks are prepared for each payee, and the proceeds are not available for the borrower to use at his discretion. The following examples illustrate when this is desirable.

Example 1

To reduce monthly debt payments to a more manageable level, the applicant wishes to consolidate four other closed-end loans. The new loan would reduce the customer's monthly debt obligations by $150, and would just satisfy the bank's debt-to-income ratio policy.

In this case, the lender wants to be sure that the existing loans are paid off. Otherwise, the borrower may exceed the bank's debt-to-income ratio and would not qualify for the loan. Separate checks are made out to each creditor, and no new funds are given to the borrower.

Example 2
To lower his monthly payments and reduce the rate of interest that he is currently paying, the applicant wishes to consolidate four open-end credit accounts.

This situation poses an entirely different problem than the one presented in Example 1. Because the accounts to be paid off are open-end accounts, the lender faces higher credit risk and more difficulty in controlling the borrower's future credit usage. Individual checks could be sent to pay off each of the accounts; however, the lines of credit would still be open and the customer could easily begin to accumulate debt once again. If that happens, his ability to pay could again be strained and the level of credit risk would be increased. Clearly, the least desirable option in this case would be to sell the customer on another open-end line of credit. Credit judgment should always take precedence over the desire to sell customers larger loans and more flexible credit arrangements.

Credit Insurance

Credit insurance protection is another important variable in structuring and selling consumer credit products. The sale of credit life, credit disability—accident and health—and credit unemployment insurance enhances the bank's profits and provides added protection for the consumer and the bank. The consumer benefits by having the loan paid off in the event of death, or having the insurance company make the payments on the loan when he is unable to work due to medical or other covered reasons. The bank benefits by avoiding delinquencies and losses associated with death and disability. Credit insurance also helps preserve customer goodwill during difficult periods.

Insurance experts recommend two basic approaches when selling credit-related insurance services. First, avoid the use of the word "insurance." The term "insurance" causes many consumers to immediately throw up all kinds of defenses and objections. Instead, use phrases such as "credit protection plan." This allows the lender time to present the benefits of these products before having to address the consumer's preconceptions about the need for "insurance." The second practice is to always quote monthly payments with the full credit protection package. Then, if the customer does not want some of the coverage, the result will be a lower monthly payment. Psychologically, it is easier for the consumer to accept some form of insurance coverage when payments are lowered as coverage is reduced rather than raised as insurance is included. Another popular approach is to quote the cost of insurance on a daily basis, which is usually just pennies per day.

The effect that credit insurance plans have on the cost of closed-end consumer loans is shown in *Exhibit 11–4*.

Notice that adding single credit life coverage, based on a premium of $.63 per $100, results in a $2.03 increase in the monthly payment and a $15.29 increase in the finance charge. Adding both credit life and disability insurance adds $7.04 and $53.22, respectively. These amounts increase greatly as the size of the loan and term increase. Full coverage on the sample $10,000 loan results in an increase of $20.10 in the monthly payment and $302.22 in the finance charge. Clearly, it is easier to sell these coverages when the highest monthly payment amount is quoted and then reduced if the customer does not want certain types of insurance coverage.

Indirect Loans

Indirect loans do not provide many opportunities for bank employees to do loan structuring or cross-selling. Loan structuring is restricted to adjusting the terms of the loan as requested by the dealer. The bank may ask for a larger down payment, change the term of the loan, approve a lower amount financed, require additional signers, or limit the amount of the monthly payment. There is no opportunity to cross-sell other services until after the loan has been made. Then, the bank may pursue an aggressive direct mail and telemarketing effort to sell its indirect loan customers on other bank services.

The lender must temper the dealer's desire to optimize sales on each finance transaction based upon the creditworthiness of the borrower and his ability to pay. If the borrower will not be

EXHIBIT 11–4
Credit Insurance Sales—Effect on Loan Payments and Bank Income

APR	*Amount*	*Term*	*Life Premium*	*CDI Premium*	*Monthly Pmt.*	*Finance Charge*
16%	$3,000	36	No insurance		$105.47	$796.92
16%	$3,000	36	$57.79	N/A	107.50	812.21
16%	$3,000	36	60.48	$139.74	112.51	850.14
12%	$10,000	60	No insurance		$222.44	$3,346.40
12%	$10,000	60	$303.97	N/A	229.20	3,448.03
12%	$10,000	60	321.66	$582.12	242.54	3,648.62

able to comfortably handle the total level of debt after the new loan, the lender must condition the approval to bring the loan within acceptable bank standards. For example, if the new loan would result in a debt-to-income ratio of 45 percent, and the bank's standard is 40 percent, adjustments would need to be made in the loan terms to bring the ratio into line. This may be done by—

- extending the term of the loan and thereby reducing the monthly payment—this is rarely an option on indirect loans since dealers almost always submit loans for the maximum term allowed by the bank
- increasing the amount of the down payment—this lowers the amount to be financed, which, in turn, reduces the monthly payment and also improves the bank's collateral risk on the loan
- approving the loan subject to a specific monthly payment that meets the bank's policy—this approach allows the dealer to restructure the components of the loan in many ways. He may elect to write the loan at a lower rate, drop the sale of insurance and/or the warranty policy, or ask for a bigger down payment.

From these examples, it is apparent that bank lenders have little control over indirect loan structuring. They are unable to do anything about the borrower's other debt obligations, nor can they truly implement the philosophy of selling the best loan for the customer and the bank. Any structuring of the customer's overall debts will need to be done in a later transaction.

A word of caution is in order at this point. Dealers count on the finance income from loans they book with a bank. Therefore, if the bank were to follow a practice of aggressively selling loans to the dealer's customers, and if this resulted in many of the dealer loans being consolidated into new loans, trouble would quickly develop since the dealer would lose finance income on accounts that were paid off early. To avoid this problem, yet still make the most of the indirect customer base, some banks follow the practice of approving indirect loan applicants for two loans. For example, they approve the indirect loan request and also qualify the customer for a credit card or unsecured line of credit. These credit products are then offered to the customer on a preapproved basis soon after the dealer loan is made.

Open-End Credit

The ability to offer loan structuring and do cross-selling on open-end credit applications varies with the type of product. Loan structuring can be an important part of selling an equity line or large, unsecured line-of-credit product. These lines may be large enough to allow the consumer to consolidate debts and to gain other advantages such as lower rates, lower monthly payments, and tax deductibility of interest. Loan structuring is not possible on most credit card programs or check overdraft plans. But cross-selling opportunities abound with open-end accounts. The monthly billing statement provides a convenient vehicle for cross-selling and may be used to supplement other direct mail and telemarketing efforts.

Loan structuring and cross-selling efforts are enhanced when open-end applications are generated via direct personal contact or over the telephone. Direct customer contact gives the bank salesperson greater flexibility in obtaining information from the customer and tailoring the sales approach to the specific applicant. The employee is able to sell any of the bank's products using "the best loan for the customer and the bank" philosophy. This may mean that the customer will be sold a closed-end loan or an open-end product different from the one initially requested.

The growing use of preapproved and prescreened credit programs allows banks to aggressively pursue new customers.

These customers may then become prospects for the bank's other services. While some banks look at these customers as only a source of profits for a particular product, others see broader potential and conduct marketing efforts to build upon the relationship. Industry statistics strongly suggest that the more accounts a customer has with the bank, the less likely that customer is to leave.

Cross-selling open-end loan products also offers an opportunity to tap different markets not served by the bank's branch network.

The Selling Process

At any given time, there are a group of consumers ready, willing, and able to purchase consumer credit products. It is the bank's challenge to market its products in a manner that will attract this group. The effort begins with an understanding of the sales cycle.

The basic sales cycle for any product or service can be broken into four elements, as shown in *Exhibit 11–5*.

The selling process begins when the consumer becomes aware of a need. The need for credit is almost always derived from the desire to satisfy some other need. For example, if a consumer's car is about ready to fall apart, he may need a new car, which, in turn, leads to the need for a loan to pay for the car. Obviously, a consumer does not need to purchase a $45,000 Mercedes to satisfy his need for a car. A Ford Escort could meet that need at a much lower price. However, some consumers have other needs, such as ego gratification or a desire to establish a certain image, both of which may result in the purchase of a Mercedes.

Once the consumer recognizes the need for funds to purchase goods or services, he may begin the process of searching for a means of satisfying the need. This may be a very brief process or it may be quite extensive, depending upon the consumer involved and the relative importance of the decision. Some consumers search no farther than the car dealer's finance and insurance office. Others respond immediately to a direct mail offering or an advertisement. Still other consumers go through an extensive process of comparing competitors to find the one with the lowest rate or the best overall product.

EXHIBIT 11–5
Sales Cycle

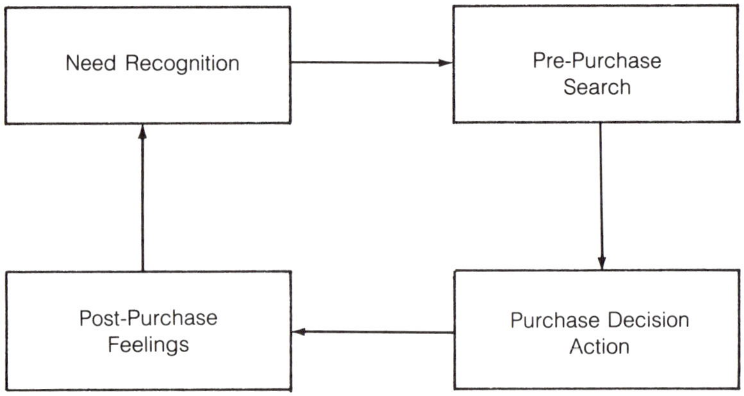

Convenience combined with sales ability are key factors affecting which product the consumer purchases. If credit products are convenient and delivered with a high level of service, they may be sold to consumers even though the bank may not offer the lowest rate in town. Skilled salespeople can also control sales and minimize "credit shopping" by consumers if they have the ability to recognize the consumer's needs and provide products that meet those needs. Another essential skill is the ability to build credibility with the consumer. Indeed, many of the finest consumer credit salespeople in the country have substantial followings by loyal customers, who trust their advice and seek them out over competitors that, from a pricing standpoint, offer more attractive products.

Another point at which selling opportunities are created is the period between when the credit application is taken and the credit decision is made. This is somewhat unique in retail sales. In virtually every other type of retail sale, the consumer makes a decision to buy, then simply presents the necessary form of payment. The transaction is thus concluded. On loans, the customer must wait for the seller—the bank—to make a decision. It goes without saying that this decision should be made as quickly as possible, but, in the interim, the lender can use the information on the application to identify possible sales opportunities.

All consumers have an opinion of the service they received when sold a product. If the consumer is satisfied with the loan product that he has purchased, and if the loan process was handled in an efficient and customer-oriented manner, he will likely think of the bank the next time another loan is needed and will probably be responsive to the bank's efforts to cross-sell other services. On the other hand, if the consumer views the loan experience as unpleasant, feels he paid too high a rate, or decides that the product did not perform as expected, then he is going to be less receptive to future selling efforts.

The sales cycle should be kept in mind as the bank reviews its consumer credit products and the lending process. It is vitally important that the consumer be the focus of product design and operational procedures. These factors should not be designed solely out of concern for the bank's needs.

Selling Skills

Effective selling involves the following skills:

- establishing rapport with the customer
- recognizing customer needs
- understanding the products
- handling and overcoming objections
- closing the sale.

Direct personal selling situations usually begin with a specific request from the borrower, for example: "I want a loan to purchase a new car." However, before the employee plunges into completing the application form, it is desirable to undertake a general conversation designed to put the customer at ease and build rapport. Rapport is undoubtedly strengthened if the customer has repeated satisfactory contact with the banker over time, but it may also be achieved if the banker is able to empathize with the customer and use good human relations skills.

The ability to identify customer needs sounds easy, but it can actually be quite challenging. The basic need—the need for funds—is obvious. But other needs are less obvious and must be determined through conversation with the borrower. Alternatively, needs can be assumed based upon the data submitted on the loan application. For example, if the customer faces a series of borrowing needs in the foreseeable future, such as to make major home improvements, the lender may satisfy the immediate need with a closed-end loan. However, a better answer might be a line of credit that covers both the immediate and long-term needs.

Another example of a hidden need is ego gratification. A basic VISA or MasterCard may satisfy the need for a convenient transaction device, but an American Express Gold Card or a Premier VISA may satisfy the higher priority need for ego enhancement demanded by some customers. Identifying these intangible needs helps to "sell the sizzle, not the steak," and to make the most of each selling opportunity.

Effective selling also involves matching the customer's needs with the product that best meets those needs. To do this, the salesperson must possess a certain level of knowledge regarding the bank's and competitor's products. This is not to say that the salesperson must have an exhaustive knowledge of all aspects of every product. That is virtually impossible in today's rapidly changing banking environment. Rather, the salesperson should have a basic understanding of the key features of each product, and know to whom to refer the customer for more detailed information.

Another essential skill is the ability to handle and overcome customer objections—often the difference between making or losing a sale. An objection raised by a customer can be viewed positively, in that it helps the salesperson identify the needs that seem most important to the customer. In response to an objection, the salesperson should empathize with the customer, clarify any misunderstanding and offer a solution to the objection. Typical objections to consumer loans and some possible responses are presented next.

Objection: "The rate is too high."
Response: "Mr. Jones, I agree that the rate is an important consideration when obtaining a loan. That is why we offer a wide range of loan products with different loan rates. You may be able to qualify for one of our lower rate plans."

Objection: "I don't want a second mortgage on my home."
Response: "I understand your concern, but a home equity line of credit offers many benefits that actually help you reduce financial risk. You will have money available to meet financial emergen-

cies, be able to control how much credit you use, and also keep your monthly payments at a comfortable level."

Closing the sale has two steps. The first step is actually getting the application. The second involves turning the application into a loan account. Skilled lenders know how to turn customer inquiries into loan applications, while less skilled employees seem unable to get past the customer's first question—"What is your rate?" A simple response to this question will almost always result in the phone being hung up or the conversation being abruptly cut short.

But getting the application and approving it is no guarantee that the sale will be completed. Sales are lost because the bank failed to respond in a timely fashion, the application was handled poorly, the customer found a better deal somewhere else, or the customer changed his mind. Lost sales are unavoidable; however, a sound consumer credit operation should minimize these missed opportunities through effective selling from start to finish.

Summary

Selling is a vital part of a consumer credit operation. The deregulated, highly competitive financial services environment has made it essential that banks emphasize strong selling skills in their personnel and implement sales programs designed to meet the needs of the consumer and the bank.

Consumer credit selling involves the use of loan structuring techniques that enhance the attractiveness of loan products to the consumer, while enabling the bank to optimize earnings, retain customers, and keep credit risk within acceptable levels. Loan structuring requires that lenders have a sound knowledge of what products the bank has to offer and how those products can fulfill the consumer's specific needs.

Finally, consumer lenders must recognize their role as full-service bankers. They must look for ways to cross-sell the full range of retail bank services and products to loan customers. These selling efforts may begin with the loan application, but they extend into sales programs designed to sell additional bank services to all of the bank's customers after loan accounts have been opened.

Questions for Review and Discussion

1. What is the distinction between selling and cross-selling?

2. Explain the meaning of this statement: A consumer lender should sell loans, not just take orders.

3. What difference in service is implied if you think of bank customers as clients?

4. Why is a direct lending transaction more conducive to loan structuring than most other types of consumer credit transactions?

5. How does an understanding of consumer psychology and the sales cycle help a consumer lender make loans?

6. If done right, determining a customer's needs is not always easy or perfectly straightforward. Why?

7. Why are a customer's objections often a helpful element in a loan interview?

8. Does your bank promote a sales culture by actively encouraging consumer lending personnel to sell and cross-sell bank products and services? Is selling mentioned in your bank's policy statements or procedural manual? If so, what is your bank's stance on the subject? Write a brief description of your findings.

12 Loan Documentation and Closing

Documentation of a loan is the process of completing and executing the forms required by the bank and by state and federal law for the type of loan being made. *Closing* a loan involves taking the actions necessary to give a successful credit applicant access to the loan proceeds or authorization to use the credit account.

A loan closing can be held at a variety of locations. Direct loans are closed in the bank's offices, indirect loans are closed at the dealer's place of business, and open-end lines of credit are either closed at the customer's home or at the bank's offices. Occasionally, loans may be closed by an attorney or service company that represents the bank.

Proper documentation is essential if the bank is to protect its investment and its customers are to fully understand the loan product they have selected. Failure to properly document loans can leave the bank exposed to unnecessary credit risk and to costly compliance violations. Therefore, many banks use a formal loan review process to ensure that all loan forms are properly completed.

A loan closing is also a stage of the lending process that offers some significant marketing opportunities for the bank. A loan closing can be used to lay the groundwork for a future sale and to create a positive image of the bank and its employees.

Objectives of the Documentation and Closing Process

Banks have five primary objectives during the documentation and closing process:

- complete all documents required by state and federal law for the type of loan being made
- comply with all applicable regulations and the bank's lending policy
- ensure that the consumer understands how the loan works
- create a positive image for the bank
- use the opportunity to sell other bank products.

This chapter will look at how each of these objectives affect both the bank and the consumer. In addition, it will examine ways to achieve the desired results.

Most banks have developed loan policy and procedure manuals detailing the documents that must be completed for each type of loan and the proper means of completing those documents. Generally, the lender relies upon the bank's legal counsel to supply documents, which, if properly completed, will be in compliance with all applicable regulations. The lender's responsibility is to ensure that the forms are properly completed and executed.

Accurate document preparation is essential to the efficient operation of the consumer credit department. Properly completed forms flow through the system without delay and without the need for expensive special handling. If, on the other hand, there are documentation errors, normal work flow is disrupted and additional time and expense must be invested to correct the problems. For example, when a branch loan officer fills in the wrong numbers for the amount of finance charges and the amount of the monthly payments, the loan has to be sent back to the branch. The branch must then contact the customer and ask that he return to the office to sign corrected documents. If the documentation error goes undetected, the bank is exposed to additional credit risk and compliance violations.

The need to comply with all applicable regulations is closely related to the objective of getting complete and accurate documents. This objective extends beyond the forms themselves to the order in which disclosures are made. For example, Regulation Z requires that federal disclosures be presented to the consumer before any documents are signed. Thus, it is a violation of the regulation to have the customer execute a *note*—the legal agreement that contains the customer's promise to repay the loan—before executing the Truth in Lending disclosure form. It is also a violation to allow a consumer access to an open-end credit account before supplying him with the necessary disclosures.

Consumers generally seem far less interested in disclosures than the regulators are. Many consumers seem happy to be getting the loan and are more concerned with getting their check than with listening to, or reading all of, the information on the loan documents. A consumer's lackadaisical attitude should not, however, lull the lender into complacency regarding proper disclosures. The lender is responsible for proceeding through the loan closing in the appropriate order and for ensuring that the consumer is aware of the required disclosures.

The third objective for the loan closing is to ensure that the consumer understands how the loan product works. Basically, the consumer needs to understand—

- when payments are due and the effect late payments will have on the cost of the loan
- the method of calculating earnings for the bank
- whether extra payments are allowed and, if so, can they be credited towards future payments
- where and how payments may be made
- the effect any variable rate feature will have on the loan
- how to access the line of credit and any restrictions, such as a minimum check size of $100
- who to contact in case of questions or problems, such as not being able to make payments when due.

If the customer understands these features from the outset, he may perform better on the loan and be encouraged to more fully utilize open-end credit accounts. For example, informing customers that their interest is calculated on a simple interest basis, and that they will pay more in finance charges if they pay after the due date, may encourage them to pay earlier. This may also help minimize the number of loans that become delinquent in their early stages.

An old saying puts it this way, "A loan well made is half collected." In other words, a good closing can prevent problems from surfacing later in the loan. Thus, both parties tend to benefit when the consumer understands how the account works. Consumers are also less likely to have customer service questions if they understand how their loan works and who to contact if they do have a problem.

The fourth objective is to create a positive image for the bank. If a loan closing is handled in a professional, consumer-oriented manner, the customer is likely to form a positive image of the bank. This, in turn, is likely to increase the customer's receptivity to future bank marketing efforts, and creates the possibility that the customer will refer other people to the bank.

Finally, the loan closing presents an excellent opportunity for the bank to sell other services. Customers are usually pleased to have been granted a loan and, if the closing is handled well, they will have a positive impression of the bank. This makes it easier for the banker to cross-sell other services that can meet the customer's needs. A sales presentation may be received favorably. At the least, the stage is set for a future sale.

Types of Documentation

The forms required to document a consumer credit transaction vary depending upon the type of loan being made and the collateral securing the loan. Following are lists of documents commonly used for several types of loans.

For direct, closed-end automobile loans, the principal documents are the—

- credit application
- Truth in Lending disclosure statement (see *Exhibit 12–1*)—this form provides all of the required federal Truth in Lending disclosures as well as some disclosures required by state law
- note and security agreement—this form combines the note, which is the consumer's promise to pay, with the security agreement, which describes the security interest in goods being pledged as collateral on the loan. The security agreement precisely describes the collateral and sets forth the rights and responsibilities of each party relative to the collateral
- insurance policy or agreement to provide insurance—these forms are used to verify that the collateral is covered by insurance and that the bank is named as loss payee. The loss payee endorsement provides that, in the event the collateral is damaged or destroyed, the bank will be named as joint payee with the borrower on the insurance check. The proceeds may be used to repair the collateral and thereby restore its value, or to reduce or pay off the balance on the loan.

EXHIBIT 12–1

Truth in Lending Disclosure Statement

(Use with Consumer Credit Installment Note / Consumer Credit Installment Note and Security Agreement)

DISCLOSURE STATEMENT REQUIRED BY FEDERAL LAW

This Disclosure Statement is provided in connection with my loan from ________ Bank, National Association.

In this Disclosure Statement, the words *I, me, my* and *mine* mean each and all Borrower(s) who sign below. The word *Bank* means ________ Bank, National Association.

ANNUAL PERCENTAGE RATE The cost of my credit as a yearly rate.	**FINANCE CHARGE** The dollar amount the credit will cost me.	**Amount Financed** The amount of credit provided to me or on my behalf.	**Total of Payments** The amount I will have paid when I have made all payments as scheduled.
%	$	$	$

My payment schedule will be:

Number of Payments	Amount of Payments	When Payments Are Due
		Monthly, Beginning / /

Security: I am giving the Bank a security interest in any monies, deposits or credits held by the Bank for or owed by the Bank to, me, and in:

☐ the goods or property being purchased ☐ the following property: ________________

Collateral from other loans may also secure my loan.

Late Charge: If a payment is more than 15 days late, I will be charged a late charge of the larger of $2.00 or 5% of the payment.

Prepayment: If I pay off early, I will not have to pay a penalty.

(e) means an estimate

Itemization of Amount Financed of	$ ________
Amount given to me directly	$ ________
Amount paid on my account	$ ________
Amounts paid to others on my behalf:	
To public officials for filing fees	$ ________
To Credit Life Insurance company	$ ________
To Accident and Health Insurance company	$ ________
To Vendor's Single Interest Insurance company	$ ________
To ________________	$ ________
To ________________	$ ________

INSURANCE

A. CREDIT LIFE AND/OR ACCIDENT AND HEALTH INSURANCE

NOTICE OF PROPOSED INSURANCE

I understand that neither Credit Life nor Credit Accident and Health Insurance is required to obtain my loan and the Bank will not provide any insurance unless I sign and agree to pay the additional cost.

Credit Life and/or Credit Accident and Health Insurance is available through the Bank with the insurer named below. If purchased, the initial amount of Credit Life Insurance is $ ________ for a total premium of $ ________ for single coverage or (if joint coverage is available) of $ ________ for joint coverage. If purchased, the monthly benefit under the Credit Accident and Health Insurance offered through the Bank is $ ________ for a total premium of $ ________. Credit Accident and Health Insurance is not available on a joint life basis.

This insurance will cover only the person(s) signing the request below for the type(s) of insurance indicated. Subject to acceptance by the insurance company, the insurance will be effective as of the date I sign the Bank's current form of promissory note ("Note") evidencing my loan and will expire on the earlier of the scheduled maturity date of the Note or the date of discharge of my indebtedness, for any reason, prior to the scheduled maturity of the Note. All benefits and proceeds of the insurance will be payable to Equitable Bank, National Association to the extent of its interest and any balance will be payable to me or my estate. Until the insurance expires, the amount of Credit Life Insurance will be the amount repayable under the Note that is not delinquent for more than 90 days. If I am jointly obligated on the Note with my wife or husband and we have both signed the request for Credit Life Insurance, death benefits will be payable only with respect to the first one of us to die. Subject to exclusions, eliminations, or waiting periods stated in the insurance policy or certificate, Credit Accident and Health Insurance is for the monthly benefit stated above for each month of total disability as defined in the insurance policy or certificate. If the Note is prepaid in full prior to the original maturity date, any unearned insurance premium will be refunded to me in the manner prescribed by law. Within 30 days after I sign the Note, I will receive a certificate of insurance more fully describing the insurance coverage. If the insurance is not accepted by the insurance company, I will receive a refund of the insurance premiums I have paid.

____

Name and Home Address of Insurance Company

I want ☐ Credit Life Insurance
☐ Credit Accident and Health Insurance

____
Borrower's Signature

I want ☐ Credit Life Insurance
☐ Credit Accident and Health Insurance

____
Borrower's Signature

B. PROPERTY INSURANCE

I understand I must maintain insurance against loss or damage to my property which is subject to the Bank's security interest, and against liability arising out of my ownership or use of such property. I have the right to choose the person through which such insurance is to be obtained, but the Bank may refuse to accept the insurer which I chose for reasonable cause. Such insurance is not available from or through the Bank. I also understand that I must maintain All Risk Physical Damage Installment Loan Insurance on my property which is subject to the Bank's security interest (called "Vendor's Single Interest Insurance" in this Disclosure Statement) but that I may choose the person through which such insurance is to be obtained. Such insurance is available through the Bank for the entire term of my loan at a cost of $ ________.

ACKNOWLEDGEMENT

By signing below, I acknowledge full understanding and agreement to all of the provisions of this Disclosure Statement and authorize all disbursements itemized above. I also acknowledge receipt of a completely filled in copy of this Disclosure Statement prior to signing any commitment letter, deed of trust, mortgage, promissory note, contract of indebtedness or security agreement.

Executed under seal this ________ day of ________________, 19____.

________ BANK, NATIONAL ASSOCIATION

By: ________________________

________________________ (SEAL)
(Borrower)

________________________ (SEAL)
(Borrower)

________________________ (SEAL)
(Borrower)

Form 952 (7-83)

White copy - original Yellow copy - file Pink copy - customer Goldenrod copy - customer

For indirect automobile loans, the principal documents are the—

- credit application
- closed-end installment sales contract—this form combines all federal and state disclosures with the security agreement
- agreement to provide insurance
- copies of credit insurance and warranty policies, if applicable—banks generally require that copies of these policies be submitted with the other loan documents.

For unsecured, open-end line of credit accounts, the principal documents are the—

- credit application or acceptance form
- open-end credit agreement—this agreement sets forth all of the contractual terms for the account. The consumer must receive the agreement before he can use the account, but he generally does not have to sign the form.

Documentation checklists are often included in the bank's policy manual as a reference source for lenders. Some loans, such as those secured by real property, require even more extensive documentation, while others, such as unsecured closed-end loans, require only the Truth in Lending disclosure statement and the note. Regardless of what type of loan is being made, controls must exist to ensure that the documentation is complete and accurate.

Establishing a Security Interest in a Consumer Loan

Although the *Uniform Commercial Code* (UCC) was first drafted in response to the need for uniformity in handling commercial transactions, it applies to many consumer loans as well. Of particular importance to consumer lenders is *Article 9* of the UCC, which governs most loans secured by personal property. The provisions of Article 9 have been adopted by every state except Louisiana.

A lender making a secured loan covered by the UCC provisions first needs to create a valid *lien* between the lender and borrower. This is accomplished by having the borrower execute a security agreement. A *security agreement* is defined by Article 9 as an agreement that creates or provides for a *security interest*, an interest in property that will secure payment or performance of an obligation. The actual document used must meet several minimum requirements. It must—

- be in writing
- provide for a security interest
- be signed by the debtor
- contain a description of the collateral.

The security agreement contains numerous provisions that stipulate the creditor's and debtor's rights and duties with respect to the collateral. To create a valid security interest, the agreement must be executed by all parties with an ownership interest in the collateral. For example, if a car is owned by John and Mary Jones, both of them must sign the security agreement in order for the bank to obtain a valid lien, even if only one of them will be obligated under the note.

Once a valid lien has been created as a result of having the security agreement signed by all appropriate parties, the lender must perfect the lien. *Perfecting* a lien involves filing it with the appropriate legal authority so that the lien is a matter of public record. Perfection is achieved when the creditor's security interest is attached to the collateral by either: placing its lien on a title, placing its lien on a mortgage or deed of trust, physically taking possession of the collateral, or filing a financing statement (see *Exhibit 12–2*) with the proper governmental authority, usually the secretary of state. When the lien is perfected, the lender, now a secured creditor, has priority over rights that the borrower's other creditors may have in the same collateral. *Exhibit 12–3* indicates the most common method of perfecting a lien on various types of collateral.

Lien perfection procedures vary from state to state. Virtually all states have automobile title laws, while only a few have title provisions for boats. Therefore, to avoid errors in the lien perfection process, lenders must be aware of the requirements in each state in which they do business.

A perfected interest in collateral provides the bank with a *secondary source of repayment*—a source of funds to help it recover its investment should the borrower be unable to repay the loan for any reason. When the bank does not properly perfect its interest in the collateral, it is in an unsecured position and the borrower is free to seek a loan from another source using the same property as collateral.

EXHIBIT 12–2
UCC Financing Statement

UNIFORM COMMERCIAL CODE — FINANCING STATEMENT — FORM UCC-1

DISTRICT OF COLUMBIA

INSTRUCTIONS

1. PLEASE TYPE this form. Fold only along perforation for mailing.
2. Remove Secured Party and Debtor Copies and send other 3 copies to the filing officer. Enclose filing fee.
3. When filing is to be with more than one office, Form UCC-2 may be placed over this set to avoid double typing.
4. If the space provided for any item(s) on the form is inadequate the item(s) should be continued on additional sheets, preferably 5" x 8" or 8" x 10". Only one copy of such additional sheets need be presented to the filing officer with a set of three copies of the financing statement. Long schedules of collateral, indentures, etc., may be on any size paper that is convenient for the secured party.
5. If collateral is crops or goods which are or are to become fixtures, describe generally the real estate and give name of record owner.
6. When a copy of the security agreement is used as a financing statement, it is requested that it be accompanied by a completed but unsigned set of these forms, without extra fee.
7. At the time of original filing, filing officer should return third copy as an acknowledgment. At a later time, secured party may date and sign termination legend and use third copy as a Termination Statement.

This FINANCING STATEMENT is presented to a filing officer for filing pursuant to the Uniform Commercial Code | 3 Maturity date (if any):

1 Debtor(s) (Last Name First) and address(es)	2 Secured Party(ies) and address(es)	For Filing Officer (Date, Time, Number, and Filing Office)

4 This financing statement covers the following types (or items) of property:	5. Assignee(s) of Secured Party and Address(es)

Check ☒ if covered: ☐ Proceeds of Collateral are also covered ☐ Products of Collateral are also covered. No. of additional sheets presented:

Filed with: ....

By: .... Signature(s) of Debtor(s)

By: .... Signature(s) of Secured Party(ies)

FILING OFFICER—ALPHABETICAL

STANDARD FORM — UNIFORM COMMERCIAL CODE — FORM UCC-1

REORDER FROM Registré, Inc.

Three common forms of secured consumer lending require additional discussion. They are mortgage lending, loans secured by airplanes, and loans secured by boats documented with the U.S. Coast Guard.

Consumer lenders may be heavily involved in mortgage lending through the offering of closed-end second mortgage loans and open-end home equity loans. Most states have well-established laws for recording a mortgage or deed of trust. The mortgage or deed of trust is recorded in the county in which the property is located. State law controls the types of mortgage loans that can be made and the terms that can be used.

While few problems exist regarding closed-end mortgages, some states have not adopted open-end mortgage provisions that fully protect the bank. For example, in Washington, D.C., if a bank grants an equity line of credit to a consumer and that consumer subsequently obtains a second mortgage, the second mortgage holder would have priority over the equity line account for all advances made after the second mortgage was made. This situation increases the bank's exposure and makes

EXHIBIT 12–3
Methods of Perfecting Collateral

Type of Collateral	*How Perfected*
Airplanes	Federal Aviation Administration title
Automobiles	Title
Boats	Financing statement Title or Coast Guard Mortgage
Household Goods	Financing statement
Mobile Homes	Title
Recreational Vehicles	
Self-propelled	Title
Other	Financing statement
Real Estate	Mortgage/Deed of Trust
Savings Passbook or Certificate	Possession
Stock	Possession

the use of open-end credit plans much riskier. Most states have now passed laws that protect lenders by establishing a priority position, up to the maximum amount of their credit line, against all subsequent lenders.

Attorneys and service companies are frequently used by banks to handle mortgage title searches, loan closings, and mortgage recordings. The cost of outside specialists can usually be passed on to the customer. Using attorneys and service companies gives the bank extra assurance that its lien will be properly perfected, and may help in spotting documentation errors that, if gone unnoticed, would increase the bank's loan risk exposure.

Loans secured by aircraft must conform to the documentation requirements of the *Federal Aviation Act*. The creditor's security agreement must be recorded with the Federal Aviation Administration (FAA) office in Oklahoma City, Oklahoma. Liens perfected with the FAA provide a very strong secured position for the lender since there is little chance the aircraft can be sold without the bank first being paid. The large amount of most aircraft loans makes it particularly important that the bank properly perfect its security interest, using the FAA documents and processing procedures.

The *Ship Mortgage Act* of 1920 established procedures for the federal documentation of vessels. Boats weighing over five net tons may be documented under the act. Vessels that will operate in international waters or in several states, and which meet the Coast Guard's requirements, should be federally documented in order to provide the strongest possible lien position for the bank. Federal documentation takes priority over state titles or UCC filings.

Coast Guard documentation is a long and relatively complex process. Therefore, many banks rely on outside documentation companies to handle this task for them. It can take up to nine months for the bank to receive notification that its mortgage has been recorded, so many lenders take the additional precaution of recording their lien via either a financing statement or state title to protect them during the interim period.

Loan Review

As part of an overall compliance program, some banks have established a formal loan review department within the consumer credit division. This department may play a key role in the documentation process, performing such tasks as—

- examining completed documents for accuracy, completeness, and adherence to bank lending policy
- following up to resolve documentation errors
- expediting the booking of new loans
- developing and maintaining management information regarding items such as documentation problems and lender performance
- maintaining follow-up for necessary lien and insurance documents.

Some loan review tasks should be performed before the loan is booked. Other tasks require continual monitoring and follow-up. For example, lien and insurance follow-up programs are essential for a bank to ensure that its collateralized loans are properly secured. The department should maintain a checklist of all necessary forms, and then record each one as it comes in from the appropriate agency—state motor vehicle department, insurance company, and so forth. Even if the bank obtains all the documents needed to properly perfect its liens, things can still go wrong. For example, the state motor vehicle department may not pick up the bank's lien and may issue a title without a lien to the borrower, or the dealer may add another name to the title, leaving the bank in the position of not having its lien properly perfected since all owners may not have signed the loan documents. These errors can be resolved with relative ease if detected early in the life of the loan.

For banks with limited resources or that elect not to establish follow-up programs, collateral insurance programs are available to protect them against the risk of having liens improperly recorded.

Management information reports developed by a loan review department can help to strengthen the bank's overall consumer lending operation. If the loan review area is able to identify problems more quickly, then the bank will be able to resolve problems before they become serious. For example, if an individual loan officer is making a lot of documentation errors, the problem can often be remedied by additional training. Likewise, if one dealer seems to be having problems properly preparing contracts or resolving contract errors, the bank can act quickly to remedy the problem through additional staff training or, in extreme cases, by terminating the dealer relationship.

Booking Loans on the Operating System

The end result of the loan documentation process is booking loans on the bank's operating system. In a sound lending program, loans are booked on a timely basis, new loan information is accurate and complete, and essential information is stored for retrieval as needed.

Summary

The loan documentation and closing process is an important part of developing a sound consumer credit portfolio. It involves the preparation and execution of loan documents that comply with all applicable regulations and provide the bank with a firm legal basis for collecting and servicing its loans.

Loan documents must be accurate and complete to establish the bank's and consumer's rights under the terms of the loan arrangement. When a loan is to be secured by collateral, the bank must establish and perfect a security interest in the collateral. This requires an understanding of specific provisions of state law regarding lien perfection, as well as special documentation requirements for real property, aircraft, and large boats.

The loan closing offers the lender an opportunity to create a positive image for the bank, ensure that the customer fully understands the loan product that he has purchased, and sell other bank services.

Questions for Review and Discussion

1. State several reasons why accurate document preparation is so important in a loan transaction.

2. Cite the minimum requirements of a valid security agreement.

3. What is the purpose of a UCC financing statement? Are there other ways to achieve the same purpose?

4. What happens if the bank does not properly perfect its security interest in the collateral pledged for a loan?

5. Does your bank include documentation checklists in its policy manual? If so, take a look at them and take note of how many and what different types of forms are required for various consumer credit transactions.

6. Give a few concrete reasons why it is important to create a positive image for the bank during a loan closing.

7. What is the principal federal law that affects the loan closing? What is its thrust?

8. How would you handle a situation in which a customer resists reading or listening to the disclosures for a loan, and just wants to hurry up, sign, and get his money?

13 Collection and Recovery

The loan collection and recovery functions are an essential part of the consumer credit operation. The collection department is charged with the responsibility of collecting payments on a timely basis from consumers who have become *delinquent*—those who are making payments later than their contractual due date. The *recovery* department, also known as the *salvage* department, is responsible for collecting money still owed on accounts after they have been charged off as a loss to the bank. These functions have a key role in preserving the quality of the consumer loan portfolio and in avoiding unnecessary losses of revenue.

We will begin our discussion of these functions by focusing on the specific objectives and goals of the loan collection and recovery areas. Next, we will discuss the Fair Debt Collection Practices Act, some of the common reasons for default, and organizational issues affecting the bank's collection efforts. Then, we will look at the collection cycle, covering the usual collection tools and common remedies for default. The discussion will provide insight into the day-to-day workings of collection personnel. Finally, we will focus on the recovery department and explore the approaches used to recoup the bank's investment after the loan has been charged off.

Objectives of Collection and Recovery

There are six primary objectives of the collection and recovery departments:

- maintain delinquencies within acceptable parameters
- maintain loan losses within acceptable parameters
- generate loss recoveries at desired levels
- provide counseling to customers experiencing difficulty handling their debts
- ensure consistency with other bank objectives
- achieve collection and recovery in the most cost-efficient manner.

Management must decide what constitutes an acceptable delinquency rate for each type of product in the consumer credit product line. These benchmarks help the bank measure the quality of its loans and evaluate the performance of the loan and collection departments. Generally, the delinquency objective is defined as a maximum percentage of the portfolio that can be in default and still be acceptable. For example, the bank may set an objective of 1.5 percent delinquency for direct closed-end loans. Lower delinquency is always welcomed by management, while higher levels are indications of problems. Portfolio delinquency objectives under 1 percent may be regarded as very conservative, while objectives above 3 percent are very aggressive or liberal.

Delinquencies tend to vary depending upon the type of loan product and seasonal factors (see *Exhibit 13–1*). Note that revolving loans have a relatively low delinquency rate. This can be misleading because consumers experiencing financial difficulties can continue to borrow against lines of credit to make payments on loans. The result may be low past due levels, but increased loss exposure on individual accounts.

Seasonal factors should be considered when evaluating delinquency levels. Each collection manager should be aware of the seasonal delinquency patterns for his particular market. Many banks experience rising delinquencies during the fourth quarter of the year, as the heavy retail buying during the holiday season puts a strain on budgets.

Finally, delinquencies can be influenced by economic conditions. Defaults and losses usually rise during recessionary or stagnant economic cycles when more people are unemployed or when inflation is outstripping gains in income. Some banks relax asset quality standards during these economic downturns. On the other hand, late payments and loss experience should improve during strong economic periods. Thus, the economy in

EXHIBIT 13–1
Consumer Credit Delinquency
Percent Delinquent—National Averages

Type of loan	*October*	*November*	*December*
Unsecured—closed-end	2.78%	3.03%	3.25%
Automobile—direct	1.07	1.10	1.31
Automobile—indirect	1.31	1.44	1.85
Second mortgage	1.36	1.38	1.57
Credit cards	2.63	2.49	2.85
Revolving loans	1.02	1.14	1.20

SOURCE: Quarterly Delinquency Report—1985, American Bankers Association.

the bank's market area should be evaluated to determine its likely effect on portfolio quality as measured by delinquency and losses. This information can then be used to justify staffing levels in the collection area and to set credit approval standards.

Management must also set loan loss objectives. These objectives are set at either the total portfolio level or the individual product level. *Exhibit 13–2* shows the variation in loan losses for different products, demonstrating the importance of setting recovery goals. The difference between the gross and net losses is the amount recovered from consumers after loans have been charged off. A significant difference can represent a large amount of money coming back to the bank. Recovery efforts are therefore important, providing a benchmark for measuring the performance of the recovery department and an additional measure of overall portfolio quality.

Economic conditions also affect loan losses. *Exhibit 13–3* illustrates the loss experience on selected loan types over time. Note that peak loan losses occurred in the early 1980s when interest rates were high. Experience has shown that charge-off rates tend to move in unison with delinquencies; thus, higher delinquencies result in higher losses.

While it is important to set quantifiable goals for the collection and recovery departments, it is also important to recognize the qualitative aspects of loan collection. Successful collectors are usually good salespeople and financial counselors. They can sell the customer on making a payment and can provide guidance as

EXHIBIT 13–2
1985 Installment Credit Dollar Losses Based on Outstandings

Type of Loan	*Gross Losses*	*Net Losses*
Unsecured—closed-end	1.36%	.97%
Automobile—direct	.54	.39
Automobile—indirect	.40	.29
Second mortgage	.39	.35
Small business	1.34	1.14
Credit cards	1.56	1.35
Unsecured—open-end	.46	.36

SOURCE: 1986 Retail Bank Credit Report, American Bankers Association.

to how that can be done. The collector's sales and counseling skills can contribute to lower loss and delinquency performance over time.

Many consumer credit managers argue that loan delinquency and loss objectives should be set in conjunction with the other product line objectives. For example, if a bank is embarking on an aggressive marketing program to promote its credit cards and is liberalizing its lending policies or using aggressive marketing techniques such as pre-approved mailings, it should anticipate a higher rate of loan delinquencies and losses. It seems unlikely that the bank could liberalize its credit standards without having some effect on asset quality.

The final broad objective is to achieve collection and recovery in the most cost-efficient manner. Before proceeding, collectors should compare the anticipated costs of collection to the potential for recovery. For example, the collector who spends $250 repossessing a car worth the same amount has wasted time and energy, while not reducing the amount outstanding on the loan. Similarly, it is difficult to justify the cost of attempting to recover a $250 loss from a consumer who has left the market area and has no job or assets. It may be better to discontinue any collection effort and, instead, concentrate on those accounts with a greater potential for recovery.

The collection department's procedures should be structured to keep costs low. Low-cost notices, such as computer-generated notices that are automatically sent to all past-due accounts,

EXHIBIT 13–3
Net Installment Credit Losses—1968 to 1985

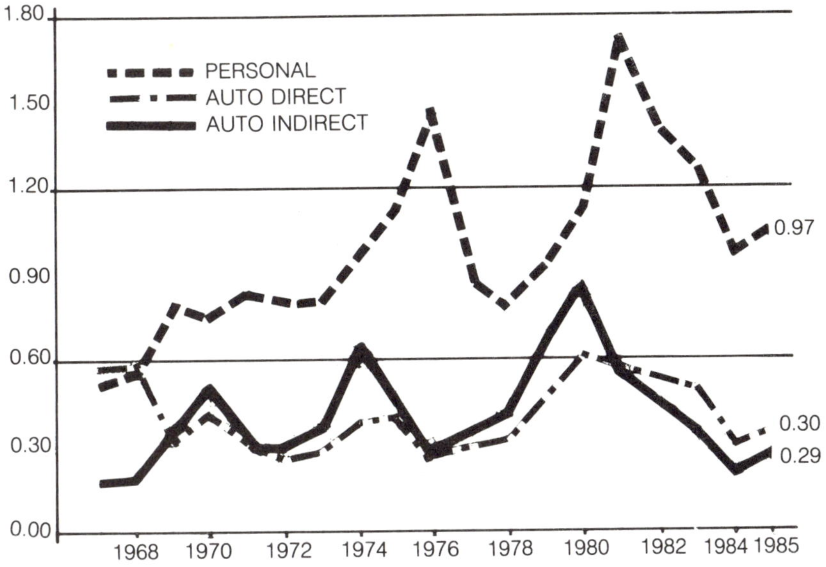

SOURCE: 1986 Retail Bank Credit Report, American Bankers Association.

can be used to reduce the number of delinquent accounts before more expensive personal contact is initiated. Automated collection systems have also helped keep collection costs under control while greatly improving the department's efficiency.

Fair Debt Collection Practices Act

The Fair Debt Collection Practices Act took effect on March 20, 1978. The act is directed primarily at independent debt collection agencies, but its provisions form a basis for identifying acceptable and unacceptable practices for bank collection departments as well. The act also serves as the basic framework for many state laws dealing with collection practices.

The act's major purpose is to—

- ensure the fair treatment of consumers by debt collectors
- define the rights of consumers
- eliminate abusive, deceptive, and unfair practices.

The collection process is, basically, a negative process. The consumer has failed to make a debt payment when it is contractually due, and the bank is trying to look out for its best interests and recover its investment. This does not pose a major concern when the customer's problem is minor, such as when he simply forgot to make the payment or had a temporary problem that is resolvable. The issue becomes far more difficult when there is no readily available solution to the problem.

In an effort to resolve the problem loans to their satisfaction, some lenders and collection agencies engaged in abusive collection practices. The Fair Debt Collection Practices Act moved to address these abusive practices by stating that collectors may not—

- harass, oppress, or abuse any person
- use any false statements
- be unfair in attempting to collect any debt
- threaten any action that cannot legally be taken.

Harassment and abuse include the use of obscene or profane language, advertising the consumer's debt, or repeatedly calling customers in order to annoy them. These are clearly unpleasant and unethical practices, and they certainly do not belong in a sound collection program. One specific limitation imposed by the act is to allow collection calls only between the hours of 8 AM and 9 PM.

The act also requires honesty in collection practices. Implying that the caller is an attorney or a representative of a government agency, implying that the customer has committed a crime and faces arrest, and misrepresenting the amount or terms of the debt are specifically prohibited.

The act also prohibits using postcards to communicate a debt, discussing the debt with neighbors, friends, or other third parties, requiring the customer to accept collect calls or pay for mail or telegrams, or depositing a post-dated check prior to the date on the check. Clearly, the practice of telling third parties about a person's debts is an odious practice. Such behavior does not belong in a bank or any other business concerned about developing and maintaining the goodwill of its customers, including those who may be experiencing problems.

Collectors are also prohibited from threatening to take any action to cure a default that is not specifically provided for in the loan contract. This provision makes it absolutely essential that collectors know what remedies are available to them on each type of loan they handle.

The regulation of debt collection practices has not had a major impact on legitimate financial institutions. Sound debt collection practices are those that enable the collector to balance the need to collect delinquent obligations in a timely fashion, while preserving the customer's goodwill. Collection efforts need not alienate customers just because they are experiencing financial difficulties. Many good customers have, at some point in time, experienced short-term problems. Once past their current problems, they most likely return to their healthy financial status.

Causes of Delinquency

To have an appreciation for the collection process, it is helpful to understand what causes customers to go into default. The major contributors to delinquency are—

- unexpected problems that change the customer's income or debt situation
- excessive levels of debt
- poor money management
- marital problems
- carelessness
- irresponsible lending
- fraud or intentional default.

A major cause of delinquency is the development of unexpected problems that lead to either a decrease in income or an increase in expenses. Examples of the kinds of problems that may lead to loan delinquency include: illness or physical disability, job layoff or termination, death, and unplanned major expenses. These changes may alter the customer's ability to repay the loan for either a short or long period of time. As such, a careful examination of the facts is necessary to determine the best possible remedy for the problem.

The ability to accumulate excessive debt obligations, thereby reducing the capacity to pay, has been enhanced in recent years, mostly due to the aggressive marketing of open-end credit products. Undisciplined consumers may easily acquire access to credit, which if fully used, will place a severe strain on their finances. When debts become excessive, the customer may be unable to make loan payments when due. At best, the consumer may only be able to make minimum monthly payments, and eventually he may need to make choices concerning which loans to pay and which not to pay.

When financial problems develop, most consumers have a priority order in which they repay loans. In descending order, the debts that are generally first paid are—

1. mortgage or rent
2. other primary residence secured loan—equity line or second mortgage
3. automobile loan
4. other secured loan—boat, recreational vehicle, and so forth
5. credit card account
6. unsecured closed-end loan
7. unsecured open-end line of credit.

This order of priority has important implications for lenders and collectors, and it helps explain the variations in delinquency objectives and the experience on various loan portfolios.

Poor money management may encompass a lot of ills. The failure to plan for financial emergencies, the failure to establish a reasonable budget, the lack of self-control when purchasing goods, and the failure to organize finances in a satisfactory manner can all contribute to problems. Poor financial management may be detected by examining the consumer's credit history and capacity at the time the loan is made, but, in many cases, this problem does not appear until after the loan is made.

Marital breakups frequently leave both parties scrambling to get out of paying debts. An income and debt structure that was in balance when the couple was one financial unit may be totally disrupted after the marriage breaks up. In many cases, one of the parties attempts to disavow responsibility for the debts, evidencing a change in character. In other cases, the marital breakup results in a reduced level of income or an increase in debts, and, consequently, the debts simply can no longer be handled.

Carelessness leads to some delinquencies. Those who have the ability to pay, but who are not strongly motivated to pay on a timely basis, are careless. This type of customer can usually be identified by credit reports that show a history of delinquencies, but no reason for paying late other than sloppiness. This is evidence of weakness in the measurement of character.

Some loans simply should never have been made. They are the result of irresponsible lenders who compromise the bank's policies or use poor judgment. The result may be the booking of loans that will result in chronic collection problems or losses.

Fraud or intentional default is significantly different from the problems already discussed because they involve the deliberate attempt to avoid repaying an obligation. Fraud is an ongoing problem for consumer lenders. Much fraud is uncovered by the collection department after the account has been set up and the customer has the bank's money. When they are detected, fraudulent accounts are typically removed from the mainstream collection effort and given to a specialist with the time and expertise needed to track down the responsible party.

Organization of the Collection Function

The collection function may be centralized or decentralized. In a centralized operation, collection specialists devote their full attention to the task of resolving delinquency problems. This approach allows for the development of high levels of expertise and lends itself to efforts to automate collection activities. Advocates of the centralized approach feel that collection specialists are more efficient and effective in handling delinquency problems.

In a decentralized environment, collection tasks may be handled by lenders and employees who also have other responsibilities. Some consumer credit managers prefer the decentralized approach because they feel that lenders use more discretion in making credit decisions when they must collect their own loans.

No matter which approach is used, the collection process must function smoothly if loan delinquencies and defaults are to be minimized. Essentials of a smooth operation are—

- a highly-automated system for handling early-stage delinquencies
- the identification of delinquent accounts as soon as they reach delinquency
- a system of tracking customer contacts and following up on repayment promises

- the development of enough information to allow collectors to work intelligently with delinquent customers
- the isolation of serious collection problems for handling by specialized collectors.

Automation of the collection function is usually desirable for large portfolios. Automated systems generally help speed up account handling, maximize productivity (as measured by the number of accounts handled per collector), and enhance efficiency by providing more and timely information to collectors.

The Collection Cycle

The bulk of consumer credit customers make their loan payments on or before the date payments are due. Of those who go into default, the majority pay within 15 days after the due date. Those who do not pay within that time are the focus of most collection activity.

In this section, we will examine the various stages of the collection cycle and discuss the types of problems and activities that take place in each stage.

Stages of the Collection Cycle

Exhibit 13–4 presents the stages in the collection cycle for a typical closed-end loan product. Open-end products generally have a longer cycle, with charge-off coming at 180 days. We will now examine these stages and discuss the collection approaches, collection tools, and delinquency remedies that are used at each stage.

Most accounts that are in default—1 day or more past due—do not pose a significant problem. The primary objective in this stage of delinquency is to eliminate as many of these accounts from a past due status as possible before the problem becomes more acute, thus allowing more attention to be directed toward those accounts that are seriously delinquent. It is also the bank's objective to hold down the costs of this collection effort.

The distribution of accounts falling into the collection cycle is demonstrated in *Exhibit 13–5*. The percentage of accounts entering the funnel may seem high, but payment is often made before the bank takes any action. Many more customers respond to notices and the imposition of late charges, paying their accounts

EXHIBIT 13–4
Collection Cycle

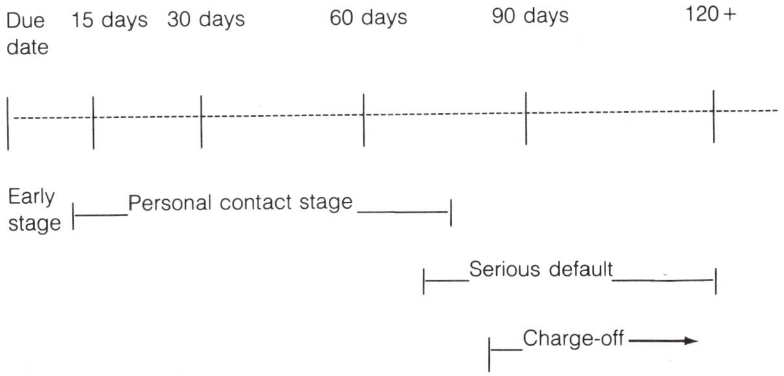

before or soon after the 15-day past due point. Thus, by the time collectors become involved, the number of delinquent accounts has been reduced to a manageable size.

Early Stage of Delinquency

The collection approach used in the early stage of loan delinquency is highly automated and requires little personal involvement. These two characteristics help to keep the costs of collections as low as possible.

The collection tools used at this stage are letters, reminder notices, late charges, simple interest, and due date adjustments. A simple, inexpensive reminder notice is sufficient to bring in many payments. This is usually the first formal action taken by the collection department. The notice may be very low key, and may even contain a sales-oriented message.

Delinquency notices on closed-end accounts are typically mailed 10 days after the due date. For an open-end account, notices are usually included on the billing statement, advising the customer that his payment is past due.

The imposition of late charges, generally 10 to 15 days after the payment due date, provides another incentive for customers to make payments on a timely basis. Simple interest also encourages customers to pay on time. If the customer understands that

EXHIBIT 13–5
Percentage of Accounts Delinquent

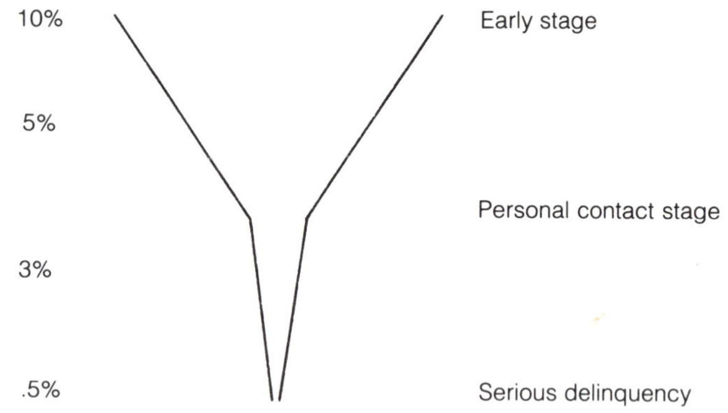

late payments will cost him more in terms of interest, he may be predisposed to make payments as soon as possible.

Due date adjustments may be possible on some types of loans. This action is desirable on closed-end loans when the due date is not appropriate for the customer's cash flow. For example, if the customer gets paid twice a month, and the loan payment is due at the same time as the mortgage payment, it may be very difficult to make both payments out of the same paycheck. By changing the due date, the bank reduces its costs, and the customer avoids late notices and late charges. This problem may not be present on open-end accounts since the customer frequently has a period of up to 25 days in which to make payments. Thus, he can correlate the payment with his cash flow.

Personal Contact Stage of Delinquency (16 days to charge-off)

The collection effort becomes more intensive once an account reaches 16 days or more past due. At this point, a collector becomes involved. Direct contact is needed to identify the problem and resolve it in a manner acceptable to both parties. The personal contact then continues until the delinquency is resolved, either by bringing the account current or by charging it off.

Problem-solving is an important aspect of successful collection practices. The objective is to first identify why the customer did not make his payment on time, then to determine how and when the payment can be made. A collector using this approach might say, "Mr. Jones, I notice that the payment on your car loan is past due. Can you tell me if you are having a problem and when you will be able to make the payment?" This is preferable to such structured questions as, "When are you going to make the payment?" or "When am I going to get my money?" The former approach is customer-oriented and is likely to elicit more information than the latter approach. The key is to identify the problem in order to find the best solution.

Some remedies available to collectors attempting to resolve delinquency problems are—

- payment collection
- extension
- refinancing
- new loan
- insurance claim
- right of offset
- consumer credit counseling.

The overwhelming bulk of delinquencies are resolved by having the customer make the delinquent payment by some mutually agreed upon date. Collectors should attempt to establish exactly when the customer will be making the past due payment, why the payment will be made on that date (for example, customer payday; other source of cash due), and how the payment will be made (for example, brought in to the bank; sent by mail). This information allows the collector to follow up immediately on broken promises. Consider the following example:

> Mr. Jones's loan payment is 20 days past due. When called by the bank's collector, Mr. Jones says he will make his payment on Friday. The collector asks, "Why Friday?" Mr. Jones replies, "That's when I get paid." The collector then asks, "How will you be making your payment?" To which Mr. Jones responds, "I will bring the payment in to your Main Street branch." This information seems reasonable and lets both parties know what to expect. The collector should review the account the following Monday to ensure that the payment has been made as promised. Timely

follow-up on broken promises is essential to a sound collection effort.

Another collection remedy is a loan *extension,* also known as *re-aging* an account. This remedy allows the customer to postpone or skip a payment. On a closed-end loan, payment may be postponed until the end of the loan, usually increasing the term of the loan by one month. Thus, the customer may skip his June payment, but resume regular payments in July. On an open-end loan, it simply means the customer is allowed to miss making a payment. The customer may be charged a fee for an extension in some states. In other instances, an additional interest cost is assessed.

Granting an extension is an appropriate collection remedy when the customer has missed one or two payments but is expected to be able to resume normal payments and eventually make up the delinquent payments. For example, if an applicant was temporarily laid off due to a short-term plant closing, he may not be able to meet all his debt obligations. After the layoff, he is able to make future payments on time but cannot make up the delinquent payment. Granting an extension resolves the delinquency and preserves customer goodwill.

The use of extensions must be controlled by the manager of the collection department and monitored by divisional management. This tool can be used too liberally by collectors who are looking for easy ways to resolve delinquencies and reduce the number of past due accounts. The result is that serious delinquency problems are hidden from management.

Refinancing—rewriting a closed-end loan to reduce monthly payments, change interest rates, or change other elements of the loan—may be an appropriate collection remedy if the customer is facing a cash flow squeeze and needs to reduce his level of debt. Sound refinancing reduces the customer's monthly payment, while possibly strengthening the bank's credit position by allowing it to gain additional collateral on the loan. This may be an appropriate solution when a customer has changed jobs and incurred a reduction in income, resulting in a high debt-to-income ratio. Assuming the customer has a good credit history and the bank is in a position to refinance the loan and reduce the customer's monthly payments, this may be the most appropriate collection remedy.

The best solution to some collection problems may be a new loan. Not only can a new loan resolve many minor delinquency problems, it can also have a positive effect on loan volume and customer relations. Consider the following example:

> Ms. Adams is 16 days late with her loan payment. In response to the collector's call, Ms. Adams says, "I'm sorry, I'll make that payment today. I just had to pay for some more car repairs; it's getting to be a real drain." The collector responds, "Ms. Adams, our new car rates are a low 9.9% now, why don't you consider a new car, then you won't have to keep pouring money into that old car and having it drain your finances." Many collectors, having the tools at their disposal to make such recommendations, are trained to think positively about their customer contacts and recognize loan opportunities.

Some delinquencies may be resolved by filing credit insurance claims. Identifying insurance claims should be an easy process. If the collector asks a customer why he has not made his payment on time, and the customer states that he has been out of work due to illness or injury, the collector should check to see if the customer has credit disability insurance. If he is covered, arrangements should be made to have a claim form processed. Potential credit life insurance claims are identified and pursued in a similar manner. To preserve goodwill, it is important that collectors act with discretion and sensitivity under these circumstances.

Some loan contracts give the bank the *right of offset*. This provision allows the bank to withdraw funds the debtor has on deposit with it, in order to make delinquent payments or pay the loan in full. Because the right of offset has repercussions for the customer's other account relationships with the bank, it should be exercised only as a last resort. To avoid creating overdrafts, immediate notification should be given to the customer when this action is taken.

Another remedy is to refer customers to a qualified credit counseling agency such as Consumer Credit Counseling, which is a nonprofit organization providing assistance to consumers who find themselves deeply in debt. The counselors work with the consumer and the lending institution to devise a payment schedule that will repay all obligations and help the consumer avoid more drastic problems like bankruptcy.

The primary methods of communicating with customers in the personal contact stage of the collection cycle are phone calls, letters, and direct contact. Direct contact is generally preferable to letters since more information can be obtained and the collector has the opportunity to work with the customer. Many collection departments have their less experienced collectors handle accounts that are 16 to 30 days past due, with more experienced collectors having responsibility for seriously delinquent accounts. Generally speaking, the further into default a loan becomes, the more time and skill are required to resolve the problem.

Serious Delinquency Stage

The serious delinquency stage does not occur at a set time. However, most collectors feel that any account more than 60 days in default is a serious problem. Serious delinquencies most often arise when customers declare bankruptcy; skip out, making contact virtually impossible; die, leaving behind uninsured debt; or simply have lost all regard for their debts. These events may occur at any stage of the collection cycle, and, in some cases, before a customer defaults.

Accounts in this category require special attention and are often handled by specialists in skip tracing, fraud, or bankruptcy. These trained personnel have both the time and the expertise to handle the accounts effectively, freeing the bank to address more routine collection activities. *Skip tracing* is the process of locating customers who cannot be found at the employer's or home address shown on the bank records. As with fraud and bankruptcy cases, time-consuming and structured follow-up are required before serious cases of delinquency can be resolved.

Occasionally, the bank may enlist the assistance of outside resources. There are, for example, agencies that specialize in repossessing collateral, a task that can be dangerous, and almost always unpleasant. Attorneys and collection agencies may also be used to handle customers who are not responding to the bank's own collection staff. Letters or personal contact from an attorney often have a stronger impact on the delinquent customer than the efforts of in-house collectors.

Collection remedies for seriously delinquent accounts include—

- repossession
- collection suits resulting in judgments
- foreclosure
- wage garnishment
- bankruptcy.

Repossession is an appropriate collection remedy when the customer is uncooperative, and the bank stands to recover some or all of its investment by selling the collateral securing its loan. Most states have laws governing how repossessions may be carried out and the customer's rights when collateral is repossessed. The customer usually has the right to redeem the collateral by bringing the account up-to-date and paying the cost of the repossession. If the customer does not redeem the collateral, the bank may sell it and apply the proceeds to the loan balance. The customer usually remains liable for any balance owed after the sale.

Another course of action is to pursue collection through the courts. If the bank can establish its claim and prove the customer is liable for the balance due on the account, it will be granted a *judgment*. This allows the bank to pursue collection by placing a claim against the assets of the debtor.

Foreclosures are the forced sale of real estate in order to satisfy a debt. Because of the consequences of this action, the procedures used are regulated by state law. The proceeds from the sale of property are distributed based upon the order of claim. First mortgages are paid in full first, then second and subsequent mortgages, and judgments last. If the proceeds cover all debts and expenses, the excess must go to the consumer. This is also true on the sale of repossessed merchandise.

Wage garnishments or *attachments* are permitted by some states to allow lenders to recover debts. A garnishment requires the customer's employer to send a certain percentage of the employee's wages directly to the bank until the debt is paid in full. This type of arrangement provides a strong incentive for customers to work out their delinquency problems before the serious stage.

Customers who are deeply in debt and unable to pay their debts when due may resort to filing for *bankrupcy*. Although it is an event to be avoided, there are occasions when, through no fault of their own, individuals find it necessary to seek protection under bankruptcy laws.

Bankruptcy laws were intended to eliminate the social stigma and other destructive aspects associated with debtor prisons. Instead, the intent was for debtors to be rehabilitated, while providing fair treatment for creditors. Subsequent legislation has attempted to balance these two objectives, with varying levels of success. Liberalized bankruptcy legislation in 1978 led to a significant increase in bankrupcy claims and to what many lenders felt were abuses of the process. These concerns resulted in revisions of the law that went into effect in 1984.

A bank may be able to recover money loaned to a customer declaring bankruptcy by filing a claim with the court and petitioning for recovery of its investment. Banks often fight bankruptcy filings when they feel the customer misrepresented his financial condition or filed a false financial statement. The court may agree to release collateral to secured lenders, allowing them to repossess and sell the goods in order to recover all or a portion of the loan balance. The court may also establish a repayment plan under Chapter 13 of the *Bankruptcy Code,* which provides for the restructuring of debts by the court in a manner that would permit creditors to be paid back over a period of time. On the other hand, the bank may be unable to recover any of its investment from a bankrupt consumer, particularly if its debt is unsecured and the customer has no assets and very limited resources.

Charge-Offs

Charging accounts off as a loss is the final stage in the loan collection cycle. It is not, however, the end of the bank's efforts to collect.

The collection manager reviews all accounts to be charged off during the month. This review is designed to check on the progress of the collection effort, evaluate alternatives to charge-off, and advise management of the dollar amount of loans scheduled for charge-off that month. If losses are lower than projected, management may elect to recognize some other accounts as losses even though they may not be at the point for required charge-off. (The Comptroller of the Currency requires national banks to recognize accounts as a loss when closed-end accounts reach 120 days past due and open-end accounts reach 180 days.) For example, an account may be charged to loss if the collateral has been sold and there is no hope of recovering the deficiency balance even though the account is not 120 days past due. On the other hand, if losses are higher than anticipated, management may elect to hold some accounts back from charge-off.

Other actions taken when an account is charged off are to ensure that the loss is reported to the appropriate credit reporting agencies and to set an action plan for future recovery efforts. The collector may give some guidance to the person in the salvage/recovery department that will help that individual begin pursuing recovery as quickly and efficiently as possible.

Accounts recognized as losses are actually charged against the bank's *loan loss reserve account* (see *Exhibit 13–6*). As new loans are made, a percent of the dollar volume is set up, or added to the loan loss reserve account, based upon the bank's historical loss experience and other factors. For example, if the loan loss rate was 1 percent, the loan loss reserve account would be increased by $10 for each $1,000 in new loan volume ($1,000 × 1% = $10). The balance in the account is reduced as individual loan accounts are charged off as losses. The loan loss reserve account is shown on the bank's balance sheet as a reduction in loans receivable.

Recovery Operations

The emphasis in the recovery department is significantly different from that of the collection department. The collection department's goals are to maintain delinquencies and losses at acceptable levels, get accounts to a current status as quickly as possible, and maintain customer goodwill to the extent practical. The recovery department is solely concerned with collecting as much of the money charged to loss as possible. This objective allows the recovery department to operate in very different ways from the collection department.

Charged-off accounts are reviewed to determine whether it is possible to recover any money on the account and, if so, who can best handle the recovery effort. Some accounts are abandoned and no further attempt made to recover the debt. For example, abandonment occurs when the borrower is deceased and there is no estate, when the balance is too small to justify further recovery efforts, or when the account cannot be collected for legal reasons such as bankruptcy. If the recovery effort is to continue, the initial effort is usually handled by a bank employee. Accounts may also be referred to outside parties such as attorneys and collection agencies. These sources either charge a flat fee or work on a commission basis, keeping a certain percentage of the amount collected.

The recovery collector or outside agent first attempts to work directly with the customer to arrange for repayment of the debt.

EXHIBIT 13–6
Loan Loss Reserve Account

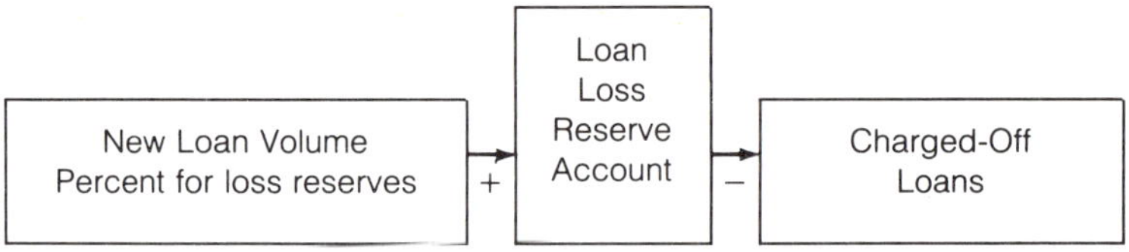

In some cases, the collector settles for a lump sum that may be less than the balance owed. For example, the collector may agree to accept $750 for a $1,000 debt if the smaller amount is paid by a certain date. However, collectors generally try to recover the full amount owed.

If repayment cannot be arranged, the recovery specialist next attempts to find any assets the customer has that may be claimed to settle the debt. The initial credit application can be helpful in this regard, particularly if it includes a personal financial statement, tax returns, or other information such as the location of bank accounts. The search for assets should focus on tangibles such as cars, homes, and boats; financial holdings such as checking and savings accounts, stocks, and bonds; and sources of income. Any of these may provide the necessary leverage needed to collect a bad debt.

Once assets are located, collection is pursued through a combination of direct contact and legal action. Common approaches to recovery include judgments, garnishments, foreclosures, repossessions, and settlements. These strong actions can help persuade customers to settle their debts, sometimes long after the loan was charged off.

The cost of recovery must always be balanced against the potential gain. It does not make sense to spend a lot of time and money on accounts when there is little chance of recovery or when the balance owed is small. Effort should be directed toward those accounts that offer the best chance of recovery and the highest possible dollar value.

Summary

The collection and recovery functions are essential to the success of a sound consumer credit operation. Well-trained and motivated collectors can make the difference between a profitable bank asset and an account that results in a loss. If the bank's loan collection and recovery departments are guided by realistic and attainable delinquency, loss, and recovery objectives, and are provided with the necessary support system, optimal results can often be achieved.

The collector has an array of collection tools at his disposal. The key task is to identify the customer's problem and then match it with the appropriate remedy. This must be carried out in a way that both encourages timely repayment and preserves the customer's goodwill. Serious delinquencies, on the other hand, require special skills to ensure that proper collection procedures are used and that strong action is taken as quickly as possible.

The recovery department operates in a less structured environment than the collection department. Its job is to recover as much of the bank's investment as possible, but it does not experience the time pressures and other constraints faced by those collecting active accounts. Money recovered on charged-off accounts can significantly improve the bank's charge-off picture and contribute directly to overall profits.

Questions for Review and Discussion

1. Do most banks expect, or at least work toward, a consumer loan delinquency level of "zero?" Explain. What goals has your bank established for delinquency on different types of loans?

2. What other roles does a bank's loan collector play besides collecting loans?

3. What is the main reason that bankers should be concerned about the requirements of the Fair Debt Collection Practices Act, given the fact that it is directed toward the activities of third-party debt collectors?

4. Give several examples of loan collection practices deemed illegal under the Fair Debt Collection Practices Act.

5. What is an advantage of the decentralized approach to loan collection in a bank? What is an advantage of the centralized approach?

6. At what point in the collection cycle does a loan collector generally become involved in collecting the debt?

7. Explain the problem-solving approach to loan collection.

8. What is the purpose of loan recovery operations, assuming the loan has already been charged off?

PART IV
CONSUMER CREDIT ADMINISTRATION

Consumer credit, like any other bank operation, must be steered by skillful hands if its potential for profit is to be fully realized. Now that you have learned all the basic, procedural, and technical information you need to function in a bank's consumer credit area, you are ready to explore the administrative aspects of the subject.

Part IV of *Consumer Lending* focuses on loan policymaking and the management of the consumer credit area. Sound policies—if clearly stated and vigilantly enforced—give the consumer credit area its mission and character. Sound management—which involves planning, organizing, directing, and controlling—gives consumer credit policy its vitality and strength. Together, skillful policymaking and management steer the bank's consumer credit operation on the road to success.

14 Consumer Credit Policies

An effective consumer credit function depends upon the development and use of a sound lending policy. A policy can be defined as a course or method of action to guide present and future credit decisions. It should be noted that the development of sound policy occurs in the context of a certain set of conditions. Therefore, credit policies should, and do, vary from one bank to the next, depending upon the specific situation.

The bank's lending policy involves a dynamic, rather than static, process. Policies are not intended to be written and then forgotten. They must reflect the bank's current philosophy and objectives, and be responsive to the rapidly changing competitive environment.

In this chapter, we will examine the purpose of a formal consumer lending policy. We will then look into the elements of a typical policy statement and survey some of the issues that must be considered when establishing a policy. Finally, we will discuss some of the procedural concerns that are closely related to the development and implementation of lending policies.

Purpose of a Formal Loan Policy

The primary purpose of a consumer loan policy is to guide decision-making in all aspects of the consumer credit operation. Informed and consistent decision-making forms the basis for an efficient and effective operation. A formal loan policy enables the bank to accomplish the following objectives:

- serve the legitimate credit needs of the bank's market area
- establish guidelines for the bank's lending staff
- increase operational efficiency
- facilitate the accomplishment of the bank's consumer credit portfolio objectives—growth, volume, profits
- ensure compliance with applicable regulations.

Commercial banks, unlike some other financial institutions, have a legal responsibility to serve the borrowing needs of qualified customers located within their primary market areas. This is required by the Community Reinvestment Act, but it is also a sound business practice.

Establishing guidelines for the bank's lending staff is vital to the development of a sound loan portfolio. In establishing guidelines, the two primary considerations are to ensure that credit decisions are made on a sound and consistent basis and that the bank develops a diverse loan portfolio that is in conformance with its overall goals.

The first consideration—providing guidelines that will result in consistent implementation of the bank's credit policies—can only be achieved by having a clear written policy and by maintaining a follow-up review to ensure lender compliance.

The second consideration—developing a diverse portfolio that conforms with the bank's goals—is always a concern of management. To ensure loan quality, an acceptable level of delinquency and loan losses must be defined by management. Banks with very conservative delinquency and loss goals emphasize the minimization of risk. They may require higher down payments, use lower debt-to-income ratios, and screen out even those applicants with minor derogatory information on their credit reports. In contrast, a bank with more liberal loss and deliquency goals may accept lower down payments, use higher debt-to-income ratios, and overlook minor negative information. Thus, the type of loan policy can help control the level of risk within the portfolio.

The loan policy should also indicate which types of loans the bank wishes to emphasize. Assuming the bank wants to aggressively promote its open-end credit products, it would, through its loan policy, encourage lenders to sell those types of loans more aggressively than closed-end products. The bank might price its open-end products at lower rates, and may even elect to use less stringent debt-to-income and credit history requirements. Achieving portfolio diversification also depends upon having the bank's goals clearly communicated and supported with specific objectives at the branch or departmental level.

A clearly stated bank loan policy can also help avoid some of the following pitfalls:

- The lender, unsure whether or not a certain type of loan can be made, must either make an arbitrary decision or take time to call someone else.
- The lender incorrectly assumes the bank does not want a certain type of business and, therefore, refuses to take an application for a loan that the bank would accept.
- The lender, biased against people employed in certain jobs, rejects loan applicants simply on that basis.
- The lender was not informed of a recent policy change and continues to operate under the old guidelines.

The foregoing are examples of some of the problems that may occur when the bank does not have a sound and well-communicated lending policy. To avoid them, the bank should specify precise loan standards. Examples of clear lending specifications are—

- minimum down payment of 20 percent of the loan
- maximum debt-to-income ratio of 45 percent
- no loans to an applicant who has declared bankruptcy in the past seven years
- no loans to an applicant living outside of the bank's trade area
- minimum credit score of 190 points.

If specifications such as these are incorporated into a bank's loan policy, the lender is spared the need to spend time on applications that do not meet the bank's credit requirements.

In contrast, unclear policy statements are those that are subject to interpretation, such as the following:

- Loans should not be made to applicants who have been at their address less than one year unless there are offsetting positive attributes. (This needs a definition of positive attributes.)
- Applicants with any major derogatory credit history should be declined. (This needs a definition of major derogatory items.)
- Bill consolidation loans should not be made unless the applicant has been cross-sold on a higher loan amount. (This is unclear as to its intent and seems a bit arbitrary.)

The bank's loan policy should be coordinated with the bank's overall portfolio objectives. Tight credit policies do not complement an aggressive loan growth objective. Likewise, relatively lax lending policies are out of place when the bank is trying to clean up its loan portfolio or improve the quality of its asset base. For example, in an aggressive growth environment, the bank may offer 100 percent financing on cars and other depreciating value collateral, while, in a conservative environment, a 25 to 30 percent down payment may be required.

Lending policies also provide protection against regulatory violations. Sound credit policies reduce the opportunity for employees to willfully or unknowingly violate regulations. Combined with sound review procedures, they help to identify inadvertent compliance violations and ensure timely correction of errors. Indeed, when defending itself against claims of regulatory violations or when undergoing regulatory audits, the bank may offer its lending policy as evidence of its intent to comply with all regulations.

Components of a Sound Loan Policy

The bank's policy statement can be brief or it can be quite extensive—depending on such factors as the size and complexity of the organization, the types of products offered, and the degree of management preference for detail. Regardless, there are a number of topics that should be addressed to some degree in all consumer credit policy statements. These components include—

- geographic limits
- types of loans desired
- credit authority
- general terms and conditions
- compliance and loan review
- collection and charge-off.

Geographic Limits

The lending policy should define the bank's primary trade area and, if appropriate, a secondary trade area. A bank's primary trade area for consumer credit products may vary with the type of product. Direct loans are generally restricted to a specific geographic area, while indirect loans and open-end products may extend over a broader geographic area.

Types of Loans Desired

The policy statement should state which types of loans the bank wishes to pursue and avoid. A clear statement should be made concerning loans to officers, directors, and employees of the bank. Federal Reserve *Regulation O* imposes restrictions on loans to the highest officers of the bank—executive vice president, president, chairman, and the board of directors—but there are generally no restrictions on loans to other bank employees. As a result, many banks view their own employees as promising candidates for loan products. When loans are made within the bank, the policy statement should define which employees are eligible, what underwriting requirements exist, and who will have the authority to approve these loan requests.

Another policy concern regarding loan types is to define undesirable loans. Management should exercise care in identifying and defining types of loans that it does not want in the bank's portfolio. Generally, loans in this category present high credit risk or are more appropriately handled by the commercial loan department. Loans fitting this description might include those for—

- bill consolidations
- speculative purposes, such as investments or new businesses
- motorcycles
- corporations or partnerships
- home equity loans secured by investment properties.

Credit Authority

The policy statement should set forth the bank's lending authority system and the decision-making approach to be used.

The power to grant lending authority is vested with the board of directors. As a practical matter, this authority is delegated to a senior operating officer or a committee. Those holding this authority are responsible for establishing lending limits for each lender and for monitoring the performance of the lending staff. Lenders who do not meet specific standards may lose their lending authority or have it reduced.

The policy statement should also specify the procedures for approving loans. The loan approval system may take the form of individual lending authorities, loan committees, or a combination (see *Exhibit 14–1*). Loan committees are generally not appropriate to the development of consumer loans, which usually require quick response times and involve lower dollar amounts and a high volume of applications. However, committees are often used for very large consumer loan requests such as airplane and boat loans over $200,000. The size and less urgent nature of these requests may allow time for committee consideration. Another option in handling larger or special loan requests is to allow lenders to combine their credit authorities. This ensures that at least two lenders have looked at a large loan request or have reviewed an adverse credit decision. The sample lending authority structure depicted in *Exhibit 14–1* provides a clear framework for handling credit decisions.

The actual decision-making system used by the bank should be described in the policy statement. Credit-scoring systems require more explanation than judgmental systems since the former is a more precise approach to lending, while the latter is, of necessity, more subjective.

General Terms and Conditions

The loan policy should define how the bank measures the applicant's capacity, character (as reflected in his credit history), and collateral risk. As capacity is a key element in evaluating credit risk, it is advisable to establish a policy for quantifying it. For example: the applicant's debt-to-income ratio may not exceed 40 percent of his gross monthly income. Thus, if the customer's gross monthly income is $2,000, the maximum amount of debt payments, including the payment on the new loan, would be $800.

The debt-to-income ratio can be calculated in many ways. The ratio may be based on gross or net income, and any outstanding revolving debt may be valued at current balances or as if the accounts were being fully utilized. Likewise, variable rate debt may be figured at its current level or at a higher level to allow for possible interest rate increases.

An applicant's credit history has been identified as one of the most important variables in predicting future behavior. However, interpreting credit history is not always a simple task. The

EXHIBIT 14–1
Sample Consumer Loan Authority Schedule

Level	*Unsecured*	*Secured*	*Minimum Qualifications*
I	$ 2,500	$ 3,500	Must complete the bank's credit training program and have one year experience in handling loan applications
II	$ 5,000	$ 7,500	Must complete the bank's advanced lender training, have one year of lending experience, and have a satisfactory lending record
III	$10,000	$25,000	Must have three years of a satisfactory lending record and complete the consumer credit review course
IV	$25,000	$50,000	Reserved for senior consumer credit department officers who have proven lending records

NOTE: Loans over the lender's authority are referred to the regional consumer credit officer. Level III and Level IV officers may combine their authorities to approve unsecured loans up to $50,000 and secured loans up to $100,000. Loans over those amounts must be submitted to the consumer credit committee for final approval. All closed-end loan applications that are rejected must be signed off by two lenders.

lending policy usually focuses on what factors in the applicant's credit should be interpreted as unacceptable and therefore lead to an automatic rejection of the application. Prior bankruptcies, repossessions, judgments, foreclosures, charge-offs, and installment loan accounts deliquent 90 or more days are often cited as reasons for rejecting a loan. If such conditions should lead to automatic rejection, the loan policy should clearly communicate that intent. However, if exceptions are to be made, the reasons for considering an exception should also be defined. For example, some lenders consider loans to applicants who have experienced bankruptcy if the bankruptcy was due to a medical

EXHIBIT 14–2
Sample Automobile Loan Policy

Automobile Loans	*Maximum Advance*	*Maximum Term*
New automobiles	100 percent of dealer invoice	Advance up to $7,500—48 months Advance over $7,500—60 months
Used automobiles	100 percent of wholesale value	Current model—48 months 1–2 years old—36 months 3–4 years old—30 months 5–6 years old—24 months

Automobile models over six years old are not eligible. All vehicles must be covered by physical damage and liability insurance coverage with $250 maximum deductible. The bank must have first lien on all vehicle loans. The suggested down payment on all automobile loans is 20 percent; however, the lender may grant an exception as long as the total advance is less than the maximum advance as just defined. Required documents:

- consumer credit note and disclosure statement
- security agreement
- copy of insurance policy naming bank as loss payee
- certificate of title
- copy of the bill of sale.

crisis. Similarly, exceptions could be made for those who have had small judgments against them, delinquencies on department store accounts, or voluntary repossessions.

Collateral risk requirements should also be spelled out in the lending policy. The kinds of collateral that are acceptable, and the amount that may be borrowed against various collateral, should be clearly itemized. *Exhibits 14–2* through *14–4* present sample loan policies that illustrate some of the detail that might be included.

Notice that the policy shown in *Exhibit 14–2* sets forth precise guidelines for determining acceptable collateral, the maximum loan amounts, terms, documentation, and insurance requirements. Note also that the lender has some flexibility on the down payment requirement on an automobile loan.

The policy statement shown in *Exhibit 14–3* is not intended to be complete, but rather illustrates a few of the unique considerations that should be taken into account when making a marine loan.

EXHIBIT 14–3
Sample Marine Loan Policy

Eligible collateral: All boats that are titled in the states of Maryland or Virginia or are documented with the U.S. Coast Guard. Outboard motors and trailers may be financed if they are purchased with the boat.

Ineligible collateral: Wooden vessels, boats to be used for charter, and vessels used for business purposes.

Age	*Maximum Advance*	*Maximum Term*
New boats	100 percent invoice	180 months
Used boats		
1–5 years old	80 percent of high book value	180 months (for advance over $15,000) 12 months per $1,000 (for advance under $15,000)
6–10 years old and older boats	75 percent of high book value or marine survey	180 months (for advance over $15,000) 12 months per $1,000 (for advance under $15,000)

Rates:
New boats: Fixed—11 percent for loans up to 60 months only
Variable—Prime + 2 percent
Used boats: Fixed—12 percent for loans up to 60 months only
Variable—Prime + 2.5 percent
Refinancing: 1 percent over the rates just quoted

Marine Survey: A marine survey is required to establish the value of all boats more than 5 years old or when the advance is $10,000 or more.

Federal Documentation: Required on all loans with a cash advance of $35,000 or more, or when the boat will be operated outside of the state. All other boats must be titled with the state.

The abbreviated policy statement shown in *Exhibit 14–4* provides clear guidance to all lenders regarding some of a bank's requirements for a home equity line account.

It is helpful to supplement a policy statement with a procedures manual that provides further guidance regarding the proper preparation and handling of all necessary documents. For example, detailed procedures may be developed to explain how to get the bank's lien on a car title and how to verify insurance coverage before the loan is made. The two items—policies and procedures—are often presented in a single manual that can provide answers to virtually any question lenders may have.

EXHIBIT 14–4
Sample Home Equity Loan Policy

Eligible Collateral: Owner-occupied homes located in Maryland, Virginia, and the District of Columbia.

Lien Position: The bank must have either a first or second mortgage position.

Maximum Advance: 75 percent of the appraised value of the home, minus the first mortgage balance, if any.

Rate: Wall Street Journal prime rate plus 2 percent.

Other Requirements:

- Property must be appraised by a certified appraiser and approved by the bank.
- Property must be the applicant's primary residence.
- Property must not be used for commercial purposes.
- Properties located in a flood zone must be covered by proper flood insurance.
- The 3-day Truth in Lending rescission period may not be waived under any circumstances.
- Bank must be named as loss payee on the homeowner's insurance policy.

Loan policies should provide clear guidelines, but they should not be so restrictive as to become straitjackets. Provisions must be made for identifying and handling situations that justify an exception to the standard loan policy. For example, although an applicant may fail to meet the bank's credit requirements, an exception may be warranted when the loan is to be fully secured by a savings account with the bank. In this case, the bank may want to make an exception contingent upon the customer having an acceptable credit history and meeting the bank's debt-to-income ratio.

Requests for exceptions often arise when the applicant is a "good" customer of the bank. In these cases, it is important that the bank define "good" by using quantitative measures such as balances in depository accounts, number of services used, length of account relationship, or profitability of the customer's accounts.

Compliance and Loan Review

Loan policy should establish responsibility for the compliance and loan review functions. A *compliance officer*—the individual charged with establishing controls necessary to ensure compliance with regulations and the bank's policies—should be

EXHIBIT 14–5
Sample Loan Charge-Off Policy

Closed-end loans: Loans will be charged off no later than 120 days past due unless one of the following conditions exists:

- the collateral securing the loan will be sold within the next 30 days, resulting in a full recovery of the balance due
- firm arrangements have been made with the customer to bring the account current or pay off the balance within the next 30 days.

Open-end accounts: Open-end accounts will be charged off no later than 180 days past due unless the line is secured, and one of the conditions just noted applies.

identified. The tasks performed by the loan review department may also be itemized.

Collection and Charge-Off

The lending policy should also define the bank's practices regarding the handling of delinquent accounts and charge-offs. Specific attention should be given to defining the point at which delinquent accounts will be charged off as a loss to the bank. More detailed collection department policies and procedures should be distributed to those responsible for actually collecting delinquent accounts. A sample policy statement is shown as *Exhibit 14–5*.

Summary

A bank's loan policy plays a key role in guiding the decision-making of lending and support personnel. A loan policy should enhance uniform decision-making and operational efficiency by clearly communicating desired actions. Lending policy should be viewed as a dynamic, rather than a static, process. To optimize results in the consumer credit market, policy may be adjusted in reponse to changing market conditions and bank objectives.

It is important that the bank's loan policy be clear and comprehensive enough to cover the major aspects of each loan type. However, policies should not be too restrictive, allowing loan officers flexibility when appropriate.

Questions for Review and Discussion

1. Why would a bank institute a formal loan policy? Does a formal policy interfere with a consumer lender's ability to exercise judgment in the lending process?

2. Give an example—from your own experience if possible—of a problem that could arise if a member of the lending staff is unaware of a matter of loan policy.

3. In what way does a lending policy help curb regulatory violations?

4. Look at your bank's written loan policy where it defines the bank's credit authority structure. Briefly summarize the various lending authorities specified.

5. Does your bank's loan policy specify types of desirable loans? Does it address the subject of loans to employees and, if so, what does it say?

6. How might a bank achieve a dynamic, responsive loan policy, given the fact that written rules tend to be static?

15 Managing the Consumer Credit Function

Managing the consumer credit business involves planning, organizing, directing, and controlling the bank's activities in the market. In this chapter, we will survey these functions in the context of the cyclical management and planning process. We will summarize the issues addressed by each function and the implications they have for the consumer credit portfolio. We will also focus on how these functions can work together to ensure that the bank builds a credit portfolio that meets all of its objectives.

The Management and Planning Process

This examination of the management and planning process for consumer credit focuses on the cyclical nature of the process and the close interrelationship of the various parts. *Exhibit 15–1* presents the elements of the process and illustrates the flow of activities.

Planning

The consumer credit management process begins with planning. The plan identifies the direction the bank wishes to go and the strategies it will use to reach its objectives. There are three basic steps in the planning process: the situation analysis, the establishment of objectives, and the development of strategies, which includes the formulation of the marketing mix.

EXHIBIT 15–1
The Management and Planning Process

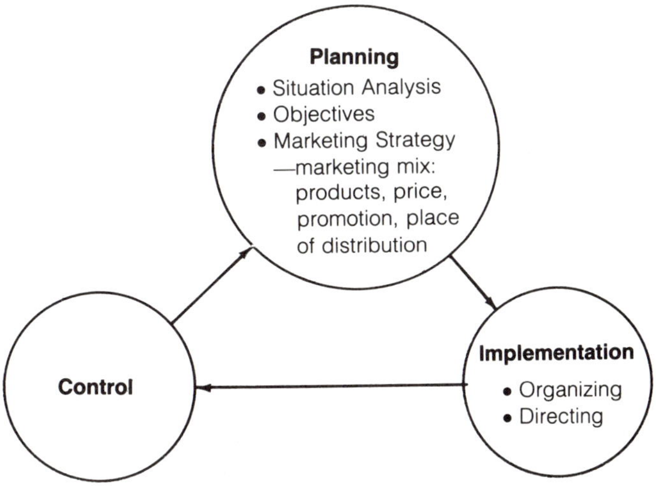

Conducting a Situation Analysis

The *situation analysis* is concerned with answering the question: "Where are we now?" Finding the answer involves an analysis of the external and internal environments in order to identify opportunities and problems.

A study of the competitive environment reveals who the major competitors are, what products they are offering, their pricing practices, and their general strategies. It is important to note that the bank's competitors may be different for each product. This analysis enables the bank to compare its products and strategies to those of the competition. It also permits identification of advantages or disadvantages the bank has in the market.

A study of the economic environment reveals the status of and trends in the economy of the bank's market area. This helps the bank focus on opportunities—such as market areas that are growing rapidly and may be underserved—or problems—such as rising unemployment or inflation possibly resulting in reduced demand for credit and an increase in delinquencies and losses. The study of the economic environment should also identify which segments of the market are growing most rapidly and which are stagnant or declining. The bank may then wish to focus on the segments it has identified and offer product lines that possess the greatest future growth potential.

A study of the social environment reveals changing attitudes, life-styles, and values that may affect the market. The trend toward smaller family units, more single-parent heads of households, and more two-income families may have some effect on the need for credit and on credit underwriting practices. Therefore, trends like these should be monitored and responded to by the bank. For example, rising divorce rates and increases in the number of women pursuing careers led many banks to change their underwriting policies in the 1960s, years before these changes were mandated by the Equal Credit Opportunity Act.

Another element the bank should study is the regulatory environment. The bank should act in an anticipatory manner to encourage changes that will help its efforts in the market and also prevent unwanted legislation. The bank must also act defensively to fight legislation that would damage its position in the market. For example, suppose a state legislator introduces a bill that would prohibit lenders from repossessing cars other than between the hours of 9 AM and 5 PM. Such legislation would greatly increase the cost of repossession and the ability of consumers to hide the bank's collateral. Consequently, banks in the state decide to join together to prevent the bill from becoming law.

The bank must also study its internal environment to identify its strengths and weaknesses. Relevant issues include staffing, training, support systems, products, asset quality, and profitability. As part of this process, the role consumer credit is to play in relation to the bank's other services should be delineated.

After analyzing its internal environment, the bank might find that its costs are lower than many of its competitors, giving it an advantage in the market. On the other hand, it may find, for example, that its home equity line product is priced higher and has higher monthly payment requirements than competing products. These findings may lead to changes in the bank's pricing practices.

Establishing Objectives

Once the situation analysis is completed, the bank should be able to establish its objectives. This stage addresses the question: "Where do we want to go?"

Objectives may be established for a number of key aspects of the consumer credit portfolio, including—

- loan outstandings
- loan volume
- delinquency and loss levels
- recoveries
- fee income
- operating expenses
- profits.

The level of detail in the statement of objectives varies from bank to bank, but it is generally desirable to establish specific objectives for each product in the consumer credit portfolio. This helps managers perform their management tasks more effectively. For example, if delinquencies and losses are higher than the objectives specify for indirect automobile loans, corrective action can be focused on that part of the portfolio without adversely affecting other products. The bank in question could change its underwriting policies only on indirect loans, or only in regard to a particular dealer, to resolve the problem.

Formulating Marketing Strategy

Having established where the bank wants to go, managers may focus on the strategies to be used. This stage addresses the question: "How are we going to get there?"

To achieve marketing objectives, managers manipulate the elements of the marketing mix—products, price, promotion, and the place of distribution. This is the creative part of the management process because it entails developing strategies to create a unique market position designed to meet the objectives. It is also a dynamic, rather than static, process since it must respond to changes in the external environment.

For example, as the 1986 Tax Reform Act moved toward final approval, many banks developed aggressive new strategies to market home equity line products. Banks that did not yet offer the product had to quickly develop one; others quickly intensified their promotional programs to bring their existing product to the attention of more potential customers. Moreover, the more aggressive banks adjusted all of the elements of the marketing mix to achieve their objectives. For instance, many adjusted their prices—offering low introductory rates and no-fee plans—and changed their place of distribution to include applications by telephone and mail.

In specifying its marketing mix, a bank blends products, pricing, promotion, and place of distribution to achieve a marketing plan that is right for it. Let us look at some recent trends in the elements of the marketing mix.

- *Products.* The consumer credit product line has expanded, with the biggest change coming in the development of open-end revolving credit products. Product features have also changed, with wider use of simple interest, simple language documents, and more flexibility for consumers and lenders in structuring loans.
- *Pricing.* Consumer credit products are now offered on both a fixed and variable rate basis by many banks. Loan fees have also become an important source of income on many types of loans. Finally, creative pricing, such as low introductory rates, loan sales, and the like have been used to achieve bank objectives.
- *Promotion.* Consumer loan products are still promoted through all available media, but the themes have changed, in many cases, to more effectively target selected segments of the consumer market. The use of direct mail and telemarketing has been increased, and banks have successfully used aggressive prescreened and preapproved promotional programs.
- *Place of distribution.* Increased emphasis has been given to providing credit to consumers when, where, and for whatever purposes they deem appropriate. Open-end products do this, but lenders have also enhanced their ability to provide nearly the same level of service on many closed-end loans. Finally, banks have moved beyond their branch and dealer distribution systems by delivering loan products by mail directly to the consumer's home.

Implementation

The implementation phase of the planning process entails the activities of organizing and directing.

Organizing

Organizing is a management task that is a part of the implementation stage of the market planning process. Organizing involves structuring the lending process to be effective and efficient. An effective organization is one that accomplishes the objectives established at the beginning of the planning process. Effectiveness involves reaching the market in a manner that generates the desired level of business and provides quality service to the bank's customers at the lowest possible cost.

The bank needs to tailor its organization to the unique characteristics of the market it serves and the products it offers. For example, in organizing the management of its direct loan portfolio, a bank might emphasize its branch network and the personal selling skills of customer-contact employees. The same bank might manage its credit card operation through a centralized department that uses direct mail with a reach far beyond the bank's branches.

The *effectiveness* of the bank's management organization is measured by the—

- growth of loan outstandings
- development of loan applications and volume
- level of delinquencies and losses
- additional business brought in by cross-sell and loan structuring efforts
- compliance with regulations and bank policy.

A successful managemnt organization is able to meet the bank's goals and objectives in each of the areas just noted. An *efficient* organization, on the other hand, is one that provides a high level of service at the least possible cost. Efficiency is measured by the—

- manner in which applications are taken
- time and expense to make a credit decision
- service turnaround times, from application to decision to loan closing
- accuracy and timeliness of loan servicing, including payment processing and error resolution
- cost of collecting past due and charge-off accounts.

Ultimately, measuring organizational effectiveness and efficiency involves both quantitative and qualitative factors that have an impact on the overall success of the consumer credit function.

Directing

Directing is the second part of the implementation stage. This task requires management action to ensure that the organization remains focused on the objectives and is moving in the right direction at the required pace. Direction begins with the establishment of policies and procedures that guide decision-making and actions, ensuring consistency and soundness in the operation. Clear and well-conceived policies result in the development of loan portfolios that enable the bank to achieve its asset quality objectives, while encouraging the development of profitable business.

Providing direction is a daily activity. It includes training and developing the skills of lenders, collectors, loan interviewers, accountants, customer service representatives, and other personnel to perform their jobs in efficient and effective ways. The task of directing also includes continually looking for ways to improve the operation.

Controlling

The controlling task is concerned with monitoring the performance of the consumer credit function to ensure that all of the elements are functioning as they should and that the bank is moving toward its objectives. The consumer credit operation has several vital control points. These include—

- the loan review group, which monitors loan documents for accuracy, completeness, and compliance with the regulations and bank policy
- the compliance officer, who reviews the bank's policies, procedures, forms, and other elements of the bank's programs to ensure regulatory compliance
- the collection department, which provides data regarding loan quality and any adverse patterns that may be developing
- management reports, which identify how lenders, branches, and the bank as a whole are performing in relation to objectives.

Deviations from objectives prompt a properly controlled operation to analyze the problem and initiate corrective action. For example:

- If the consumer credit department is not meeting its objectives for loan outstandings and volume, it may need to reduce its rates, increase promotional efforts, or pursue other segments of the market that offer greater growth potential.
- If the indirect loan department is not meeting its service objective to provide three-hour turnaround on all applications, it may need to increase staff or improve the flow of credit investigations.
- If delinquencies and losses on unsecured lines of credit accounts are higher than targeted, the bank may need to change its underwriting policy or improve the quality of the collection effort.
- If a particular loan employee is making an unacceptable level of documentation errors, he may need additional training or be relieved of this responsibility.

Proper resolution of deviations from objectives should result in an efficient and effective consumer credit operation and the attainment of the bank's profit objectives.

Summary

The management and planning process is a dynamic one in which the bank constantly adjusts to the market while remaining focused on key objectives. The process affects every aspect of consumer credit; indeed, it ties all of the various tasks, functions, and strategies into a meaningful whole.

Sound management and planning systems are critical considerations in assuring the bank's success in an increasingly challenging and complex consumer credit market. As the market continues to evolve, it is clear that the successful bank will need to effectively manage change and find a niche in the market that will enable it to meet its short- and long-term objectives.

Questions for Review and Discussion

1. What does a situation analysis look at?

2. How specific should the objectives set by management be for the consumer credit portfolio?

3. Briefly define the four elements of the marketing mix.

4. Distinguish between organizing and directing—the two components of the implementation phase of management. Which one is a daily activity?

5. What are some control tasks built into a typical consumer credit operation?

6. Talk to your bank's consumer credit manager about the management techniques he or she employs. Write a brief summary of your impressions regarding the formality and comprehensiveness of the management procedures used.

Glossary

A

account balance The difference between the total credits and the total debits to an account.

account holders The owners of an account who have the authority to deposit and withdraw funds.

accounts receivable The amount of money owed to a business by its customers for goods and services already provided.

accrue To accumulate between payments. In consumer credit transactions, interest charges accumulate from the date one payment is due until the due date of the next payment.

acquisition costs The amount of money spent to make a loan, including marketing, interviewing applicants, investigating the credit risk, gathering and processing documents, and making the credit decision.

actuarial interest Interest costs that allow a lender to take the amount of a missed or insufficient payment and add it to the unpaid principal of the loan. All subsequent interest charges are calculated against this new sum and not the original principal.

add-on interest A method for calculating interest costs by taking a percentage of the desired loan amount and adding this to the principal to calculate the total amount the borrower will repay.

adverse action The refusal to grant credit either in the amount or according to the terms requested by the applicant.

adverse action notice A document that explains to an applicant the reason credit has been denied.

amortization schedule A table that shows the amount of principal and interest due for each loan payment and the remaining unpaid balance after each payment is made.

annual percentage rate (APR) The total interest costs of a loan expressed as an annualized percent and computed by multiplying the periodic rate of interest (the rate charged each billing period) by the number of periods in a year. Truth in Lending regulations set specific formulas for computing the APR.

applicant A person or business that requests or receives funds from a lending institution.

appraisal A report prepared by an expert estimating the current market value of a property.

appreciating value collateral Assets pledged as collateral that increase in value over the life of the loan.

Article 9 The sections of the Uniform Commercial Code that govern the documentation of loans secured by personal property.

B

balance sheet A detailed listing of the financial condition of an individual or a business at a given point in time, including total assets, total liabilities, and net worth.

Bankruptcy Code The federal laws that govern legal proceedings of those who are no longer able to pay their debts. Under Chapter 7 of the code, the debtor is relieved of financial obligations and assets are liquidated to pay creditors. Chapter 13 of the code allows the debtor to "reorganize" the debt and make partial or full repayment over a 5-year period without fear of legal action from creditors.

basis point A change in interest rates or yields expressed as 1/100th of one percent.

bill consolidation The borrowing of funds with the purpose of paying off multiple and often overdue debts. The borrower then owes only one creditor with loan payments usually extended over a longer period of time.

billing cycle The period between regularly scheduled dates or days when customers' bills are mailed.

blockbusting The practice of directing prospective home buyers to a specific neighborhood in an effort to scare property owners into selling at below market prices.

block steering The practice of directing a prospective home buyer away from a specific neighborhood.

bond A certificate of debt issued by a corporate or municipal organization, usually with a maturity of 5 years or more, that promises to pay interest at regular intervals and to repay the principal at a future date.

book To enter an account or loan into a bank's records.

brokerage firm A financial company that handles the purchase and sale of stocks, bonds, and other securities for its customers.

buy rate The rate of interest a bank will charge on loans it buys from dealers of consumer goods such as autos and mobile homes.

C

call provision A clause in a loan contract that allows the lender to demand payment in full at anytime.

captive finance company A finance company owned by a large corporation for the purpose of financing consumer purchases of the parent company's products.

cash flow The amount of money available to a company or individual for spending after operating expenses are deducted from gross income.

cash management account (CMA) A customer account that combines traditional brokerage services (the ability to buy and sell stocks and invest in money market funds) with traditional banking services (check-writing privileges, a credit card, and a line of credit). The CMA was first introduced in 1977 by Merrill Lynch.

cash value life insurance The value of an insurance policy based on the dollar amount of premiums paid.

certificate of deposit A document issued when funds are deposited into an interest-bearing account at a financial institution for a specified time ranging from 7 days to 7 years.

charge off The process of writing off debts that a bank no longer expects to be able to collect.

chattel mortgage A loan made for personal property, such as equipment or automobiles, rather than for real property, such as buildings or land. In these loans, the personal property is pledged to the lender to guarantee that the debt will be repaid.

check overdraft line A line of credit on a checking account. Checks that exceed the balance of the account are paid out of the line of credit and not returned because of insufficient funds.

Civil Rights Act of 1968 A law prohibiting discrimination on the basis of race, color, religion, sex, or national origin.

close The process by which all pertinent loan documents are signed and funds are disbursed to the borrower.

closed-end loan A credit arrangement in which the borrower and lender agree on the total amount being loaned and the number, size, and due dates of each payment.

closing costs The costs a borrower must pay when a mortgage loan is finalized, including an origination fee, title insurance, attorney's fees, a property survey, and prepaid expenses, such as taxes and insurance.

co-applicant A person who joins with one or more others in requesting or receiving funds from a lending institution.

collateral Assets pledged by a borrower to a lender to guarantee a loan. These assets become the property of the lender if the borrower fails to repay the borrowed funds.

co-maker A person who signs for a loan made to another person. The co-maker does not receive the funds but is jointly and equally liable for repaying the debt if the borrower fails to do so.

commercial bank A financial company with chief functions of accepting deposits and making loans.

commission Compensation computed as a percentage of new business or sales for which an employee is responsible.

community property Property that is owned jointly and equally by a husband and wife as a result of marriage.

Community Reinvestment Act (CRA) A law that encourages financial institutions to meet the credit needs of their local communities, especially the needs of low- and moderate-income neighborhoods. Regulatory agencies are authorized to evaluate CRA performance when considering an application from an institution. The law, Title VIII of the Housing and Community Development Act, became effective November 1978.

compliance program The policies and procedures followed by a financial institution to assure it is obeying all federal and state laws and regulations.

Comptroller of the Currency A federal office responsible for chartering, examining, and regulating national banks.

consumer credit market The segment of the population that borrows money for personal purposes.

consumer credit outstanding The total dollar amount of unpaid balances on all consumer credit products, including loans, lines of credit, and credit cards.

Consumer Credit Restraint Program A Federal Reserve Board program announced in March 1980 as part of a general government program to curb inflation. The action imposed restraints on certain types of consumer credit and increased banks' reserve requirements.

consumer credit transaction The transfer of funds by a financial institution to an individual for personal use. The funds are made available for a specified period and the borrower agrees to pay a sum of money to the lender for their use.

Consumer Leasing Act A 1976 law requiring that those who lease property for personal, family, or household use receive clear and accurate information about the item being leased and the terms of the lease agreement.

consummation The point in time when the contractual relationship between borrower and lender begins.

cost of funds The price a bank must pay to have funds available for loan, including factors such as the amount of interest it must pay on deposits and on funds it borrows from investors. This figure is an important consideration in setting loan interest rates.

counteroffer A proposal to grant credit on terms different from those requested by the applicant.

coupon book A set of forms that the borrower encloses, one at a time, with each loan payment. Each coupon includes the borrower's name, loan number, and amount of payment due.

credit clinic A company in the business of advising consumers on how to improve their credit rating and resolve bad debts with lenders.

credit decision The process of determining whether to grant credit, to offer credit on terms other than those requested, or to deny credit.

credit disability insurance Insurance offered to loan and credit card customers that will pay the balance of their debt if they become unable to earn an income.

credit life insurance Insurance offered to loan and credit card customers that will pay the balance of their debt if they die before completing their payments.

credit limit The maximum allowable unpaid balance on open-end credit such as credit cards or lines of credit.

credit record A history of a prospective borrower's ability and willingness to pay debts on time.

credit report A confidential report prepared for lenders that provides factual data about a prospective borrower's financial condition and standing with creditors.

credit-reporting agency A company hired by a lender to prepare a report on a prospective borrower's credit history and creditworthiness.

credit scoring A statistical formula used to evaluate and rate credit applicants.

credit standards Guidelines used by a lending institution to determine if an applicant is eligible to receive credit.

credit union A financial institution formed by depositors with a common affiliation (for example, the same employer) in order to promote savings and offer short-term personal loans. A credit union is a cooperative organization in which the depositors are called members and their deposits are treated as shares of ownership.

cross selling The practice of promoting financial services in addition to the one being used by an existing customer.

C's of credit Criteria, all beginning with the letter *c*, used by lenders to evaluate an applicant's creditworthiness. The number of criteria varies but generally includes character, capacity, capital, collateral, and conditions.

curtailments Payments required by a bank from a dealer who has received a floor plan loan because the merchandise financed has depreciated to a value below the amount owed on it.

D

daily periodic rate The interest rate that a creditor imposes on a daily basis on the outstanding balance in open-end credit such as a credit card or revolving charge account.

dealer floor planning A loan for financing a retailer's inventory. The bank disburses funds to the dealer after specific goods sitting on the showroom floor are pledged as collateral. When this merchandise is sold, the lender is repaid.

dealer plan of operation A business arrangement in which a financial institution buys loans from a dealer who sells consumer goods, such as automobiles and boats. The consumer buys and obtains financing from the dealer but deals with the financial institution to repay the loan.

dealer recourse The right of a bank to collect funds from a dealer who sold it a loan that has gone bad.

dealer reserve account An account set up by a bank to hold the funds that accumulate because a dealer is granting loans at one rate of interest and selling them to the bank at a lower rate.

debt service The total amount of interest and principal due on borrowed money.

debt-to-income ratio A measure of creditworthiness computed by dividing the dollar amount of debts by total income.

default The failure to pay a debt.

delinquency The failure to make a loan principal or interest payment on time.

demand loan A loan that does not have a specific due date but is repaid when the creditor asks for payment or when the borrower decides to make payment.

deposit base The total dollar amount of customer deposits held by a financial institution.

depreciating value collateral Assets pledged as collateral that decrease in value over the life of the loan.

depreciation The process of decreasing in value or usefulness.

deregulation The process of removing or liberalizing legal restrictions to promote competition. In recent years, the financial services industry has experienced price deregulation (removal of interest rate ceilings), product deregulation (regulatory approval to offer more diversified products and services), and geographic deregulation (expansion across state lines).

direct loan A two-party lending arrangement in which the borrower obtains financing by dealing directly with a financial institution.

direct verification An investigation of an applicant's credit history conducted by direct contact with creditors and employers.

disburse To pay out money.

discount rate A method of calculating interest costs by deducting the interest charges from the total amount of money being loaned.

Discover Card An all-purpose credit card with related services created in 1985 by Sears, Roebuck and Company and marketed to merchants and consumers nationwide.

disintermediation The flow of funds out of interest-bearing accounts in financial institutions into other types of investments that yield a higher return.

disposable personal income The amount of an individual's income available for spending and investment after payment of taxes.

dollars outstanding The total dollar amount of all unpaid debts.

double financing The fraudulent practice in which dealers or other borrowers apply for and receive loans for the same customer from two different banks.

dowry The property that a woman brings to her marriage.

durable goods Items, such as appliances, automobiles, and furniture, purchased by individuals for their use over a period of time, generally 3 years or longer.

E

economic cycle A pattern of fluctuation in economic activity characterized by the four stages of expansion, contraction, recession, and recovery.

effective yield The real as opposed to the quoted rate of interest. For example, a rate quoted as 8 percent may actually mean an annualized rate of 12 percent.

endorsor One who either signs or rubber stamps the back of a financial instrument that bears his or her name, such as a check or money order, in order to transfer the right to those funds to someone else.

Equal Credit Opportunity Act A law that prohibits discrimination against credit applicants on the basis of their race, color, religion, national origin, sex, age, marital status, or receipt of income from public assistance programs. This law was passed as Title VII of the Consumer Credit Protection Act when it was amended in 1975.

Equal Housing Lender poster A poster lenders must publicly display declaring that their lending practices comply with both the Fair Housing Act and the Equal Credit Opportunity Act.

equity The difference between the amount of unpaid loan principal on a property and its current market value.

escrow account An account established during a real estate transaction into which a borrower deposits funds either to cover future payments, such as taxes and insurance, or to put on hold until certain conditions of the contract have been met.

F

Fair Credit Billing Act A law that requires creditors to notify customers of their rights and the procedures for making complaints about billing errors. The act, a 1974 amendment to the Truth in Lending Act, also sets requirements for resolving these errors within a specified time.

Fair Credit Reporting Act A 1971 law that gives an individual the right to examine his or her file at a credit-reporting agency and establishes procedures for resolution of any errors in that file.

Fair Debt Collection Practices Act A law prohibiting abusive and deceptive practices by debt collectors. It is Title VIII of the Consumer Credit Protection Act, which went into effect in 1978.

Fair Housing Act A section of the Civil Rights Act of 1968 that prohibits discrimination on the basis of race, color, religion, national origin, or sex when making mortgage, construction, or home improvement loans.

family life cycle The progressive stages of a family's spending and investment behavior as identified by marketers. The stages include single person, young married couple, young married couple with children, older married couple with older children, older married couple with no children at home, and widow or widower.

Federal Aviation Act A 1958 law that contains documentation requirements for loans secured by aircraft.

federal box A model format, in the shape of a rectangular box, that is used to inform borrowers of the annual percentage rate, total finance charges, amount being financed, and total amount of payments in a loan transaction.

Federal Deposit Insurance Corporation (FDIC) An independent government agency organized in 1933 to insure depositors' accounts at all national and most state-chartered banks. The FDIC also has the authority to supervise state banks that are not Federal Reserve members and rule on merger and branching applications.

Federal Reserve System The central banking authority established in 1913 to monitor and regulate the commercial banking system, to set U.S. monetary policy, to provide a nationwide check collection and payments system, and to serve as financial agent for the federal government. The system consists of 12 Federal Reserve banks, each in a different region of the country, and a board of governors in Washington, D.C.

fee-splitting The illegal practice of paying someone to refer potential loan customers.

fictitious loans The fraudulent practice by automobile dealers and other borrowers of submitting loan applications from nonexistent people or real people who do not have a sales contract with the dealer.

finance charge The total interest costs a consumer pays to obtain credit.

finance charge income Income received from interest charges on unpaid credit balances.

finance company A company that specializes in making small- and medium-sized loans to consumers, especially those who might have trouble obtaining credit otherwise.

first mortgage loan The real estate loan that takes precedence over all other mortgage loans on a property. If the borrower fails to pay, the first mortgage lender has first claim against the property.

fixed rate loan A loan with an interest rate that remains the same over the life of the loan.

Flood Disaster Protection Act A law authorizing lenders to make federal flood insurance a requirement on loans secured by real estate located in a flood zone.

floor planning A loan for financing a retailer's inventory. The bank disburses funds to the dealer after he or she has pledged specific goods sitting on the showroom floor as collateral. When this merchandise is sold, the lender is repaid.

fluctuating value collateral Assets pledged as collateral that rise and fall in value over the life of a loan.

foreclosure A legal procedure allowing a creditor to sell real estate property given as collateral on a defaulted mortgage loan.

full recourse A dealer recourse option requiring the dealer who sold a loan to reimburse the bank the full amount if the borrower defaults.

Functional Cost Analysis An annual sampling survey conducted and published by the Federal Reserve Board, which compares various asset, income, and cost ratios for banking functions, such as trust, installment lending, commercial lending, and safe deposit.

G

gross monthly income The total dollar amount of income before taxes, insurance, and other deductions.

guaranteed loan A loan, made by a financial institution to an eligible business or individual, that is guaranteed against default by a federal agency.

Guaranteed Student Loan Program A program sponsored by the U.S. Department of Education, which guarantees a loan made by a financial institution to a student against default. While the student is in school, the department also makes interest payments on the loan.

guarantor One who takes responsibility for the debts and obligations of another. The guarantor becomes liable only after all attempts to convince the first person to pay or perform fail.

H

hologram A three-dimensional image, created by a technology using lasers and precision optical equipment, that appears on credit cards and makes them difficult to counterfeit.

home equity line of credit A line of credit based on the borrower's equity in a home, for example, the market value of the home minus the amount of mortgage principal remaining to be paid. The borrower can access all or any part of this credit by writing a check or using a credit card.

Home Mortgage Disclosure Act A 1975 law requiring lenders to make public the geographic location of their mortgage loans.

Housing and Community Development Act A 1977 law implementing federal housing policy and programs and containing the provisions of the Community Reinvestment Act.

I

index rate A leading economic indicator, such as the prime rate or the 90-day Treasury bill rate, that is used as a benchmark for setting variable loan interest rates. As the index rate rises and falls, the loan rate follows.

indirect loan A loan involving three parties including the borrower who obtains financing from a merchant who then sells the loan to a financial institution.

indirect verification An investigation of an applicant's credit history conducted by contacting a third party such as a credit bureau.

inflationary spiral An economic condition where higher prices for goods and services mean higher costs for buyers, which results in demands for higher wages and, eventually, results in still higher prices from producers and suppliers paying those wages.

insolvent The inability to pay debts when due.

installment loan A loan that is repaid in two or more periodic, fixed payments.

interchange fee A handling charge collected by either the merchant's bank or the card-issuing bank for processing credit card transactions that have occurred outside their local market area.

interest-earning assets Bank funds that are invested in loans, Treasury bills, municipal and corporate bonds, and other investments that earn interest income.

interest rate The price one must pay to borrow money. The rate is generally computed on a percentage-per-year basis.

interest rate sensitivity The degree to which behavior is influenced by fluctuations in current interest rates. For example, interest-sensitive consumers borrow money when loan rates are low and invest more funds in certificates of deposit (CDs) when CD rates are high.

interest subvention program A program through which a manufacturer of goods pays a portion of the bank's loan interest charges so that the company can offer below market rates to its customers.

K

kickback An illegal payment by the borrower to the lender in return for granting credit.

L

leasing A contractual arrangement through which the owner of property or goods, such as automobiles and equipment, rents them to someone else.

lessee One who rents and uses property or goods owned by someone else.

lessor The owner of property or goods that are rented to someone else.

lien A legal claim giving a lender the right to take possession of collateral if a borrower fails to repay the loan.

limited recourse A dealer recourse option requiring the dealer who sold a loan to provide partial reimbursement to the bank if the borrower defaults.

line of credit The amount of money a financial institution is willing to lend over a specified period without requiring additional loan applications. The customer can borrow, repay, and borrow again any or all of the credit extended and may be required to keep a certain level of funds in the bank or offer personal property as security.

liquid assets Assets that can be easily and quickly converted into cash without a loss in value.

liquidation costs The amount of money spent to remove a paid-up loan from the bank's records and return the note to the borrower.

liquidity The ease with which assets can be converted into cash without a loss in value.

loan balance The total amount still owed on a loan after deducting the total amount of payments made.

loan contract The written agreement between borrower and lender that spells out the amount and terms of the loan.

loan decision The outcome of determining whether to grant a loan, to offer credit on terms other than those requested, or to deny credit.

loan documentation The process of gathering and completing all the papers necessary to secure the lender's interest and comply with the legal requirements of making a loan.

loan loss rate A measure of a lender's previous experience with bad loans computed by dividing the dollar amount of total losses by the dollar amount of total loans made.

loan policy A written statement of the goals, guidelines, standards, and procedures a lender follows in determining who will receive credit and under what specified terms and conditions.

loan portfolio The total of all loans held by a financial institution and managed as a collective whole.

loan shark A person or firm that lends money to a poor credit risk at an excessively high or illegal rate of interest.

loan structuring The process of constructing a loan interest rate that results in enough income to cover the costs of lending and earn a reasonable profit.

loan volume The total dollar amount of loans made in a given period.

loans outstanding The total dollar amount of unpaid balances on all types of loans.

loss exposure The amount of money a lender could lose if loans go bad.

M

maintenance costs The amount of money spent to maintain a loan until its maturity date. This includes overhead expenses (such as rent and utilities), salaries for loan processors and customer service representatives, coupon books and other office supplies, and computer expenditures.

margin account Credit provided by a brokerage firm to its customers to enable them to pay for stocks and other securities they may want to purchase. These funds can only be a portion of the total sale and interest must be paid to the broker for the use of the borrowed funds.

marginal loan A loan that is considered a borderline credit risk.

mass market To offer and promote a product or service to the general public.

MasterCard International An independent, for-profit corporation that contracts with financial institutions to offer an internationally accepted credit card, credit insurance, traveler's checks, and other related credit card services to their customers.

maturity date The date a loan is due.

maturity structuring The process of determining a loan maturity date that results in enough interest income to cover the cost of lending and to earn a reasonable profit. Common maturities are 36, 48, and 60 months.

merchant discount The amount a merchant pays to a bank for processing its credit card transactions, generally figured as a percentage of the dollar amount of each sale.

money market rates The interest rates paid on short-term private and government obligations, such as Treasury bills, commercial paper, and tax-exempt securities.

Morris Plan bank A type of financial institution that was first established in 1910 by Arthur J. Morris to make small- and medium-sized unsecured loans to consumers who could convince two others to co-sign the loan with them. Since most banks in that day only made loans to businesses, Morris Plan banks were one of the earliest institutions that provided consumer credit.

N

net investment The total expenditure to acquire or use an asset minus the value of the asset.

net worth The value of an individual or a business after deducting the total of liabilities from the total of assets.

nonrecourse A dealer recourse option where the dealer who sells a loan has no liability to the bank that bought the loan if the borrower defaults.

note A written promise to repay a specified amount of money by a specific date.

O

open-end loan A credit arrangement allowing the borrower to make purchases and take cash advances up to a previously agreed limit. Repayment is made at fixed intervals and will vary in size depending on the amount of credit extended. Lines of credit and credit cards are two examples.

over-limit charge A fee paid by a credit card holder who charges more than the authorized credit limit.

P

pay down To reduce a debt by making payments.

pay out To pay off a loan before its due date.

payroll deduction plan A plan allowing an employee to authorize that specified sums of money be deducted from his or her pay to be credited to financial obligations, such as health insurance, loan payments, or savings programs.

perfect a lien A procedure for protecting a lender's claim to loan collateral in the event of default. When collateral is handed over to the lender, as in the case of stocks and bonds, the claim is secure. When the lender does not have possession of the collateral, the lender must file a financing statement, which describes the collateral and the terms of the loan agreement, with the appropriate legal authorities. By taking this step, a security interest is "perfected."

periodic rate The interest rate that a creditor charges on a daily, weekly, or monthly basis on the outstanding balance in open-end credit such as a credit card or revolving charge account.

periodic statement A summary, usually mailed monthly, of the activity in an open-end credit account, including the previous balance, new transactions, finance charges, new balance, and minimum payment due.

personal banker A bank employee assigned to provide personalized customer service to highly valued customers. Personal bankers are banking professionals who are informed about the financial needs of customers and have the authority to handle all nonroutine transactions.

personal loan company A company that specializes in short -term small- and medium-sized loans to consumers.

point-of-sale (POS) verification terminal An electronic device, found at retail locations but connected by telephone to a bank's computer system, that checks a customer's account to verify that adequate funds are available to pay for goods or services. Some POS terminals are also capable of transferring the funds from the customer's to the merchant's account in the same transaction.

portfolio liquidity The ease with which a financial institution's collective holdings can be converted into cash without a loss in value.

prescreening The practice of examining credit bureau files for individuals who meet credit requirements and targeting efforts to market at these consumers.

primary borrower The person who receives the direct benefit of borrowed funds in a loan signed by one or more co-makers.

prime rate A benchmark from which a bank computes an appropriate rate of interest for a loan contract. Generally, the benchmark is based on numerous factors, including the bank's supply of funds, what it costs the bank to keep those funds, its administrative costs, and competition from other suppliers of credit.

principal The amount of a loan or deposit excluding fees and interest.

principal balance The amount of unpaid balance of a loan excluding fees and interest.

product line A group of products that are closely related because they have similar functions, for example, passbook savings, statement savings, and money market savings accounts.

product packaging The practice of marketing a group of financial services as a single customer product. For example, a product package may include free checking and a line of credit accessed by the bank's credit card.

profit margin A ratio computed by subtracting expenses (or total dollars of expenses) from the sales price (or total dollars of sales) and dividing the result by the sales price (or total number of sales).

purchase money loan A mortgage granted by the seller to the buyer of the seller's property.

Q

qualify To meet a lender's criteria for granting credit.

R

range of balances The lowest to the highest dollar amount on open-end credit balances that will be charged a specific rate of interest. When the range changes to a new low and high dollar amount, the rate changes. For example, on a balance from $1 to $2,500, a monthly interest rate of 2 percent will be charged, but this rate drops to 1.5 percent on a balance of $2,501.

rate cap The maximum allowable interest rate a financial institution may charge on a loan.

rate floor The lowest interest rate a financial institution will agree to charge on a loan.

rate subsidy program A program in which a manufacturer of goods pays a portion of the bank's loan interest charges so that the company can offer below market rates to its customers.

re-age an account An arrangement for allowing a delinquent borrower to skip one or more payments and then extending the life of the loan by the same number of payments.

real estate broker A licensed professional authorized to represent clients involved in real estate transactions and to facilitate the sale or leasing of a property.

Real Estate Settlement Procedures Act A 1975 law that requires lenders to provider borrowers with accurate and timely information on the costs of the real estate settlement process and protects borrowers against abusive uses of their escrow funds.

rebate To return interest to the borrower because the loan has been repaid early.

recession proof The ability to maintain a level of consumption despite a general slowdown or decline in economic activity.

recovery department The offices within a lending institution responsible for getting whatever repayment is possible on a defaulted loan.

redlining The practice of restricting or refusing to make loans in certain neighborhoods because they are considered a bad investment.

refinance The process of obtaining a new loan, usually at a lower interest rate, in order to pay off an existing loan and reduce monthly payments.

regional banking The establishment of a banking presence in nearby states by merger, acquisition, or new charter.

Regulation B The Federal Reserve rule that prohibits credit discrimination, sets guidelines for gathering and evaluating credit information, and requires written notification when credit is denied. Regulation B implements the Equal Credit Opportunity Act.

Regulation C The Federal Reserve rule requiring financial institutions to make public the geographic locations of their mortgage loans. Regulation C implements the Home Mortgage Disclosure Act.

Regulation O The Federal Reserve rule that prohibits a bank from making loans to its executive officers and officers at banks with which it does business.

Regulation U The Federal Reserve rule that governs the amount of money a bank may lend for buying stocks.

Regulation X A rule of the Department of Housing and Urban Development that requires full and accurate disclosure of credit terms in real estate transactions. Regulation X implements the Real Estate Settlement Procedures Act.

Regulation Z The Federal Reserve rule that requires disclosure of credit terms, including finance charges, service charges, and payment schedules, and sets procedures for resolving billing errors. Regulation Z implements the Truth in Lending Act.

relationship banking A program designed to develop long-term client relationships with bank customers by offering them a package of products that serves their total financial needs.

repayment period The time interval between when a debt begins and when it is due.

repossession The act of claiming property or goods given as security on a loan when the borrower has defaulted.

repurchase recourse A dealer recourse option requiring the dealer who sold a loan to repurchase it if it becomes delinquent within the first 90 days.

residential loan A loan in which real estate, such as an owner-occupied home, is pledged as security.

residual value The value of an asset at the conclusion of a lease agreement.

retail banking Products and services offered by a bank to individual consumers as opposed to those offered to businesses or other organizations.

retail installment loan A loan made to an individual for personal use and repaid in periodic, fixed payments.

retail paper Dealer installment loan contracts that are sold to banks.

retention rate The rate of interest a bank will charge on loans it buys from a dealer.

revolving loan A prearranged line of credit that can be activated by writing a check or using a credit card. The payment due is always less than the total balance due and any unpaid balance is subject to finance charges.

right of offset A provision in loan contracts that allows the lender to use funds deposited in the borrower's accounts for payment of delinquent loans.

right of rescission The right of a borrower or buyer to cancel a contract within 3 business days without penalty and with refund of all deposits. This privilege is a provision of the Truth in Lending Act.

rule of 78s A method used to determine how much interest to refund to the borrower when a loan is repaid early.

S

sales draft A multipage sales slip used in credit card transactions to document that the card holder owes money to the card issuer.

salvage department The offices within a lending institution responsible for getting whatever repayment is possible on a defaulted loan.

savings institution A financial institution that accepts savings deposits and invests them by offering long-term mortgage loans. This is a general term that refers to savings and loan associations, savings banks, and credit unions.

second mortgage A loan on a property that was made after the first mortgage loan. If a borrower fails to pay off loans, the second mortgage holder must wait until the claims of the first mortgage lender have been satisfied.

secondary market A national market where a financial institution's loans, primarily mortgages, can be bought and sold to other investors. The secondary market enables the institution to convert long-term loans back into cash.

secured loan A loan requiring the borrower to pledge specific assets that become the property of the lender if the loan is not repaid.

securities Documents that show evidence of ownership or indebtedness. Stocks and bonds are two kinds of securities.

securities broker One who acts as an agent for others in the buying and selling of stocks and bonds.

security agreement A document signed by a borrower establishing a lender's right to take possession of loan collateral in the event of default.

sell up To convince a borrower to accept a loan for more money than requested.

service To perform those activities related to collecting loan payments, including handling and securing loan documents, sending billing statements or coupon books, receiving payments, responding to customers' inquiries, and following up on delinquencies.

Ship Mortgage Act of 1920 A law that sets documentation requirements for loans secured by seagoing vessels.

short-term equity advance A loan granted for a short period on the basis of the equity in the borrower's home.

simple interest A method of calculating a loan interest rate by taking a percentage of the loan balance each month, not including previous interest charges, and expressing this figure as an annualized rate.

skip tracing The process of locating borrowers who have stopped making their loan payments and cannot be located at their last known address or employer.

stable value collateral Assets pledged as collateral that remain constant in value over the life of a loan.

statement of waiver A document signed by a borrower relinquishing rights to rescission (privileges to cancel a loan contract within 3 working days).

stock A certificate showing evidence of ownership in a corporation.

straw purchaser An individual who allows someone with a poor credit rating to use his or her name and credit report to obtain a loan.

surety A person who agrees to be responsible for the debts and obligations of another.

T

tangible assets Property and goods that are in a physical form and can be touched or seen, such as an automobile or a piece of land.

term The period between the commencement and termination of a debt or contract.

thrift A financial institution that accepts savings deposits and invests these funds in long-term mortgages. The three types of thrifts are savings and loan associations, savings banks, and credit unions.

tie-in selling The practice of offering a buyer products or services in addition to the one requested.

transfer of title To change ownership from one party to another.

triggering terms Words or phrases that, when used in bank advertising, "trigger" or set off certain Truth in Lending disclosure requirements.

Truth in Lending Act The law that requires clear and accurate disclosure of credit terms in a lending transaction, including interest, fees, and all other costs. Truth in Lending is the popular name of the Consumer Credit Protection Act of 1969.

Truth in Lending Simplification and Reform Act A 1982 law designed to streamline the original Truth in Lending legislation by easing and simplifying disclosure requirements so that disclosure statements can be more easily understood by consumers.

U

unauthorized transaction The illegal use of a credit card or bank account by someone other than the card or account holder.

underwriting guidelines Criteria used by a lending institution to determine if an applicant is eligible to receive credit.

Uniform Commercial Code (UCC) A set of laws drafted to give consistency to the legal aspects of business and financial transactions, including bank deposits, the sale of goods, stock transfers, and secured loans. Every state except Louisiana has adopted the UCC.

uniform disclosure A standardized format for informing consumers about the terms of a credit agreement.

Uniform Small Loan Law A law adopted on the state level that spells out uniform guidelines on maximum allowable interest rates, loan size, and the licensing of small loan companies. A model of this law was drafted and promoted by the Russell Sage Foundation to encourage consistency and credibility in state consumer credit legislation.

unsecured line of credit The amount a financial institution is willing to lend over a specified period of time without requiring additional loan applications. The borrower can withdraw all or part of the amount, repay and withdraw again on the basis of his or her credit history and ability to repay, and not because he or she has pledged specific assets to the lender.

unsecured loan A loan made on the basis of a borrower's credit history and ability to repay and not on the requirement of pledging assets to the lender.

unsolicited credit card A credit card issued to a consumer who has not requested it. The practice of issuing unsolicited credit cards is now prohibited by law.

usurious interest A rate of interest on a loan that is higher than that allowed by state law.

usury law A law that sets the maximum interest rate that can be charged on different types of loans.

usury limit The maximum interest rate allowed by law.

V

valuation guide book A reference book used by lenders to determine the market value of collateral that may depreciate over time, for example, used cars, mobile homes, and boats.

variable rate loan A loan with an interest rate than can change over the life of the loan. The loan rate is tied to an important money market indicator, such as the prime rate or the 90-day Treasury bill rate, and rises or falls with that rate.

Visa International An independent, for-profit corporation that contracts with financial institutions to offer an internationally accepted credit card, credit insurance, traveler's checks, and other related credit card services to their customers.

W

wage attachment A court order for seizing a person's wages as security for his or her debts.

wage garnishment A court order requiring an employer to withhold a portion of an employee's wages to pay his or her creditors.

warranty A guarantee of quality made by the seller of a product or service.

End Notes

1. Michaelman, Irving S., *Consumer Finance: A Case History in American Business*, Frederick Fell, Inc. (New York, 1966), p. 88.
2. Ibid., p. 88.
3. Ibid., p. 89.
4. Ibid., p. 90.
5. Ibid., p. 90.
6. Plummer, Wilbur C., "Consumer Credit in Colonial Philadelphia," *The Pennsylvania Magazine of History and Biography* (October, 1942), p. 396.
7. Michaelman, op. cit., p. 74.
8. Osthaus, Carl R., *Freedom, Philanthropy, and Fraud: A History of the Freedman's Savings Bank*, University of Illinois Press (Urbana, 1976), pp. 122–23.
9. Michaelman, op. cit., p. 78.
10. Ibid., p. 80.
11. Ibid., p. 108.
12. Fousek, Peter G., "Prerequisites for the Growth of Consumer Instalment Credit," *Journal of Finance*, Volume 13 (May, 1958), pp. 166–67.
13. Porter, Sylvia, *New Money Book for the 1980's*, Doubleday & Company, Inc. (Garden City, 1979), p. 78–79.
14. Tobin, James, "Consumer Debt and Spending: Some Evidence from Analysis of a Survey," *Consumer Instalment Credit*, Volume I, Part II, p. 543.
15. Dunkelberg, William C., and F.P. Stafford, "Debt in the Consumer Portfolio: Evidence from a Panel Study," *American Economic Review*, Volume 61 (September, 1971), p. 611.
16. Berry, Leonard L., and James H. Donnelly, *Marketing for Bankers*, American Bankers Association (1975), p. 11.

Index

D

E

F

G

H

M

N

O

P

R

S

T

U

V

W

Consumer Lending

Date: ______________

This questionnaire is designed to get reader opinions on the adequacy and relevance of the text. Your comments, both positive and negative, will influence the design and content of future AIB textbooks. Thank you for your assistance.

I. Background Information

A. In this course I was a(n): ☐ instructor ☐ student

B. Highest educational attainment:
☐ High School ☐ Some College ☐ BA/BS Degree ☐ Advanced Degree

C. I am a(n): ☐ Officer ☐ Non-Officer ☐ Non-Bank Employee

D. Asset Size of Bank:
☐ $0-100m ☐ $101-500m ☐ $501-1b ☐ Over $1b

E. My major job responsibility is ______________________________

F. I am pursuing an AIB diploma: ☐ Yes ☐ No

II. The Materials

Please rate the text according to the criteria below. Check the box that most closely corresponds with your opinions.

Thoroughness:	☐ covers too little of subject	☐ Covers sufficient content	☐ Covers too much unrelated content
Difficulty Level:	☐ Too basic	☐ Appropriate for level of course	☐ Too difficult
Interest Level:	☐ Dull and uninteresting	☐ Acceptable	☐ Very interesting
Organization:	☐ Sequenced logically	☐ Not in logical sequence	
Timeliness:	☐ Most content was current	☐ Most content was outdated	
Practicality:	☐ Too theoretical	☐ Has sufficient practical application	

Please rate the *overall effectiveness* of the text by circling the number which represents your opinion.

Very effective as a learning aid — Ineffective as a learning aid

5 4 3 2 1

III. Comments

A. Can you make any suggestions for improving the book?

____

____

____

B. Would you recommend this book to someone who needs to know this information?
☐ Yes ☐ No

FOLD IN HALF AND STAPLE

FOLD HERE

No Postage
Necessary
If Mailed
In The
United States

BUSINESS REPLY MAIL

First Class Permit No 10579 Washington, D C

Postage Will Be Paid by

Educational Planning
Education Policy & Development Group
American Bankers Association
1120 Connecticut Avenue
Washington, D.C. 20036